STARTING RESEARCH

Education is what survives when what has been learnt has been forgotten.

(B.F. Skinner, *New Scientist*, 1964)

STARTING RESEARCH

AN INTRODUCTION TO ACADEMIC RESEARCH AND DISSERTATION WRITING

ROY PREECE

PINTER
PUBLISHERS
LONDON, NEW YORK

Distributed exclusively in the USA and Canada by St. Martin's Press

Pinter Publishers
25 Floral Street, Covent Garden, London, WC2E 9DS, United Kingdom

First published in Great Britain, 1994

Distributed exclusively in the USA and Canada by St. Martin's Press, Inc., Room 400, 175 Fifth Avenue, New York, NY10010, USA

Roy Preece is hereby identified as the author of this work as provided under Section 77 of the Copyright, Designs and Patents Act 1988.

British Library Cataloguing in Publication Data
A CIP catalogue record for this book is available from the British Library

ISBN   1 85567 090 9 (hardback)
       1 85567 091 7 (paperback)

Library of Congress Cataloging-in-Publication Data

Preece, R. A. (Roy A.)
   Starting research: an introduction to academic research and dissertation writing
Roy Preece
   p. cm.
   Includes index.
   ISBN   1-85567-090-9. — ISBN 1-85567-091-7 (pbk.)
   1. Report writing. 2. Dissertations, Academic. 3. Research.
   I. Title.
LB2369.P69 1994
808'.042—dc20   93-48992
                                                                      CIP

Typeset by Saxon Graphics Ltd, Derby
Printed and bound in Great Britain by Biddles Ltd of Guildford and King's Lynn

CONTENTS

FIGURES AND TABLES

Figures

Table

PREFACE

This book has been written in the context of a number of changes in higher education; this is not the place, however, to argue whether all of these changes are or are not desirable. They include, for example: a student population drawn from a wider range of age, background and experience; larger numbers of students, larger classes and a decline of individual tuition; a possible devaluation of the first bachelors degree and a move to the American system of increasing numbers of masters and post-graduate courses generally; more exacting deadlines for submission of dissertations and less time for initiation, self-discovery, planning and reflection; movement across disciplinary boundaries and the development of inter-disciplinary programmes; in short, a more fragmented, though in some ways more intense, and, it may be, more abbreviated education.

All degrees, other than the now uncommon pass degree, require the preparation, at the student's initiative, of a dissertation which, even if it is not considered strictly to be a piece of research, has much in common with research. It therefore seemed useful to produce a text which in one volume would comprehensively and conveniently introduce the principal aspects of research thought and activity required for dissertation writing, particularly at the masters level but of value to both first degree and doctoral students also. Special importance has been placed on readability while maintaining, it is hoped, rigour and accuracy. I have been aware throughout of the possible dangers of simplification, and of Dr Johnson's stricture on the matter; but, even so, experience shows that what is presented here exceeds the theoretical and methodological content of many student dissertations which could be substantially improved in these respects. Further, once a comprehensible overview has been obtained, students may overcome the resistance which in many cases they display to this type of material and feel confident to tackle some of the works recommended for further reading on individual topics.

Some explanations: I have for clarity followed the practice of respected academic writers and the *Oxford English Dictionary* in using the term 'dissertation' to embrace the term 'thesis'; I have naturally drawn many illustrations, though not all, from my own experiences and teaching, but readers should usefully seek analogies in their own disciplines; and I have followed the practice, again of comparable texts, in not referencing every point exhaustively. Referencing has been used as a courtesy only where names or quotations are given though all sources used are included in the bibliography and are here gratefully acknowledged, not least for the interest and enjoyment which many have afforded. Lest any misunderstanding arise, however, it must be emphasized that a student dissertation should be comprehensively and extensively referenced, as set out in Chapter Nine.

The need for a glossary has been eliminated by the definition of all special terms used as appropriate in the text. The location of these definitions is indicated by bold type in the index.

I particularly wish to thank Dr Roland Newman, formerly Reader in Architecture at the Oxford Brookes University and my colleague for many years, who has been a constant and ready source of encouragement, penetrating criticism and useful advice and whose rigorous teaching has to some extent shaped this book. Special thanks are due to Lin Paris who has typed and re-typed the manuscript and whose goodwill and efficiency have substantially facilitated the progress of the work. I am grateful to Alan Preece who provided valuable criticism of an early draft; also to Val Bacon, to Augustin Rodriguez-Bachiller, to Catherine Tranmer and to Pete Smith who have each made helpful comments on parts of the text, and especially to Roger Mason who kindly offered to apply his sharp legal mind to the whole work. The School of Planning at Oxford Brookes University has provided not inconsiderable help with production up to the final manuscript stage. I would naturally like to thank my wife Wendy for her support and tolerance during the inevitable disturbances caused by preparing a book. I am indebted also to the following individuals and organizations for kind permission to reproduce portions of previously published works on the pages shown: the Editor of the *New Scientist* (p.ii); David Higham Associates Limited, for the extract from Sir Herbert Read's

Reason and Romanticism, Faber and Faber; John Murray (Publications) Ltd, for the extract from Sir Kenneth Clark's *Civilisation* (p.96); Dr Robert Browning of the Department of Classics at Birkbeck College for the passage from *The Byzantine Empire* (p.186) and Curtis Brown and John Farquharson for the extract from Eric Hebborn's *Master Faker* (p.209).

INTRODUCTION

Student dissertations can usefully add to our general systems of knowledge. Indeed contribution to knowledge is a requirement of work carried out and presented at doctoral level. Any good dissertation, at whatever level, should be of interest and relevance, even if only at a local or particular scale. But the educational purpose of producing a dissertation is wider than this and is concerned with understanding the nature of knowledge itself. Investigation and writing for a dissertation provide, according to its level, an introduction to or a training in research, not just in the techniques of a particular discipline, but in the general principles of how knowledge is won.

A student who has successfully completed a substantial dissertation feels, rightly, that significant steps forward have been taken in knowledge, competence, awareness and intellectual maturity. The student will have more appreciation of the great efforts which others have put into the advancement of knowledge but will also be more critical of much that is purported to be knowledge. He or she will be alert to selective evidence, to inadequate or unrepresentative samples, to the dangers of seeing what we want to see, to invalid argument, to the patterns of probability and coincidence, to poor design in experiment or survey, to leading questions and much more; distinction will be made between information and systems of knowledge, and facility and exactness of expression will be enhanced. In short the student will have significantly advanced his or her education for life.

This book provides an introduction to the principal areas of research thought and activity. It begins with the distinction between research, in the sense of work within and contributing to systems of ideas, and mere collection of information, chronicling of events or even immediate problem-solving. It continues with an account of how philosophers over the centuries have developed concepts and arguments in an attempt to distinguish objective fact from feeling and to investigate relation between events, particularly that of cause and effect. These principles are then applied to procedures for the systematic collection of primary information in terms of experimental design and the organization of surveys. In particular, some of the problems in the measurement of attitudes are examined, and requirements for the preparation of information for computer analysis is outlined.

Chapter Seven provides an outline both of the principles and of some commonly used procedures of statistical analysis, drawing attention to the strength and to the limitations of such information; the procedure for testing the null hypothesis is set clearly within the general philosophical arguments established in earlier chapters. With this basic understanding it is possible to go on to consider the criteria for selection of suitable and realistic research questions and hypotheses and the preparation of a research proposal; the concept of originality is examined here. In the last chapter are considered both the psychological and practical problems of organizing and writing a research dissertation, and the requirements for a successful and worthwhile dissertation are explained. In the appendices are set out, first, some further details of statistical procedures and, second, in the light of declining standards of English, some basic points on clear style selected from experience of common student errors and queries.

Clearly, single chapters or parts of chapters cannot be complete substitutes for whole books on philosophy, documentary analysis, survey design, statistical analysis or the writing of English. Accordingly, further recommended reading is appended to each chapter. Nevertheless, what is set out here goes beyond what is achieved in many student dissertations, even at a doctoral level, and full cognizance of this material would significantly improve both the supervision and final quality of student dissertations generally. Further, while the sheer hard work and frequent perplexities involved in rigorously searching for new knowledge can scarcely be appreciated other than by attempting it, it is hoped that, as a result of reading this book, anyone can acquire a more critical and realistic view of the multiplicity of information and ideas which bombards us today.

1
WHAT IS RESEARCH?

'Reason is a very difficult word to use without confusion.'
(Herbert Read, *Reason and romanticism*, 1926)

'Do some research into the jolly train time-tables would you Jeeves?'
Thus, the fictional Bertie Wooster, intending to visit a neglected
friend in the country, might have instructed his long-suffering butler.
The knowledgable Jeeves, however, probably would have replied, 'I
do not think we would want to dignify such an activity with the use
of the term *research*, Sir. Mmmmm . . . Nevertheless........'

Who is correct, Bertie or his butler? In different senses, each is
right, but Jeeves is the more precise. What then is this activity called
research?

The nature of research

Research is an exciting and fulfilling intellectual activity; definitions
appear to be dull. But definitions are always worth examining carefully. This is not to be excessively precise, or pedantic, but for the
much more important purposes of thinking about and discussing,
from a common ground, the meanings of the ideas which the words
represent. It is very important in research to be clear about the particular ideas or concepts which are being used in investigations (see,
for example, the discussion of concepts in Chapter Two). A popular
English dictionary defines research as: 'systematic investigation
towards increasing the sum of human knowledge'. By way of introduction, let us examine the ideas used in this definition.

Research within a system of ide

First, in research, investigation is systematic. This does not mean only that the investigation should be well-organized, though it ought to be that also, but that it is carried out within a *system* of ideas. Jeeves, for example, already has in his mind the ideas of trains, stations, connections and links; otherwise the time-tables would be meaningless to him. We might even, naturally, suppose that no serious research project would pay someone to wander around vaguely hoping to discover just anything. Nevertheless, serendipity does sometimes play a valuable role in advancing human knowledge, as when, in the late eighteenth century, Dr Edward Jenner, chatting to a pretty young woman, wondered why milkmaids in particular rarely caught the common and disfiguring disease of smallpox. This chance observation led Jenner's trained mind to the discovery of vaccination. A discovery of this sort is not as unsystematic as it might at first sight appear. Although the individual observation itself was, in this case, not the result of any organized study, yet Jenner's mind had been trained to recognize certain systems or pat-

I wonder.....

Important discoveries are sometimes made by the impression which a chance observation produces on a trained and systematic mind.

terns of occurrences and to be alert to departures from such patterns. Further, he had, by the standards of his day, an idea of the
general physical relationship of cause and effect and some ability to
test specific relationships experimentally and systematically.

The importance of a system of ideas, or a discipline, for any subject is thus two-fold. First, only a systematically trained mind is
likely to be aware of the possible significance of any chance observation; that milkmaids did not get smallpox had long been well known
to country people. From such observation the trained mind develops an intuitive idea: in everyday terms, a 'hunch'. This mental
process is an example of what is known as induction. The discoveries of penicillin and of microbes are two other important illustrations of this process. The nature and value of inductive thought will
be examined further in Chapter Three. Second, the inductively
formed ideas must be tested systematically according to procedures
which are in part general to all disciplines but are also to some
extent specific to individual subjects. Much of the rest of this book
is concerned with such procedures and the arguments which under-
lie them. In passing, and by contrast, it may be pointed out that a
medieval monk trained in theology might have reasoned that milkmaids were especially favoured by God – since Christ was born in
an ox's stall – and pursued the matter no further. There are also
many examples in the physical sciences of observations whose
importance was not recognized until the appropriate discipline had
developed sufficiently to provide a context within which their significance could be seen.

Increasing the sum of knowledge

So far, Bertie and Jeeves would both appear to be right, but their
ideas are soon seen to diverge when we consider, next, the idea of
the *sum*, or totality, of human knowledge. For Jeeves' investigations
will not add to the sum of knowledge. Railway time-tables are published for anyone to see. Although not everyone might be acquainted with this information, it is nevertheless already part of the
storehouse of available information. The mere transference of information from one place or publication to another does not in itself
constitute serious research, though it may of course be a useful
thing to do (Chapter Four). The organization and cataloguing of
existing information is, however, certainly an essential foundation of

research activity; it both furnishes the setting or context, or system of ideas, within which the research will take place and often provides the material itself which is to be researched. This would be especially true where the information was already so disorganized or remote, or inaccessible for any reason (for example, not translated from a dead language) as in effect not to form part of human knowledge in the present. But even the re-arrangement of what is already known is not in itself the essence of research unless it leads on to the development of patterns or classification systems which, as in evolutionary biology, do reveal new knowledge about relationships and which prompt further research and testing.

The notion of the sum of knowledge raises another point; if this sum is to be increased, what is the nature of the addition? Can it be more of the same, more apples to a basket of apples so to speak? Or should it be something different, original, a new and exciting fruit? In fact both operations are valuable, though the second can be much more so and is, of course, much more rare; few doctoral theses can have had as much impact as Marie Curie's original account of radioactivity. But there is value also in the accumulation of knowledge which is broadly similar in nature; that is, the amount, the repetition or replication and the generality of knowledge are important. This is more true in some fields of investigation than in others (Chapter Four).

Universality and relevance

A third term in our definition is human – *human* knowledge. The word human can scarcely have been chosen in order merely to exclude that knowledge, mostly we suppose instinctive, which exists in the rest of the animal kingdom, if indeed that is knowledge at all as we understand it. It is likely, rather, that the word has been selected to imply the universality of knowledge, its applicability to the human race. This raises the vexed question of the relevance of research. Is research to be generally useful and beneficial? A railway itinerary to some remote rural station would have no relevance to anyone but Bertie and a few others, and of course may be relevant only for one period in time. But Jeeves' perusal of the time-table could have led him to something else if he had started with a different question – what we might call a research question – and if he had had a lot more time. He could, though it is unlikely, have derived a method of prediction of which trains are most likely to be late or, even better, an explanation (or causal mechanism, whether mechanical or human) of *why* trains are late, and perhaps a solution or two. Such information might be thought to begin usefully to add to the sum of human knowledge, though it could be argued that this sort of investigation belongs more in the realms of consultancy or management than in research.

A distinction between consultancy and research is not always clear and, in addition to the question of the relevance of research, raises further issues of pure research as distinct from applied research and, it may be said, of a sort of intellectual one-upman-ship. Nevertheless, there is no need to apologize for distinguishing between, on the one hand, one-off problem-solving, or even infor-mation-gathering and, on the other, work which introduces new ideas, or concepts, and adds to our *system* of knowledge. The world and its inhabitants are very complex; we can only comprehend or know them if we have patterns of reference and a more or less common kit of ideas, or concepts, in order to organize this knowl-edge. Even when treating people as individuals, as we should, we draw on this common system of knowledge much more than per-haps we realize.

Relevance is, of course, relative. A useful piece of research for a village local history society would have no relevance to a national defence budget (though cumulative personal attachment to place might have relevance to the will or motivation for national defence). In between these extremes are all sorts of levels of relevance. 'Useful', in research terms, usually means useful to the intellectual progress of the relevant discipline or subject, but is Classical Histo-ry, for example, useful at all? The usefulness of the research and the usefulness of the subject are two different concepts which need to be treated in different ways (and which are often confused) but the second concept does not concern us here, except to point out that research which is useful within a subject may not be regarded as socially useful in the sense that it would attract public funds. Nor does usefulness necessarily imply practical, applied or economic usefulness. Useful research, in purely academic terms, means that which is carried out within the system of knowledge of a particular subject or discipline and contributes to or modifies or even casts doubt on – in fact tests – that system. This important idea of research as the testing of ideas is examined further in Chapter Two.

Research as Discovery

To aim to increase human knowledge in any systematic or universal way appears to be an over-ambitious, even daunting, objective for a single research project – as indeed it is. Use of the word 'towards' suggests, rather, that systems of knowledge are built up incrementally; they become accepted, or rejected, as a result of the cumulative – and sometimes conflicting – evidence from many research projects. This idea will be examined further in the discussion on hypothesis formulation (p.66). Clearly, complex relationships such as those between smoking and lung cancer, or between television viewing and violence, cannot be investigated conclusively by one project; the concepts involved are too general and the possible variables are too numerous. Social science research degree proposals often display over-ambition in terms of scope, while those of the physical sciences are usually more limited and researchable. In any case it is essential that a research proposal or dissertation should clearly show how the specific project relates to the present general state of knowledge in the area (Chapter Eight) and how the results might tend towards the support or rejection of existing ideas. However, even though today much ground in research work is well charted, and the destination or outcome often largely predictable, there is always the expectation and the possibility that some new aspect, something unknown, will turn up. Research aims *towards* increasing human knowledge, and that word sums up the challenge and excitement of even the smallest research undertaking.

Research as a quest for explanation

Bertie was not entirely wrong, at least linguistically, in his use of the term research. For another acceptable definition is, simply, a careful search. Nevertheless, looking for a lost wallet, however carefully, is not research. The idea is, though, not over-fanciful since the word research relates to search, which in turn comes from an Old French word meaning to go around in a circle; research presumably means to go around in circles – again. Research has, of course, come to mean much more than this, though it does retain an obsessive element.

We tend particularly to admire in any quality the development to an extreme of its intrinsic nature: in movement, of speed; in lifting, strength; in speech, fine singing, and so on. The development of human thought can be seen as an increasing ability to deal with abstract ideas; that is, to conceptualize links or patterns – what we think of as explanations – which appear to relate between concrete events or things. Academics, who are, in part, society's paid thinkers, tend to deal in abstract ideas: that is, not so much with day-to-day problems as with questions about principles which are largely independent of time or place. Thus, questions which do not appear immediately relevant are dismissed as mere 'academic' questions by people such as consultants or politicians who have to get things done. But academic research is not necessarily concerned with individual problem-solving as such, nor with technical brilliance (nor, to take an illustration from the arts, with story-telling); in so far as these things are done, however, they will be done within, and by utilizing, an existing system of knowledge. Often it is only these wider systems of knowledge which can provide the explanations for everyday events or the means for solving immediate problems. Academic life has thus tended to elevate this form of research to be the highest form of activity. The best students have generally been encouraged into research (indeed a traditional criterion of a first-class student was one who was particularly suited to research); the best departments have been seen as those most successful at research. Anyone wishing to obtain an academic research qualification should bear the nature of academic research carefully in mind.

There are, though, many different kinds of searching or investigation or of problem-solving which are extremely useful and may perhaps be dignified by the term research. Finding out why one particular car will not start on a particular morning may not be research (though it is an admirable logical investigation, (see Chapter Three); finding out what causes regular traffic jams may be 'road research'; managing the proverbial brewery is not research; so-called 'operational research' for the efficient planning of a new project may be; asking your friends what soap powder they use may not be; asking 1,000 people is called 'market research'. The common distinctions between these two levels of activity appear to be that: (a) the research activity uses well-tested logical methods of investigation; (b) there is, perhaps, something significant about the scale or generality of the investigation; (c) there is a level, admittedly ill-defined, at which the outcome is of public rather than personal relevance; and (d) the investigation is related, both in approach and outcome, to the wider system of knowledge of the particular subject or discipline.

It cannot be emphasized too strongly, once more, that to say that research is set within a system does not mean it should merely confirm that system (see Chapter Three). It probably will – new systems of knowledge are very rare – but occasionally something new, though apparently peripheral, comes along – every researcher's dream. Marie Curie's work on radioactivity was little valued at the time, and her thesis was strongly disputed; its relevance was not understood. Einstein's theory of relativity undermined the apparently absolute and reliable system of Newton's explanation of the universe. Yet both Curie and Einstein stood, so to speak, on the shoulders of others: Curie on the traditional chemists, and Einstein on Newton and Galileo. More recently the calibration or adjustment of radio-carbon dating by the counting of tree-ring formation back over time (dendrochronology) has fundamentally changed the accepted system of the stages of development of civilization. None of this work was independent, unrelated to what had gone before, but it was nevertheless new and revolutionary.

While individual ideas or concepts (and new concepts) are not merely useful but essential parts of thinking and understanding, it is the systems of thought by which they are linked which provide real power. Explanation, understanding, relationships, cause and effect, prediction and control come from these links or systems or patterns. When, in the 1840s, Dr John Snow plotted on a map the locations of cholera outbreaks in London he saw, though he had no concept of germs or bacteria (that was to come with Pasteur's work), that all the outbreaks were linked by a single water source (long put underground) which supplied drinking water to the victims and which proved to be polluted. The idea, now so obvious to us, met with great scepticism at the time, not least from those who supplied the water. In a quite different example, Galileo and Copernicus and others, observing the complex movements of the planets, deduced from the system of movement that the earth must go round the sun, though the Church thought otherwise. But Newton was able to go further and *explain* the system by his laws of mass and the inverse square of distance relating to gravitational force; centuries later this understanding can be used to control and predict the flights of spacecraft. There are other systems, less spectacular but no less interesting, to be identified and explained: the migration of birds, the location of leukaemia, changes in weather patterns, the incidence of mental disease, the decay of inner cities, holiday destination and travel, and so on. Unfortunately many of these events are less regular, less researchable, less predictable than physical happenings. Whether social systems can, or ever should be, researched in scientifically conventional ways is examined in Chapter Two.

But, returning to Jeeves' problem for a moment, let us fancifully suppose that trains ran in an apparently arbitrary and possibly random fashion and that there were no such things as time-tables. It might be possible by many observations, at many places and by many people, to infer the system by which trains ran, in fact to write a time-table from scratch. This would involve the activities of identifying, cataloguing, counting, checking, rechecking, corresponding, correlating but, above all, of working out the patterns. Research, essentially, is rather like writing time-tables for systems which already exist.

The results or outcomes of research are not, of course, usually like train time-tables, which have been used here only as an illustration or analogy; but, most important, these outcomes are not produced in the same way. There are perhaps, ideally, three main stages in time-tabling an actual railway system. First would come an analysis of where and when people wished to travel. In practice, this information is usually limited to desired variations in existing travel patterns, but, if explored systematically to produce explanations, such investigations could be considered useful social research. Second, time-tables would be devised which provided as far as possible for the desired travel patterns. This stage can be seen essentially as problem-solving, though again if problem-solving techniques of more general application were developed in the process this aspect could be useful research. Third, the time-tables themselves would be prescriptive, that is they would prescribe how the railway was to be organized, which in turn is a management and implementation problem. To suggest that much of this work is not research is in no way to deny the high levels of intelligence and application which it needs, nor its social value.

But the outcomes of research, in terms of systems described, whether physical or social, which we have not very accurately referred to as time-tables in research terms, are not prescriptive. They do not say what ought to be, but what is; they are the result of discovery, not of deliberation, though knowledge of what *is* may of course change our ideas of what *should* be (but see the discussion of normative and positivist values in Chapter Three). To call such knowledge merely descriptive however would be to undervalue the quality of thought involved, though description and ordering of information do have an important place in research, and most disciplines go through a necessary descriptive stage before systems and explanations can be inferred.

As suggested above, physical and social patterns can be likened to unknown railway systems, waiting to be discovered. They cannot be discovered by reading time-tables, since usually there are none, but only by painstaking and logical empirical research. This is unlikely to be the work of one person; an individual researcher may achieve no more than the equivalent of knowing what happens at one station for one hour, when perhaps no trains run at all. Although apparently rather negative, even this is useful knowledge of a sort for, by slowly putting it together with that from other stations, eventually the whole system can be known and, above all, explained and understood.

These time-tables, or systems or patterns of events, are what could be called the subject matter of human knowledge. But research is concerned not only with the systems of particular disciplines but with the more general system of knowledge itself, what is sometimes called *epistemology*, below. The nature of knowledge, the fifth element in the definition of research, is the subject of the next section.

The problem of knowledge

Throughout the ages knowledge has been seen as a source of power. If this were true we might expect the world to have been ruled by philosophers. This is clearly not the case. What then is knowledge? Certainly it is not just the random collection of facts which lead to success in a popular quiz-game aptly named 'Trivial Pursuit'. This sort of knowledge might *indicate* an intelligent and well-read mind (for the importance of indicators in research see Chapter Five), or it might not; but it is not the same thing.

The type of knowledge which is sought in research might be better expressed as understanding – which after all only means to know thoroughly. This is summed up by a common phrase, 'To know one's stuff'; that is, to have a deep knowledge of principles and their application. In terms of power it is the sort of knowledge which can be applied to give the ability to conquer, to manufacture, to heal, and to create; to teach and to share; in personal and, especially, academic terms it gives the satisfaction of true insight. It is knowledge of a system of related information.

But let us digress a little from the subject of the content of knowledge – what is known – and think about the essential nature of knowledge itself; that is, how do we know it, and what is meant by knowing? This question of course underlies all research activity, but it also has a particular bearing on the somewhat tense debate about the distinction, if any, between scientific and social-scientific research. More generally it raises questions about the whole direction of civilization at present, in respect, that is, of the balance between material and non-material progress.

If we are to know something, then surely it must be real? So at any rate argued the philosopher A.J. Ayer (1956). Not that knowing it, or thinking that we know it, *makes* it real, but that it must be real *in order* that we can know it. If we think we know something, but that thing is not real, that is, it does not actually exist, then what we have is not knowledge. We may of course *believe* anything we fancy, but that should not, as so often it is, be confused with knowing. Wanting something to be true does not, of itself, make it so. A common error in research is to set out to find what we want to find, and to find it, or think we have (Chapter Three). How do we know what is real?

The system of thought that attempts to investigate ultimate reality is metaphysics. It is not a science in the modern physical sense but rather a part of what remains of philosophy from the Middle Ages. Physics, indeed any modern discipline, assumes the world is real, and gets on with discovering how it appears to work and what are its systems. But metaphysics reminds us that we cannot take reality for granted and has prompted philosophers and scientists over the centuries to develop rigorous arguments and procedures which continually test what we assume to be reality. Just because, in a general way, these procedures have become largely routine, does not mean that we should ignore their fundamental importance or allow them to be overborne by any form of ideology nor even diminished by individual egotism. For they form part of the foundation not only of material progress but of freedom of thought and action.

Mostly we do not go around doubting that the world and ourselves, as part of it, are real. When we get up each morning it looks much as it did the day before; it is consistent. If we kick it around a bit it reacts in a more or less predictable way. Only occasionally does an event occur which makes us wonder if we are dreaming; then tests of reality are needed other than consistency and predictability. The seventeenth-century philosopher and mathematician René Descartes addressed himself to the problem of existence, of reality. He concluded that since he could doubt or question his existence this was proof that he *did* exist; that he existed because he thought, because he was aware, not because he believed he existed but because he doubted it.

This is a start, but only a start. It may demonstrate that a mind exists, but is there existence outside of it? In one sense we can never know and it is best not to enquire too far, not because the question is frivolous but because to pursue it would lead to disorientation and despair. Some philosophers have questioned whether mere physical objects exist when there is no mind there to be aware of their existence. Not that these thinkers are seriously suggesting (are they?) that the objects cease to exist, but they are making the point that we can never know for sure that they do. The object may always be there when we go back to look, other people may tell us that it was there when we were not. But do we know? We think we know that physical objects do not move around of their own volition. If a chair was in a room, and no one has been in, then the chair must still be there. When we find it is not we conclude that someone must have moved it unobserved, for chairs do not vanish into thin air. But there have been and are societies where the second explanation would seem quite plausible, and there are objects whose behaviour is not as predictable as a chair.

If we cannot be sure even that a chair is in a room at any particular time how then can we investigate elusive sub-atomic particles such as the near-legendary quark, or be sure where Charles II was at 12 noon on September 15 in the year 1651, or whether racial prejudice exists in education? How does the individual researcher know that what is observed is real – not imagined, not dreamt, not the product of his or her bias or wish? And how does some other person assess the accuracy and reliability of the first person's work and decide that it does indeed add to the sum of human knowledge?

Researchers do not of course go through an agonizing metaphysical struggle each time they embark on research, though perhaps those atomic physicists, mathematicians and astronomers who work at the boundaries of reality do so. We assume that, subject to appropriate tests, the world of which we are aware is real, and that by the application of rational processes of observation, argument and experimentation we can discover more real things about it. In fact we soon find that apparently straightforward questions and problems to do with the physical world can be extraordinarily difficult to answer in a convincing rational manner, and that some of the most important things in life, such as feelings, may not, for the present at least, be susceptible to strict research at all. We also expect that fellow researchers work with integrity and report truthfully; note that we expect this and do not merely assume it – it is in fact a duty of research.

But the metaphysical struggle did take place and the outcome is now part of a heritage of rational thinking, so that the man or woman in the street may display insight which eluded the best brains of a few centuries ago. Rational thinkers needed first to convince themselves (as did Descartes). Then they needed to convince others. For example, when the metal lead was heated by alchemists in their vain attempts to turn it into gold, it could clearly be seen to lose something in the form of sparks or flame. The problem was that the burnt substance weighed more than the original. Some of the best brains of the past accepted as explanation that the supposed substance lost, called phlogiston, had negative weight (this sounds rather like some modern concepts in economics). In the late eighteenth century Joseph Priestley and Antoine Lavoisier were able to show, by rational experiment, that the increase of weight is caused by the burning substance combining with a portion of the air (familiar now to us as oxygen) though no one had ever seen oxygen (nor have they to this day, except as a few molecules under an electron microscope). Similar work was needed in the nineteenth century to establish the causes of diseases such as cholera. Although the phlogiston theory now seems ridiculous, the capacity for self delusion still exists.

Some limitations of scientific knowledge

Application of rational thought, as expressed through scientific method and experimentation, appeared to be so successful in overcoming superstition and ignorance, in improving material welfare (anyone who questions this may care to imagine having a painful gallstone removed without anaesthetic) and to some extent increasing economic freedom, that the scientific approach came to be seen as the only proper way of thinking, and quantifiable knowledge as the only desirable form of knowledge. Certainly it is very useful and powerful and, indeed, persuasive. There is developing currently however a reaction against science and its methods. In some ways this disillusion is justified, in some not. In so far as science dispels ignorant and harmful superstitions, it is liberating; if it diminishes human and spiritual values, it is harmful; if it brings bodily well-being, it is good; if pollution and destruction, it is bad; if it provides an example of the power of free and rational thought, it is beneficial; if it is dogmatic and exclusive, it is harmful.

In the somewhat contentious matter of the application of scientific method to social questions, and not least because the question of the place of a materialistic science in society is of great importance, it is well to consider briefly what science both is and is not since the protagonists for and the reactionaries against science each tend to overstate its scope and claims. This is a natural tendency, and makes for good academic and journalistic and, even, political fun but it can oversimplify the issues.

First, scientific method owes much to the ideas of thinkers who were not primarily scientists in the modern sense, but philosophers using logical thought processes – men like John Locke at Oxford in the seventeenth century who argued that all knowledge comes from experience rather than from pure thinking. This doctrine is known as empiricism (Chapter Two) and has come to be equated with the narrow idea of experience as scientific experiment, or at least as measurement, but this is not necessarily so. Another influential thinker was John Hume in Edinburgh who, in the eighteenth century, attempted a rational treatment of the relation between cause and effect, or causality.

Second, scientists do not claim that the whole of potential human knowledge is their subject matter. To be dismissed as unscientific is certainly a criticism of a scientist, but not, for example, of a novelist. Certain types of problem and certain subjects are susceptible to scientific investigation: many, so far, are not. Although scientists may give the impression that theirs is the most important subject there is, they are probably no different from others in this respect.

Third, and most significant, the application of scientific method describes and explains the time-tables of the physical world, above; it does not follow that anyone has to use them. Of course, if a scientist feels he knows how to cure a disease he would be remiss *as a citizen* (as would anyone) if he did not try to apply that knowledge; he acts because he is a scientist (and has the concomitant knowledge) but not *as* a scientist. But generally the application of scientific knowledge should be subject also to broader considerations, to what might be called the collective wisdom of our decision-making processes. A crisis of conscience arises for the scientist however when he or she knows that some potential discovery, such as atomic fission, embryo research or genetic mapping, is likely to be abused. By a long tradition, going back to Galileo's battle with the Church and beyond, and including on the way the human mind-centred philosophy of Descartes, the scientist may assert that no restriction should be placed on the development of thought and knowledge. But in doing this, whether right or wrong, he is scarcely more arrogant than is the playwright or author who rejects any censorship.

Indeed the scientist might turn the debate round by arguing that if the development of wisdom and ethical principles (of which his critics seem to claim to be the guardians) had kept pace with the development of scientific knowledge many problems would not arise: if for example education in the humanities and design produced a more satisfactory alternative to materialism (or even indeed a satisfying materialism); if Christianity was more true to its ideals; if Locke's empiricism and belief in the study of human nature was not replaced by ideology or instant political solutions; if Hobbes' warnings about the potential jungle of human society were more heeded; or if John Stuart Mill's distinction between liberty and freedom were applied, for example, to acts of pollution.

Another misunderstanding of science is to suppose that it deals in certainties. By its nature it is implicitly and explicitly constrained by reservations and conditions which popular journalism rarely understands. The most apparently certain edifice of all, Newtonian physics, was undermined by Einstein's theory of relativity which in effect says that nothing is absolute: this idea was revolutionary in art and morals as well as in science. All that scientists claim is that theirs is the best possible understanding of a system for the time being, and until something better is discovered this one appears to work, more or less. We do not always know if the chair is still in the room but we have always assumed it is and this assumption has not yet let us down. Newtonian mechanics still works as an explanation for everyday events within the solar system.

This very brief outline of some aspects of scientific method and knowledge, in the broadest sense, has been included here for two purposes. One is to give some idea of how scientific method, and

rational thinking generally, developed within a world that was largely irrational and non-empirical, and often hostile, and how this
development has not only produced much material well-being but
has also provided powerful ways of thinking and knowing which
have at least some connection with freedom of thought itself. The
second and apparently contradictory purpose is at the same time to
acknowledge, indeed to emphasize, the limitations of the scientific
process even when it is practised with generosity of thought and not
with its inherent perils of narrow-mindedness or dogmatism. If a
balanced view of the strengths and weaknesses of scientific method
can be attained this will greatly ease any consideration of the prob-
lematical issue of its application to social problems which is introduced in the next chapter.

Conclusions

In research work, as in any advanced or specialized activity, terms
are used which have both a broad popular meaning and a precise
restricted one. Linguistically, the word 'research' covers any careful
search or investigation, but among academics it has come to have a
more particular meaning, what may be called advanced research,
which we will simply revert to calling research. It has a number of
characteristics or qualities.

Such research is conducted within a system of knowledge or
understanding, but it should always be probing or testing that
system. It aims towards increasing a common heritage of knowledge, though sometimes it will fail. The increase of knowledge may
be something entirely new and original or, more commonly, it may
consist of checking, testing, expanding and refining ideas which are
themselves still provisional. In particular, research should continually question the nature of knowledge itself, what it is and how it is
known. Each discipline has its own systems of acquiring knowledge
but in fact they all have much in common. The two most familiar
are, broadly, scientific method, as developed in the physical sciences, and the quasi-judicial system traditionally used in historical
study. The principle of English law that a person is innocent until
proved guilty 'beyond reasonable doubt', and even the ordinary citizen's idea of giving the 'benefit of the doubt' in a case, finds a more
formal parallel in the logical scientific argument of the null hypothesis (Chapter Seven). More recent disciplines such as anthropology,

psychology and sociology have largely adapted established systems to their own use although this adaptation is not always acknowledged. What all research disciplines share, or should share, is a common ground of rational thought founded in logical argument and ultimately in Lockian common-sense.

It would be an error however to infer from all this that research method is relevant only to a small number of specialized workers. For at all levels of education, even at primary school, there is a large amount of project work which, even if it is not research in the advanced sense, simulates research and often partially uses research procedures such as social surveys. Although these exercises are thought of as being of a practical nature they are, or should be, to some extent at least, exercises in thinking, and it would be well if this was treated explicitly as part of an intellectual heritage. At degree level, both under-graduate and post-graduate, quite substantial investigations are carried out which simulate research procedures, are intended as training in research and in fact are often useful small pieces of research. Research degrees of course, by definition, must display the characteristics of advanced research.

At the popular level, research affects so much of our lives that any educated, indeed thinking, person needs a knowledge of its procedures. We are subject to so much information in the newspapers and from television and radio about the latest discoveries, latest environmental crises, opinion polls, new products and so on that sensible decisions, opinions even, can only be formed if we understand something of the intellectual, as distinct from merely technical, processes involved.

CHECK LIST : Chapter One

You should know and understand:

- the full definition of research
- the significance of each of the terms in this definition
- the need for research to take place within a system of ideas
- the criteria for 'useful' research
- the distinction between discovering new knowledge and collecting existing information
- the idea of research as providing explanation
- the idea of research as discovery of patterns or systems
- the distinction between knowledge and belief
- the limitations of scientific knowledge
- the need for a critical attitude to information in everyday life

Further reading

Ayer, A.J., 1956, *The problem of knowledge*, Penguin, Harmondsworth.

Barzun, J. and Graff, F., 1985 [1957], *The modern researcher: the classic manual on all aspects of research and writing*, 4th edn, Harcourt Brace Jovanovich, New York, Parts I and II.

Hansen, N.R., 1965, *Patterns of discovery*, Cambridge University Press, Cambridge.

Hobbes, T., 1968 [1651], *Leviathan* (ed. C. Macpherson), Pelican, Harmondsworth.

Leedy, P.D., 1980, *Practical research: planning and design*, 2nd edn, Macmillan, New York, pp.1–40.

Losee, J., 1993, *A Historical Introduction to the Philosophy of Science*, Oxford University Press, Oxford.

McCrone, J., 1993, *The myth of irrationality: the science of the mind from Plato to Star Trek*, Macmillan, London.

Murdoch, I., 1992, *Metaphysics as a guide to morals*, Chatto & Windus, London.

Walker, K., 1950, *Meaning and purpose*, Pelican, Harmondsworth.

Wilson, S., 1973, *Truth*, Arts: third level course, problems of philosophy, Units 9–10, The Open University, Milton Keynes.

2
ELEMENTS OF SCIENTIFIC METHOD

'The human understanding when it has once adopted an opinion draws all things else to support and agree with it. And though there be a greater number and weight of instances to be found on the other side, yet these it either neglects and despises, or else by some distinction sets aside and rejects; in order that by this great and pernicious predetermination the authority of its former conclusions may remain inviolate.'
(Francis Bacon, *Novum organum*, 1620, aphorism xlvi)

A student may 'know' that he or she is going to fail the big Finals examination. The tutor, on the other hand, drawing on long experience that if a student of average ability does a reasonable amount of work he or she will pass, and being acquainted with the student's record, predicts with a high degree of probability that the student will pass. They can scarcely both be right, and the odds are in favour of the tutor. The student's assessment of the future has been affected by deep-seated feelings of inadequacy, personal fear of the unknown outweighing rational thought. Or maybe there is a primitive caution that premature pride, what the Ancient Greeks knew as *hubris*, might somehow invite disaster from the gods. Thus the student's 'knowledge' in this case can, to a large extent, be discounted since it has been distorted by personal emotion and is based on inadequate experience (though it could be a self-fulfilling prediction if fear leads to breakdown). An average tutor, we may assume, is largely unaffected by emotion in this situation, other perhaps than by a desire to appear reassuring. Even so, he or she cannot predict the future with 100 per cent certainty.

There are a number of ideas contained here which deserve to be examined in outline at this stage. The student is being *subjective* in that personal feelings are being allowed, however understandably, to influence rational thought. The tutor, though making an assessment as an individual, is nevertheless being *objective* by reasoning from experience and not being influenced by personal considerations, and it is therefore probable that any other rational person with the same information would reach the same conclusion.

Strictly, although we may try to predict it, we cannot know the future. This would be to assume that the future will operate exactly according to the same relationships and conditions as the past. However much experience may lead us to expect this, it is, ultimately, a matter of trust or belief. The fact that the sun has unfailingly risen on a million consecutive mornings does not prove that it will do so tomorrow. Indeed it is thought that one day even the sun will die and become a red dwarf. On the whole though, the idea that the future will operate according to the same rules as the past seems more likely to be true for physical events, such as sunrise and eclipses, than for biological ones such as the course of a disease, and is perhaps even less certain for social or economic events, as in the development of an economic recession.

Considerations of why social events are less certainly predictable than physical ones stand at the heart of the debate about the application of scientific method to social questions. One explanation is that human beings are much more variable than are atoms and molecules, being made up of millions of these put together in a uniquely complex way. Another reason is that mere molecules are not influenced in their response by reading a newspaper or by what someone said in a pub. It is easier, too, in the case of physical objects, to ensure that the act of observation does not itself change the behaviour which is being observed, a process known in the social sciences as the Hawthorne effect. While the nature of purely physical objects may change they are not generally so rapidly adaptable nor indeed so idiosyncratic or even mobile as humans. There is, also, an ethical distaste for studying people as though they were physical objects rather than individuals, and when we come to contemplate the control of human behaviour for experimental reasons (p.25) there may be practical and even moral objections.

Where objections to the scientific study of social events are not over-riding there can be distinct advantages to human welfare in studying people as a population of objects rather than as individuals. In this way patterns of events may become clear and provide beneficial knowledge. Such appears to be the case, still under investigation, of the use of the anti-breast-cancer drug tamoxifen (Chapter Seven). This is not to deny however the value of individual and sympathetic counselling and the study of a sufferer's needs and lifestyle.

Part of the difference between prediction of the future of human behaviour as opposed to that of inanimate objects is that the latter are simply more consistent. Since we can predict that, in normal circumstances, a stone released a few metres above the earth's surface will always fall to the ground we can also predict that this will be true for any *one* stone. We do not need to know anything about it except that it is a stone. We could predict with almost equal certainty that 60 per cent, say, of heavy smokers will die of lung cancer; the difference is that we cannot say, in the present state of knowledge, which particular individuals will succumb. This does not, however, mean that the information is without value.

A tutor can predict with some confidence that a student will pass Finals because the academic system is so arranged that students who are unlikely to pass are normally weeded out at early stages. Even so, the tutor makes certain assumptions: that the examination has not been made more difficult, that the student's mental and physical condition is unchanged, and that earlier results are not aberrant. Most statements of fact involve such conditions and assumptions but often these are not stated because they are so constant. We do not distinguish between past experience and future prediction when we say stones fall to the earth since it is such a well-attested phenomenon. What we are really saying is that our experience has been that stones invariably fall to the earth when dropped and we therefore predict that, assuming the somewhat mysterious force of gravity continues to act and that there is no other stronger force acting on the stone, and that there is nothing intervening, a stone will fall. This is strictly an empirical statement: that is, it is based on experience; it does not result from theoretical reasoning nor is it subjectively influenced by a consideration of the location of one's toes. That there are other ways of reasoning about this same phenomenon will be discussed later.

A tutor might wish to be more precise and attempt to predict the class of degree which a student will obtain. This is certainly what is of most interest to the students themselves who have reached this stage of their studies. The prediction might be based on the student's academic record, but also on factors such as temperament, family background, type of education, age, and so on. Essentially what is being sought is a relationship between these factors and the student's ultimate performance. But the only way this can be done is by looking back at *other* students' records and achievements to see if there is a reasonably consistent pattern or relationship which might be used for prediction. The usual procedure would be to develop a mathematical equation, often called a *model* (see Chapter Seven), using the simple computer programs now available. Such a model would, ideally, both contain all the important figures or variables and express the nature of the relationship (if any) between them.

A model relationship can be tested and refined, or calibrated, by gathering information or data on students who are about to take their Finals, predicting the results and then checking the actual results against the predictions. This form of experimentation is fairly neutral but it would be possible to interfere actively in the students' progress by varying, say, the method of teaching or the subjects covered to see what the result might be, or even to treat different batches of students differently to obtain a wider range of evidence.

Ethical questions arise here. At a general level, the idea of forecasting an individual's performance from past records might seem to reduce that individual's status to a mere bundle of statistics. It could appear to deprive the individual of a sense of free-will and, perhaps, of motivation. Though in a sense it is doing no more than organizing or structuring the tutor's intuitive interpretation of experience, it *seems* to be more impersonal. Further, such apparent pre-knowledge might influence other people's attitudes to an individual, though scientists could argue that that is not an argument for rejecting scientific knowledge but a matter of maturity, values and judgement which lie largely outside the realms of science. Objections become more serious at the more specific level of interfering with a student's education for experimental purposes in a way that could be detrimental. This is the dilemma faced by medical research. A further, scientific, objection is that some factors which influence the results cannot readily be quantified, or be measured at all, in such a way as to be incorporated in a mathematical prediction. Some scientists might choose to ignore items such as motivation, persistence or determination as not being capable of measurement; others might include rather crude indicators of these qualities. In fact, for these sorts of reasons, quantitative predictions of student performance have not proved to be very accurate. The tutor, however, will form intuitive judgements about the extent and effect of these intangible qualities, and these judgements may in fact be reasonably accurate.

It is a mistake to take extreme positions on scientific and non-scientific methods. If more was known about the stone – its mass, shape, height above the earth – we could predict not merely its fall but the likely effect of its impact. Recent developments in gene mapping, unimaginable a few decades ago, mean that it may in fact be possible to predict which individual heavy smokers have the potential to contract lung cancer. A scientist might argue that if everything was known about a person we could predict his or her future. While it seems unlikely that we could know and *measure* everything about a person's character, it would be wrong to assume that what we cannot measure is unimportant or, alternatively, that we can measure nothing. Either way the non-scientist may see scientific investigation of social affairs as a threat to human value and individual worth. But this would be to deny the potential of much useful investigation. *The most important thing is always to be clear about the assumptions, conditions and limitations within which any investigation, scientific or social, is taking place.*

So far we have noted some of the difficulties and objections involved in applying scientific research to the social activities of human beings: their variability, their complexity and their changeability as social entities. There are too the problems of measuring the many attributes of personality and character. Experimentally there are the practical problems of controlling human behaviour, even temporarily, so that consistent observation can take place. And last, there are the ethical and human problems of experiments with personal behaviour, and of reducing individuals to mere statistics or stereotypes. On the other hand scientific research has much to offer human welfare. Theoretical development in science has been aimed at overcoming some of the problems of knowledge discussed in Chapter One (what is knowledge, how do we know it?) and also the related question of how far subjective feelings may influence what we think of as knowledge. In the next section the nature of scientific methods of acquiring knowledge is examined.

What is science?

Science means, literally, knowledge. But it is knowledge which has been critically examined, rigorously tested and ordered into a system of ideas. A science implies a method of assessing and understanding knowledge. The natural sciences include the physical sciences which deal with non-living substances, the biological sciences which are the study of living things, and medicine in so far as it studies humans as biological systems. It was these natural sciences in particular which were able to develop rigorous and objective methods for the acquisition of new knowledge which would be of universal application in the development of modern civilization. While other disciplines were not necessarily less rigorous or less logical in their discourse, science has come to be identified particularly with both innovation and experimentation. Thus the term science has become almost invariably identified with natural science. It is meaningful to answer, in a general way, the question, 'What is biology?' with, 'It is a science,' for this produces an image of a definitive type of activity.

While it is perfectly proper to speak of political science or the science of economics, or to describe sociology as the science of men and women as social beings, the use of the term science in this way does not have the same connotations as in the case of the physical sciences. There are those who feel, as did Sir Keith Joseph, a former Minister of Education and Science, that the so-called social sciences should operate more as the physical sciences do. Others take the view that this is not only impossible, partly because of the larger numbers of variables involved (see Chapter Six), but also undesirable for the sorts of reasons outlined above. What then is the definitive nature of the natural sciences and what, if anything, might be learned from them?

First it may be said that the thought processes of the natural sciences are by no means exclusive to them but that they are applied – perhaps more easily can be applied – more rigorously, exclusively and consistently here than elsewhere. Second, while the principles of scientific method can be stated quite simply, they rest, like all great ideas, on a considerable foundation of original thought which is necessary to a proper understanding of their operation.

Accordingly, some of what may be called the components, or elements, or principles of scientific method will be examined first in outline here with brief comment on their relative usefulness and on their applicability to the natural or social sciences. The essence of scientific method will then be explained in Chapter Three and the nature and use of these components will be treated further and in more detail there.

Experiment

Science is seen above all as experimental. This conjures up images of dotty men in white coats producing explosions in laboratories. But experimentation is not essentially a physical activity, though in practice it usually is. An experiment is anything done to test an idea, or theory, or to discover something unknown. (In passing, it must be said that the use of the term theory in this sense, for what is in fact a hypothesis, is not universal, see Chapter Three.) The important idea here is that of testing. We all know how it is possible to persuade ourselves that something must be true, or something will work, either because we want it to or perhaps simply because there is an untested, if plausible, assumption somewhere in our line of reasoning. This determination, faith even, is a valuable attribute of the human spirit in achievement and healing, but scientists at least do not accept that it can over-rule the forces of impersonal nature. It may, in individual cases, appear to change the actions of human nature but whether it can change, other than temporarily, the aggregate behaviour of men or women as social beings is an open question. Belief may be what drives an individual scientist, against all the odds, to persist in experimentation and invention. But he or she will not blindly persist in the construction of theoretical systems in isolation from the real world of experience, but will be continual testing the ideas involved, even if failure is frequently the result.

It is of course possible, to some extent, to test ideas with other ideas; a scientist will do this naturally before incurring the trouble and expense of physical experiment. A mathematician can scarcely test in any other way but by the axioms, accepted theorems and logic of his discipline; if his equation requires two plus two to equal five, so to speak, he knows he is wrong. But the ultimate test is in what we think of as the real world. An architectural historian may test the idea that Charles Barry, part-architect of the House of Commons, was much influenced by his extensive travels in the Middle East. Do Egyptian forms appear in his work? If so, were they there before his travels? Are they truly Egyptian? What did Barry himself say, or his friends? What do his travel sketches show? The idea has to be tested against the evidence. But while a historian discovers his evidence (but could misinterpret it) the natural scientist in his experiments makes his own evidence, which is why he must be so rigorous if he is to avoid self-delusion or even dishonesty. One of the problems of social and economic investigation is that evidence may be hard to define and is often inconclusive. Logical problems associated with testing and the assessment of evidence will be examined in more detail in Chapter Three.

Measurement

A second important activity of science is that of measurement, or more generally of description and identification. This is essential if evidence is to be acquired. Mere description is often regarded as a lower form of activity than actual experimentation but it is the foundation of knowledge and, particularly in the activity of classification, has its own mental skills and discipline. If a scientist is studying the effects of whaling on the world population of minke whales he has to know a minke whale when he sees one, not mistake it for some other species. Further, scientists all over the world have to agree what is a minke whale. Chemists all over the world must know that what, for example, they call potassium cyanide is always the same thing.

The theories of evolution or of stratigraphy could not develop until enough scientific descriptions of the varieties of animals and plants or of rocks were available for general comparisons to be made. If modern scientists had followed the practice of medieval chroniclers and artists and sat indoors drawing mythical monsters which no one had ever seen, or painting imaginary land forms, no progress in these sciences would have been possible. In a sense the acts of exploration and accurate observation from nature were experimental – they were testing experience of the real world against myth, and discovering new knowledge.

Unbiased and unambiguous observation and description are important activities in scientific training; they are perhaps more difficult to achieve in social studies, and can result in simplified stereotypes. Physical scientists attempt to use natural relationships as an objective basis for classification that is free from personal values. In the social sciences, natural groups, if they exist at all, are less clearly defined; it is more difficult to avoid bias in the selection of categories used for recording causes and effects and thus possibly influencing the apparent results (Chapter Four). It is important, as with other concepts (below), that classification systems and categories have as much reality and common acceptance as possible.

An important aid to objective description and reporting is, of course, measurement. While not absolutely necessary for experimentation in the broader sense, measurement has been essential for the development of modern natural sciences; the famous American scientist Clark Maxwell asserted that science *is* measurement. Again, the properties of electro-magnetism, Maxwell's particular field, are in some ways much easier to measure than ill-defined social concepts such as aggression, privacy, vandalism or happiness.

Relation

Observation, experimentation and more observation are necessary to discover relationships. The meaning of this word has been distorted in recent years to express what was formerly dignified by the term common-law marriage. Essentially it means the state and mode of being related or connected, one thing with another; are they related and how? This is the most important sort of scientific knowledge, and possibly of that of other disciplines too. Why is this so?

It is understanding of the way one thing is related to another which makes knowledge powerful. If we know the causes of disease maybe we can remove them; if we know the effect of treatment perhaps we can produce a cure. If we know the relationship between low barometrical pressure and bad weather we can predict and prepare for it. If – a big if – we know the causes of economic depression or of poverty maybe we can avoid these social ills. A knowledge of relationships therefore gives us not only understanding but, potentially, the power both to *control* and *predict*. It is a mistake, however, to assume that all observed relationships, or correlations, are causal (Chapter Seven).

Practically all useful knowledge can be thought of in terms of relationships. When Newton discovered gravity he did not come upon it as an isolated entity, like a rare flower in a jungle. When, apocryphally perhaps, the apple fell on his head he reasoned that this event was connected or related to some other phenomenon, that it indicated the existence of something else. Experiment showed that physical objects have a mutual and invisible force of attraction one for the other – which is why stones fall to earth. Even relationships which have no effect on life or death, good or ill, can add greatly to the interest of our surroundings; so Barry's early nineteenth-century tour of the mystic East apparently finds expression in an obscure Midlands church design (All Saints, Stand, Prestwich). Much work in the social sciences however could be seen as essentially description, albeit with an impressive statistical base; explanation is often little more than speculation based on prevailing ideologies of left or right which scarcely even merit being called hypotheses (Chapter Three). So, for example, practitioners of town planning and architecture have engaged in large scale and disruptive social change with very little theoretical, let alone empirical, base; though it could be said that what passed for theory in this case far outweighed experience or even common sense. The idea of common sense, as will be seen, is not unrelated to that of experimentation.

Concepts

If we are to investigate relationships between things it is important to ask, 'What sort of things?' and even, 'What is a thing?' This apparently curious philosophical question has most important implications for research and, again, is perhaps more difficult to answer for the social sciences than for the natural sciences. A thing is whatever can exist independently in space and time, as opposed to an idea which requires one or more minds in which to exist. Physical objects are most obviously things, but so are events, actions and the products of minds when expressed externally as in writing or speech. A concept on the other hand, a term much used in research work, is formed or imagined or thought in the mind. The two, thing and concept, can be seen to be related as follows: a piece of furniture, table A, is a separate thing from table B and indeed from all other tables. We know this since if table A were to be taken away or destroyed table B remains itself. But in the mind we form a concept, 'table', which links all forms and designs of tables. If we are looking for a table to use it is probably a matter of indifference whether we use table A or table B. A concept is thus a general notion of a thing formed in the mind. But if we use a box or a stone as a table, does it become a table? In our minds, in a sense, it does; in another sense the idea is ridiculous. It is necessary to be very wary about the possibility of commuting one concept into another. The validity, or soundness, of the general notions or concepts used in research into relationships is crucial to the question of the universality or general application of the results.

Today we do not follow medieval philosophers in their theoretical concern about whether *universals* exist only in the mind, or in reality, or perhaps not at all. But for practical purposes the validity or soundness, or otherwise, of the *universal argument* is very important; if we discover something about a thing, or a few things, or a sample of things, does the discovery apply universally to all other similar things which we include in the same concept? Conversely, when we discover a new thing, into which concept or class does it fit? When an archaeologist discovers a flat stone structure, is it simply a crude domestic table, or is it perhaps a sacrificial altar? With suitable training we may indisputably recognize a minke whale or potassium cyanide. But how universal is human behaviour? Is what one researcher understands by stress or by aggression the same thing as that to which another researcher gives the same name? How do we distinguish ambition from selfishness?

This problem of the universality or generalization of scientific work is today seen not so much as a theoretical or, rather, a philosophical problem but as a practical one. It is dealt with in two ways. First, by the careful *classification* or sub-division of things into more or less homogeneous, distinct and recognizable categories, classes or concepts. This is done both by careful *description* and by *standardized tests* for identity. In a general way these two procedures apply equally to things as diverse as a simple chemical substance or a complex personality trait such as introversion or depression. But clearly the processes are likely to be less exact when dealing with human attributes. Second, especially where there is considerable variability within a class of things, care is taken to obtain *representative samples* for experimentation. Even with relatively simple things like chemicals, impurities may vary from batch to batch. The refinement of concepts for the purpose of exploring relationships is discussed further in Chapter Three under hypothesis formulation. Procedures for sampling are examined in Chapter Six.

Universality of the concepts used is essential to what is called the *external validity* of an experiment or investigation. While an experiment may be conducted perfectly rigorously within itself (that is it has *internal validity*), it has external validity only if the results can be applied to other similar, but external, situations. It is clearly important that we are talking about the same concepts, minke whales, not porpoises, tables not altars, myalgic encephalomyelitis, not chronic fatigue syndrome. This is one of the reasons why accurate reporting and description of experiments is so important, not just of the concepts under investigation but of all those other things or concepts which make up the background or conditions under which the experiment has been conducted. Thus a very close fit, or correlation, may be obtained between measurements of a group of students' records and personality traits and the students' final degree results. But will the equation apply to other groups of students, or to students in other institutions? Do examinations having the same

'And it also cuts grass, sir'

It is necessary to be very careful about the possibility of commuting one concept into another.

Cartoon: © The Telegraph plc, London/MATT, 1993

subject title examine in fact the same things? Are measures of personality traits used for one group appropriate for another group? The external validity of experiments in the more controlled natural sciences is usually greater than that of investigation in the social sciences. On the other hand, experiments performed consistently in the uniform conditions of laboratories *in vitro* – literally 'in the glass (test tube)' – may not work in the more varied conditions of real life, *in vivo*. Most social investigations can, of course, only be performed *in vivo*. This matter of experimental validity is discussed further in Chapter Five.

Cause and effect

So far we have, for the sake of argument, somewhat uncritically referred to the relationship known as cause and effect as though it could be taken for granted. Philosophically this is far from the case, though in practice it often is. Nevertheless, a consideration of some of the philosophical problems associated with *causality*, that is the general relation of cause and effect, provides a caution against too readily assigning simple causes to events.

Joseph Hume, the amiable eighteenth-century Scots philosopher and historian, gave a great deal of thought to the nature of cause and effect (Hume, 1896 [1739]). How could this relationship be recognized? Does it indeed exist, or do things just happen? Hume clearly intimates his bafflement that such an important relationship could be recognized in only two ways: that the cause must come before the effect, and that cause and effect should exist together or in contiguity – though he did admit of distant causes working remotely through a chain of cause and effect. He could think of only one other characteristic, and that was that cause and effect should be observed together on successive occasions; that is, the evidence is to be based on experience of repetition. Hume appears almost apologetic about advancing this last proposition since he was a good enough thinker for his time to know that the fact that something has occurred on several occasions is in itself no logical guarantee that the same thing will occur in the future. As to whether cause and effect relations do in fact exist generally, Hume can only assert that it is self-evident that everything which exists must have a cause.

Despite being expressed in elegant language Hume's observations on cause and effect scarcely get us beyond the Dark Ages.

While his three tests do apply to real causes and may eliminate some errors they can apply equally to many false causes too. Unless tempered with a liberal dose of common sense they do not eliminate false argument or even superstition. The ways in which modern scientific philosophers attempt to identify cause and effect, the essence of scientific method, will be examined in Chapter Three. But before leaving the discussion of causality here it will be useful to look briefly at some ideas of John Stuart Mill.

Mill was a noted nineteenth-century economist and philosopher. Drawing on the work of others, such as Hume, he tried to develop logical rules to determine the cause of any event. Accepting that there might be a number of conditions surrounding an event or effect, he argued that the true cause might be found by a process of elimination. In order to do this it was necessary first to experience a number of occurrences of the effect and to list possible causes. Then, he argued that: (1) any condition which was not present when the effect occurred could not be a cause and, conversely, (2) any condition which was present when the effect did *not* occur could not be a cause. This latter proposition assumes that the existence of a cause is sufficient for the corresponding effect to occur. At first sight this all sounds very reasonable or plausible, but is in fact wrong.

Unfortunately, as we now understand, Mill's last assumption was incorrect (Trustead, 1979); as also was the implication that an effect has only one cause. Today we accept that for an effect to occur may require a number of causes or conditions to be present. (In this context cause means the same as condition.) Causes are rarely simple, and if they appear to be so it is usually because we take many of them for granted. Further, two types of cause may be distinguished: necessary and sufficient. A *necessary cause* is a condition which must be present for an effect to occur but is not in itself sufficient to precipitate that effect. Thus, contrary to what Mill thought, an essential or necessary cause may be present without the relevant effect taking place. A *sufficient cause* on the other hand is one which, if the necessary conditions are in place, is sufficient to bring about the effect. This cause may also be present without the relevant effect if the necessary cause is not present too. Furthermore, since any one of a number of different sufficient causes may alone bring about the effect, the effect may occur when a particular sufficient and effective cause is absent, again contrary to Mill's ideas. Thus, two sufficient causes for a boulder to roll down a mountain may be either that someone levers it out of place or that natural erosion undermines it. We tend to forget that a necessary condition or cause would be that the boulder was on the mountain in the first place, whether placed by human or natural agency; we assume also that the condition of gravity is present.

Hume and Mill were great thinkers. Yet today the man or woman in the street, having acquired something of our intellectual heritage, may exhibit an understanding of cause and effect as good as or better than theirs. When someone points out that the (sufficient) conditions are in place for an event to surely happen – 'Not necessarily,' is the reply.

In 1988 there occurred the tragic capsize of the Channel ferry *The Herald of Free Enterprise*. This event furnishes a whole catalogue of causes. At the purely physical level the ferry capsized because there was 'free' water sluicing around inside and upsetting the equilibrium of the vessel. The water was in the boat because (a) the bow doors were open and (b) the vessel put to sea in that condition. The bow doors were open because the man responsible for closing them was asleep. He was asleep because no one woke him up. The vessel was put to sea in that condition because the captain did not check whether or not the doors were closed. He could fail to do this because there was no automatic warning about the doors built into the controls. This was because the managers had refused to fit one. The design of the boat was unstable because normal rules of naval design had been suspended to enable quicker movement of cars. This was to reduce turnround time at the port because ferry operation is a competitive business and because holidaymakers want the quickest possible crossing. We could go further and say the loss of life occurred because of management attitudes reflected in the refusal to listen to a subordinate's advice, or to save money. We could blame the English class system or the free enterprise capitalist economy (forgetting that disasters occur in other political systems also) or the impatience of holidaymakers. It is clear that while an individual may be blamed for not fulfilling his particular role here, it is too easy to say that that was *the* cause. At the level of boat operation we could say that the absence of an automatic warning system was a necessary cause; with such a system in place the accident could not have happened. Given this necessary cause, or condition, the failure to close the door and the failure to check were, together, sufficient causes. If such a relatively straightforward event can have such a complex of causes (and the account here is much simplified) it seems obvious that we cannot expect to find simple causes for complicated social phenomena.

Objectivity

Philosophy and grammar have a common interest in meaning. Take for example the apparently simple statement, 'The tourist saw the smooth grey back of a hippopotamus in the river.' Grammatically and philosophically we take the tourist as the subject of this statement, the one who does the seeing. The hippopotamus is the object, the thing seen. Did the tourist in fact see a hippopotamus? Maybe the tourist was simply in error, short-sighted, or colour blind, or too far away. Perhaps he could not distinguish a hippopotamus from a mud-bank. Or perhaps he was biased, maybe he wanted to boast he had seen a hippo; or maybe he was afraid of hippos and hoped that what he saw was really a mud-bank after all. Maybe he was expecting to see a hippo, and so he saw one which was in fact a mud-bank; or he was not expecting to see a hippo and so saw a mud-bank which in fact was a hippo. Does the statement mean that the tourist *said* he had seen a hippo or that someone else had told him that what he thought he saw as a mud-bank was actually a hippo?

While all these dubious observations are going on we assume that the object, whether mud-bank or hippopotamus, remains just that. The observer, the subject, was we say being subjective; what he believed he saw was determined by his own mind and consciousness, or by his own tastes or views or prejudice. Meanwhile the object was, well, objective – that is external to the mind, real, existing in nature in contrast with what is ideal or exists only in the mind. This property of being real we can transfer to the observer's judgement if he is being impartial, detached, realistic, not allowing his observation or judgement to be influenced by prejudice or personal taste; we say he is being objective, or that the observation is objective.

Natural sciences make much claim to being objective. Clearly, if we wish to discover general truths about the physical world we cannot use observers who are afraid to discover a hippopotamus or ashamed to have discovered only a mud-bank, who exaggerate danger to justify public expenditure or, conversely, who play down

Philosophy and grammar have a common interest in meaning.

risks to avoid spending money. These latter may be legitimate activities of politics or of business but they are not science.

Scientists attempt to be objective in two main ways. We say attempt since it is not clear that complete objectivity is always, or indeed ever, attainable. First, great care is taken to observe, identify and measure, as outlined above. This is aided by corroboration where possible, whether by other observers or by mechanical means such as photographs. Obviously such corroboration is not infallible. The issue is rarely one of dishonesty, but of realistically acknowledging that observation may be in error, and that different individual accounts of an event may in all honesty vary, particularly so in the case of social conditions, opinions or attitudes. It may simply be very difficult in some situations to observe objectively. The second main way in which scientists try to be objective is in the logical treatment of procedures used to discover and define relationships (Chapter Three).

To avoid any confusion it may be pointed out that, in actual experimental situations, use of the terms subject and object is different from that set out above. A person or persons who are used for an experiment are known as the subject or subjects of the experiment, and not as the objects of the experimenter (though in a sense they are), since it is their actions or reactions as subjects which are to be observed. The experimenter is, theoretically at least, a neutral observer. The term object, on the other hand, is often used in the sense of the aim or purpose of the experiment.

Empiricism

An outline of the elements of scientific method would scarcely be complete without mention of the idea of empiricism itself which runs through all that has been said here so far. In philosophy, empiricism is defined as a system of thought which regards experience as the only source of knowledge. This is not at all to deny the value of thought. The conception of molecules or of genes, years before either had been seen, was a triumph of scientific thought and indeed of imagination. To predict the existence of the planets, Neptune and Pluto, from their gravitational influence on the movement of other planets, before telescopes were powerful enough for either to be seen, was similarly remarkable. These mental achievements were, however, initiated by observation and subsequently tested in the same way.

Though the essential idea of empiricism, above, had been put forward by Sir Francis Bacon as early as 1606, it is particularly associated with the work of John Locke who taught at Oxford towards the end of the seventeenth century. The noted philosopher, Sir Isaiah Berlin, says of him that he is the father of the central philosophical and political tradition of the Western World: a substantial claim. Locke based his work on normal powers of empirical observation, on trial and commonsense judgement and may, as Berlin suggests, almost be said to have invented the notion of common-sense (Berlin, 1956). Locke encouraged man only to study his own nature, not perhaps merely as an individual but as a species. His call for self-awareness is not for self-indulgent introspection but for honest examination of our own attitudes in relation to the world and our fellows to reach a better understanding of common human values in all their complexity. Locke was a *pragmatist* rather than a theoretician: that is, he saw practical consequences as the test of truth. It is unlikely that he would have endorsed theoretical systems which did not take account of human nature, and, like Mill, he would have considered it improper to tell people what they should think or believe. The questioning, experimenting, doubting, even 'cussed' nature of Western society which has led to its relative technical and political progress has roots here.

Empiricism, then, can be seen, in a sense, as being the opposite of subjectivity, and closely allied to objectivity. However, an emphasis on experience as opposed to pure thought has sometimes come to mean experience which is devoid of thought altogether, at least in the form of value judgements. So-called scientific proof is sought, empirical 'facts' are called for, independent of feelings or, even, informed judgement. Emotion is suspect since it brings into doubt the validity of any findings. The use of numbers, or quantification, is often seen today as the only way of being truly empirical or objective, indeed the terms are sometimes seen, wrongly, as being synonymous. But this is to stray some way from the original meaning. Numbers may in any case be selected and interpreted subjectively; where they are produced as estimates it may be difficult for even the

'Do you have the feeling that other people are answering more sex surveys than you?'

An objective judgement is one made by testing in all ways possible one's subjective impressions.

Cartoon: © The Telegraph plc, London, 1993

most honest worker to avoid bias, or they can simply be wrong. The essence of objectivity or empirical evidence lies in the testing of ideas against experience, and though measurement is an excellent and indeed desirable way of doing this it is not the only way. A simple historical example concerning the architect Charles Barry has been outlined above.

Two American historians, Barzun and Graff, have attempted to put the genie of subjectivity back firmly into the bottle, in the individual mind of the first person singular, the subject, where etymologically he belongs. If, they ask, an individual looking at the night sky perceived an image of the moon on his brain, how can he know that the moon is real, whether it has an existence outside his subjective impression? The most usual test is to ask someone else if he or she can see it also. The existence of the moon is so well objectively attested that it is taken for granted. But what about a pink elephant or a flying saucer – or a hippopotamus? A natural reaction is to say, 'Is it real, can you see it too?' and then, can other people see it? Thus Barzun and Graff (1985 [1957]) state that an objective judgement is made every time a capable mind attends to the evidence before it, and that an objective judgement is one made by testing in all possible ways one's subjective impression. The possible tests include corroboration, confirmation – subject always to the rules of logic – and falsification (Chapter Three), experience of human nature, probability (Chapter Seven) and so on. If quantitative tests can be applied, then they should be; but these are not essential to objectivity which is a matter of competence and intellectual rigour, of accuracy, reliability and validity, and not necessarily of quantification.

Quantitative and qualitative methods

Qualitative and quantitative methods of enquiry each have advantages and drawbacks. While some disciplines have come to be associated particularly with one or other of these approaches, both find a place in most fields of study. *To qualify* is to ascribe a quality, or to describe a thing. The study of literature, for example, could be seen as largely qualitative. Quantity, however, is an amount that can be counted or measured. *To quantify* is used in the sense of to ascribe a quantity to a thing, and the process is known as quantification. Recently a quantitative element has crept into literary studies where computer analysis of word frequency, or even of style, has been used as evidence in cases of disputed authorship (did Shakespeare write all the plays attributed to him?). Chemistry, in contrast to literature, appears to be a quantitative subject, involving much weighing and measuring. But qualitative analysis in chemistry is just that, determining the nature or qualities of components rather than their relative (or quantitative) proportions. Qualitative methods, however, should not be seen as mere description. Though numerical procedures are not essentially involved, logical testing and argument are just as important in, for example, history and law, or the qualitative parts of geography, as in more quantitative disciplines. Quantitative methods generally have developed further to include not merely counting and measuring but also the powerful analytical procedures of statistics and many other techniques such as mathematical modelling and linear programming.

So far, so good; qualitative and quantitative methods can be seen as complementary, with different emphases in different disciplines, but sharing a heritage of logical thought and empiricism. Unfortunately, as in Swift's satirical Kingdom of Brobdignag where the end on which one chose to crack an egg became a matter of political significance, these two approaches have become associated with other differences in social and academic attitudes and values. In the 1970s geographers seemed about to tear their discipline apart in a heated debate over quantitative as against qualitative methods. These differences can become particularly acute when the investigations, whether medical, sociological, psychological or political, involve human beings. It has been seen in this chapter how certain elements appear to be necessary to build up rational, universal and objective knowledge; these elements include measurement, a logical analysis of cause and effect relations, an empirical or experimental approach, testing and objectivity. It has also been seen that there are problems and limitations in the application of all these principles in any ideal way, especially where investigations about people are concerned.

It is of course possible, indeed it is very common in research, to investigate qualitative characteristics in a quantitative manner. this may be done by using arithmetical *measurement* of a quality, such as height. However, quantitative research is particularly characterised by the *counting* of the occurrences or frequencies of qualities, or by determination of their mean values for numbers of individuals. It will be seen that statistical techniques, in addition to usefully summarizing and comparing quantitative information, also introduce a further element of objectivity when properly applied. The quality being investigated does not necessarily have to be measurable in the arithmetical sense (though, if it is, experimentation and analysis can be more rigorous). Some examples are: the frequency of black swans in a swan population; the proportion of voters who say they would support the ecology party; the proportion of potential suicides in the unemployed population. The essential thing is to be able to identify the presence or absence of a quality in individuals, so that they can be counted, either by direct observation or by the use of various indicators. The scientists' philosophical aim of universal knowledge, and the needs of mass societies for prediction and organisation both require the quantitative description of populations and their relationships rather than of the qualities of individuals.

Following the sorts of criticism already outlined above (p.25) of this quantitative or scientific method, a number of social investigators have chosen to emphasise the so-called qualitative method of research. This seeks a more intimate acquaintance with the feelings, motivations and qualities of a few individuals, using, for example, ethnographic techniques, or series of long unstructured interviews which would be too expensive to apply to large populations. The aim has been expressed (Bryman, 1988) as an attempt to see and understand situations as they are seen by the individuals being studied. It may be that 'qualitative' is not the best term for making this distinction since, as has been seen, all research is essentially about qualities.

Extreme positions are sometimes taken on the merits of qualitative and quantitative research. Qualitative research can be accused of being unscientific, unrepresentative, open to bias and, even, to manipulation, conscious or unconscious. Clearly, if a researcher is to achieve the ideal of seeing as the subject sees then the researcher would need to lose any external frame of reference and to understand no more than the subject; this seems neither possible nor desirable. Conversely, quantitative methods can be criticized as reductionist, as using pre-conceived or half-understood concepts, and thus as open to bias or manipulation in a different way. In short, each side may accuse the other of producing a distortion of the 'truth'.

While conflict often usefully serves to highlight principles, there is usually much value in accommodation, and the two approaches, qualitative and quantitative, are increasingly seen as being complementary. In social investigation, the former method is useful in providing material for hypotheses, in helping to define complex concepts more rigorously and realistically (see, for example the simple illustration on p.45 below), and subsequently in suggesting possible causal mechanisms and as a caution against over-simple interpretations. Quantitative approaches are valued for hypothesis testing, for their logical rigor, for universal argument, or generalisation, and for their apparent objectivity.

Reductionism

One way of attempting to deal with the above limitations in complex situations has been to reduce and simplify characteristics to a level where they *can* be measured, controlled and tested. This approach, known as reductionism, can produce powerful results but could, in some applications, be seen as denial of the complexity of life: thus some medical practitioners may recognize the existence of physical symptoms only, ignoring so-called psychosomatic conditions (where the state of mind, or *psyche* is thought to affect the physical body, or *soma*); researchers may deny that animals suffer stress or even pain; scientists generally may reject 'unscientific' knowledge as having little meaning. Town planners may assume that physical comfort and convenience are sufficient to produce happiness and well-being, at least in other people. The architect Le Corbusier's idea of a house as 'a machine for living in' may be contrasted with the complex concept of a home with all its personal, aesthetic and spiritual associations. But it was seen in the introduction to this chapter how a tutor may appear to have a better understanding of his or her students than is provided by a complex though essentially reductionist mathematical equation. When we add to this the awareness that society does not seem to be sufficiently mature, morally and emotionally, to deal with scientific discoveries such as atomic power or embryo research, a reaction against science and scientific method is at least understandable.

Science on the other hand sees itself, with good reason, as a rational process which has benefited society by opposing itself to superstition and authoritarian dogma. It has not merely established the true relation between the earth and the sun (which knowledge admittedly has little effect on day-to-day living) but by rational argument has eliminated such diverse scourges as the persecution of harmless old women as witches, of death from child-bed fever, cholera, polluted water and food, or painful operations without anaesthetics. More recently, the careful scientific observation, measurement and establishment of cause and effect relations have dramatically increased awareness of the damage being done to the planet by the economic activities of both capitalism and communism. Rational scientific thought originally found itself opposed by religious dogma, and more recently by pseudo-scientific and political ideology whether of fascism, Marxism, socialism or capitalism. Scientific thought was seen to liberate society not only materially but politically. Mill's *System of logic* (1972 [1843]) forms the basis for modern scientific experimentation, while his seminal rationalist essay *On liberty* (1929 [1859]) performs a similar role for the value of individual thought in human affairs. To say that each person has an equal right to voice an opinion is not however to say that everyone's opinion is always of equal value or is equally informed.

Social reality

Social science has attempted to overcome the admitted shortcomings of natural science by to some extent adopting other methods. Emphasis may be given to holistic, or whole, social reality rather than to the possible distortions of reductionism. So-called *ethnographic* methods may be employed. Originally used by Western anthropologists to study other cultures by living with them, sharing their conditions and so attempting a deeper understanding of their lives, these methods may now be used to study sub-cultures within Western society itself. A classic case was a study of drug sub-culture in America in this way rather than by external observation. An example of a much simpler case will illustrate the point. Some local authority forestry officers were surveying mature trees adjacent to a Glasgow Council housing estate when the surveyors were attacked by teenagers throwing rocks. One teenager was chased and caught (not perhaps an ideal ethnographic technique). He claimed his behaviour was caused by his concern that the trees were to be cut down (partly true). 'But you don't like trees,' he was told, 'when we plant them you tear them up.' His reply was two-fold. 'Och they're nae trees – are they? You mean they'll grow up like this?' He pointed to the large mature trees. 'Anyway, you never asked us if we wanted them!' There are two points here. First, authority was imposing a pre-conceived landscape ideal, ideology even, on individuals without consulting their views. Second, growing up in a Glasgow slum had produced no concept of young trees and their potential growth into maturity. A social survey of attitudes to tree planting therefore might in any case have been misleading since surveyors and surveyed would not have had shared the same concept of a newly planted tree. This is the sort of misunderstanding which qualitative methods (above) attempt to deal with, though there is always a concern that preliminary investigation might in itself influence attitudes.

Acquaintance with the philosophy of natural science however raises suspicions about ethnographic and social-reality approaches to knowledge. Claims of 'empathy' and 'richness' do not appear to suggest objectivity. It is so difficult to know what someone means even if they are being truthful, which for many reasons they may not. Honest observers may produce quite conflicting accounts of what was said at a meeting, even when conducted in their own language. Human communication is such a subtle *two-way* process that what we 'hear' can be much influenced by what we expect or wish. If only one observer is present what corroboration is there? Margaret Mead's (1930) classic ethnographic study *Growing up in New Guinea* is now regarded as suspect. Is the 'experiment' repeatable? The influential psychologist Sigmund Freud (whose work on sexual motivation appears to be indispensable to so much modern literary criticism) is now suspected of having misrepresented his results (Fisher, S., and Greenberg, R., 1977). In such circumstances it may be very easy for workers with strong political convictions to find evidence which tends to confirm their own views of society. Is their professional 'insight' in fact bias? We all incline to think that it is only other people who are biased.

Some social investigators do not just acknowledge the problems of being objective but would deny the possibility or even desirability of objectivity. It is sometimes argued, quite correctly, that often the choice of subject to study and the questions asked reflect a subjective preference; this would not seem to preclude objectivity as an ideal *within* the study, indeed it would appear to make it more necessary. Does social investigation then become merely a branch of politics in which every person has a right to shout his or her corner? Or is it a branch of social literature without the style of a Gaskell or a Dickens or a Zola? If people in a position of *scientific* trust consciously (or even unconsciously through sloppy methodology) interpret events according to their own preferences is this not a form of censorship or of authoritarianism?

Ideological influences

In the nineteenth century it was religion and imperialism which attempted to twist experience to suit preconceived notions. Thus aboriginal people, it was argued, were not human; freedom of thought did not extend to non-Christians, and so on. In the twentieth century, Marxism has similarly been criticized for its re-interpretation of facts in order that its own apparently all-sufficient theory should not be questioned or tested. For this reason the scientific philosopher Sir Karl Popper has likened Marxism to a religion rather than to the rational scientific system of thought which it claims to be. An extreme example may be found in Russian science. Communism claims that a person's life is not determined or limited by birth or breeding but that everyone has the potential for ultimate improvement. The argument is an attractive and humane one in essence, correctly questioning whether a so-called nobleman is necessarily a better or more worthy person than a peasant. But the plant-breeder Lysenko took ideology to the extreme, claiming that the important genetic difference between strains of spring and winter cereals could be over-ridden by environmental treatment or programming, against all objective evidence. Lysenko's ideas found favour with his political and non-scientific masters (who were trying to do something similar with millions of people) with disastrous effects, for a time, on Russian agriculture. (It could be argued, conversely, that a genetically determined individuality may in a sense be more human than an infinitely programable personality.) If such distortions can occur in the relatively objective field of natural science how much more easily can they take place in the field of social science investigations where nuance and value judgement may be subject to pressures from the left or the right of politics? There have been, for example, suggestions that commercial television interests have monopolized, suppressed and distorted investigations on harmful effects of television, especially in the USA (Eysenck, H. J., and Nias, D.K.B., 1978). Why is it that surveys commissioned by an organization nearly always produce results favourable to that organization?

Conclusions

This chapter has shown in outline how the more rigorous procedures of physical science, such as experiment, measurement, use of common concepts and universal argument can be difficult to apply to research on the complex subject of people as social beings. Both the scientists' solution of reductionism and the social scientists' search for social reality equally have their disadvantages.

Faced with the inherent disadvantages of both the natural and the social sciences we might feel, like Voltaire's Candide, that the only true wisdom lies in cultivating a garden. But the reality of peasant toil is unlikely to please a society accustomed to material and social progress. If, as seems likely, our society continues to engage in a quest for knowledge about our environment and ourselves it is essential, whatever particular methods of investigation are used, that we satisfy as far as possible the general criteria of logical and empirical rigour; that we are clear about the assumptions, questions and limitations which our methods involve, and above all that we tread a path between the extremes of technological imperative or of a new dark age of uncritical thought.

CHECKLIST : Chapter 2

You should know and understand:

- the distinction between objective judgement and subjective feeling
- the problems of scientific study of human beings
- the advantages of scientific study of human beings
- the need to make clear the limitations and assumptions in any investigation;

- the nature of physical science:
    experiment
    testing

measurement
description
identification
classification
relation
- the distinction between a concept and a thing
- the importance of commonly agreed concepts
- the importance of universal argument
- the distinction between internal and external validity and the importance of both;

- the use of a knowledge of relationships to control and predict events
- the cause and effect relation
- necessary and sufficient causes
- the idea of mathematical modelling of a system or relationship;
- the need for objectivity in observation
- the nature of empiricism
- the distinction between quantitative and qualitative investigation
- the reasons for and dangers of scientific reductionism
- the reasons for and dangers of social reality research
- the possible influence of ideology on research

Further reading

Barzun, J., and Graff, F., 1985 [1957], *The modern researcher: the classic manual on all aspects of research and writing*, 4th edn, Harcourt Brace Jovanovich, New York, Parts I and II.

Berlin, I., 1956, *The age of enlightenment: the eighteenth century philosophers*, Books for Libraries Press, New York.

Bryman, A., 1988, *Quantity and Quality in Social Research*, Contemporary social Research Series, Martin Bulmer, (ed.), Unwin Hyman, London.

Fisher, S., and Greenberg, R., 1977, *The scientific credibility of Freud's theories and therapy*, Harvester Press, Hassocks.

Hansen, N.R., 1965, *Patterns of discovery*. Cambridge University Press, Cambridge.

Hobbes, T., 1968 [1651], *Leviathan*, (ed. C. Macpherson, Pelican, Harmondsworth.

Hume, D., 1896 [1739], *A treatise of human nature* (ed. Selby-Bigge), Clarendon Press, Oxford.

Leedy, P.D., 1980, *Practical research: planning and design*, 2nd edn, Macmillan, New York, pp.1–40.

Locke, J., 1924 [1690], *An essay concerning human understanding* (ed. Pringle-Pattison), Oxford University Press, Oxford.

McCrone, J., 1993, *The myth of irrationality: the science of the mind from Plato to Star Trek*, Macmillan, London.

Mead, M., 1930, *Growing up in New Guinea, a study of adolescence and sex in primitive societies*, Penguin, Harmondsworth.

Mill, J.S., 1972 [1843], *A system of logic*, Book III Longman, London.

Mill, J.S., 1929 [1859], *On liberty*, Watts and Co., London.

Murdoch, I., 1992, *Metaphysics as a guide to morals*, Chatto & Windus, London.

Reynolds, P.D., 1971, *A primer in theory construction*, Bobbs Merrill, Indianapolis.

Skinner, Q., (ed.) 1985, *The Return of Grand Theory to the Social Sciences*, Cambridge University Press, Cambridge.

Trustead, J., 1979, *The logic of scientific inference: an introduction*, Macmillan, London.

Walker, K., 1950, *Meaning and purpose*, Pelican, Harmondsworth.

Wilson, S., 1973, *Truth*, Arts: a third level course, problems of philosophy, Units 9–10, Open University, Milton Keynes.

3

THE LOGIC OF SCIENTIFIC METHOD

'It is the fashion of the present time to disparage negative logic – that which points out weaknesses in theory or errors in practice; but as a means to attaining any positive knowledge it cannot be valued too highly.'

(J.S. Mill, *On liberty*, 1859)

Scientific knowledge is not absolute. That is to say it is not free from limits or conditions, nor is it unalterable. There was perhaps a time when so-called scientific fact was thought to be absolute and final; Newton's gravitational laws of motion are a case in point. Today any knowledge, even the most precise, is thought of as being relative: relative to other present knowledge, relative to present powers of measurement, relative to whatever tests have so far been applied. Knowledge is seen as provisional: that is, subject to revision and subject to obsolescence; though not untrue, present knowledge may be superseded by more useful and relevant knowledge. Even in precise subjects like physics, measurements cannot be made with one hundred per cent accuracy. It is part of the beauty and wonder of physics that so many natural phenomena, such as the time of swing of a pendulum, can be described by simple mathematical expressions usually involving whole numbers rather than fractions. But experimentally the whole number, or integer, is inferred from the average results of many trials, each one of which only approximates closely to the central value. Or events may occur with such a very high probability that they can be taken as 100 per cent certain.

The vibrations within certain crystals, which have replaced the pendulum as the regulator in modern clocks, are accurate to a second or so in thousands of years. If social data are less accurate and have lower probabilities than physical phenomena, are they essentially any different in their nature?

A problem with conceding that all knowledge is relative is that, ultimately, it seems to imply that there are no absolute standards and that one person's view may be as good as another's. This, in the arts, is the doctrine of relativism which asserts for example that *Bugs Bunny* may be as valuable as *A Midsummer Night's Dream*. This may be acceptable in the arts, but when it comes to the people who build our bridges or perform operations on us, or who plan our economic and social life, we trust that they have a fairly consistent and reliable common knowledge. Thus scientists *aim* for absolute knowledge while accepting that it is unattainable; as in Plato's *Theory of Forms*, it is an ideal which we all recognize as an abstraction but by which we evaluate performance in reality (Field, 1949).

Before going on to examine how scientific method aims to acquire and test knowledge it is necessary to look briefly at the nature of logical argument.

The nature of argument

Most people, when asked, appear to think of an argument as an altercation, slightly unpleasant, between two people. Such a dispute may involve argument, though it is more likely to have arisen because of the lack of calm reasoned argument. In logic an *argument* is simply a reason or series of reasons put forward in support of an assertion or opinion. Each reason, or piece of evidence, and the final assertion, or conclusion if the argument is a sound one, are usually in the form of a statement, thus:

> Statement A (= reason 1)
> Statement B (= reason 2)
> Therefore,   Statement C (= conclusion)

A sound argument is one whose form and content correctly support its conclusion. In logic a sound argument is called a *valid* argument and the conclusion is also said to be a valid conclusion or, simply, valid. An unsound argument is said to be *fallacious* and the unsound conclusion a *fallacy*. An unsupported statement is known as an *assertion*; it is not necessarily untrue but does not become a valid and acceptable conclusion until sufficient evidence is presented to support it in the form of a valid argument. Note that the same form of words or statement may have different qualities according to its logical status and that this status may be changed by argument. Thus a statement may be an assertion until shown to be a valid conclusion; it may be the conclusion of one argument or a correct statement of evidence in another. It may be shown to be a fallacious conclusion or fallacy, and it may be a piece of incorrect evidence in another argument.

Validity

What then is a valid argument? A sound argument has two main general features. First, each piece of evidence should be correct in itself; its correctness may depend on a subsidiary argument or it may be considered self-evident. Second, the evidence or reasons should be related to each other and to the conclusion in a valid logical manner; that is, the argument should have a valid form. Logicians have for centuries studied different forms of argument and have distinguished those forms which are valid from those which are fallacious. Thus an argument may have a valid form but incorrect evidence and so be unsound; on the other hand it may have correct evidence but an invalid form and so also be wrong.

It is not difficult to recognize most forms of argument when they are set out formally, but in writing or speech this may not always be so. The conclusion may be stated first, in which case it is merely an assertion or proposition, or it may be stated in the middle of the argument. Some evidence may be out of logical order or only implied and not stated. The argument needs to be re-arranged before it can be assessed for validity.

Syllogism

A common and apparently straightforward form of argument, much used in research work, is known as the syllogism. It consists of a first general statement, called the first or major premise, a second particular or minor premise, and a conclusion. It is instructive to use obvious cases at first to make the argument quite clear. For example: (1) All employees have a right to be consulted; (2) Joan is an employee; (3) Therefore Joan has a right to be consulted. The truth of the conclusion rests on the correctness or truth of the evidence or premises. Thus: (1) All cats have tails; (2) The Manx cat has no tail; (3) Therefore the Manx cat is not a cat. Since we think we know that the Manx cat is a cat, either the first premise is wrong or we have to modify our concept of what a cat is.

Not only have the premises individually to be correct, they must have a correct logical relationship to each other. For example: (1) All cats have claws; (2) This animal (say it is an eagle) has claws; (3) Therefore it (the eagle) is a cat. Both premises are correct but the argument falls down in this case because the second premise is not a particular, or concrete, example of the first general, or abstract, statement. An animal is not a particular example of a cat, though a cat is a particular example of an animal, and the Manx cat is a particular example of a cat. This type of fallacy is a common one, where the relationship of the premises is not correct, and may typically be used (wrongly) to support prejudice or even persecution as in: (1) All pirates have black beards; (2) This man has a black beard; (3) Therefore this man is a pirate. Even if the first premise is correct, which it probably is not, the conclusion is fallacious since man is not a particular case of pirate. 'I knowed 'e were a pirate 'cos 'e 'ad a big black beard', is the same argument stated informally.

A premise may not be quite what it seems. Consider: (1) Only elephants have trunks; (2) This animal has no trunk; (3) Therefore it is not an elephant. This is a correct argument yet 'animal' is not a particular case of 'elephant'. The key in this case lies in the word only. The first premise really says, No animals, except elephants, have trunks.

Deduction

A syllogism is an example, and there are others, of what is known as deductive argument, or simply deduction. One quality of deductive argument which makes it particularly attractive to scientists is that, if the argument is valid at all, then the conclusion is 100 per cent certain. Given the premises, the conclusion follows as inevitably as the final line of noughts and crosses. The obverse of this quality is that the conclusion tells us nothing which is not in effect already contained within the evidence, it is not a creative or imaginative argument which produces new ideas. A third characteristic of the deductive argument is that it requires a sufficient amount of evidence but no more; additional evidence does not add to the strength of the argument which, as stated, is absolute within its own terms. We will return to the uses of deductive argument later.

Induction

A second type of argument is known as inductive argument or induction. It has qualities opposite to those of deduction: the conclusion is not certain, merely probable, but the conclusion does contain new ideas; that is, a creative leap may be necessary to reach the conclusion. Also, additional supporting evidence strengthens the conclusion. Consider for example the following inductive argument:

1. These people have cholera.
2. These other people do not have cholera.
3. Those who have cholera all used the same water source.
4. Those who did not use that source do not have cholera.
5. Some who used the source do not have cholera.

This argument suggested to Dr John Snow in a cholera outbreak in the London of the 1840s that the water source had some connection with the cholera disease (Harrison, 1963). But the answer was not conclusive. The conclusion seems obvious to us now but some creative imagination was required to reach it in the 1840s. The possible conclusion was strengthened by further evidence:

6. When the water source was shut off no further outbreaks of cholera occurred.

But of course Snow did not have this evidence when he first argued for the supply to be shut off. The reason that the cause of the disease seems more obvious to us today is that we have two more pieces of evidence which were not available to Snow and which have not yet been stated:

7. Cholera is caused by a bacillus.
8. This bacillus lives in polluted water.

Extra evidence makes the conclusion more forceful, that the polluted water source caused the cholera, but it is still not conclusive in the way that a deductive argument is. There could have been some other cause which also ceased when the water was turned off; after all, not everyone who drank the water caught cholera (point 5 above). Note that different bits of evidence may point to different conclusions. Nevertheless, the balance of the argument leads us to believe that the polluted water was the cause. It is the best conclusion we can draw from the given evidence since it seems the most likely; however, it is a great mistake to assume that the most likely conclusion or explanation is necessarily the correct one. Because the conclusion of an inductive argument is never absolutely certain, some logicians (for example, Salmon 1984 [1963]) prefer to reserve the term 'valid' solely for sound deductive arguments, referring to apparently sound inductive arguments as being only 'correct'.

The example also illustrates the use of different types of evidence. Reasons 1 to 5 are empirical only, being based on observations and experience, and the possible relation of cause and effect rests largely in Hume's first two reasons, particularly on the contiguity of the act of drinking the water with the development of the disease. Reason 6 is, in addition, experimental, a result of testing by shutting off the water supply. Reasons 7 and 8 are of a different nature; these are general, if not universal, truths about the *causal mechanism* of cholera which have been derived from other experiments and observations external to this particular case. An understanding of causal mechanisms greatly aids the powers of control and prediction. Thus while experience alone tells us that a stone will fall to the earth, an understanding of the causal mechanism of gravity enables us to predict what will happen where we have no experience, on the moon for example, or on a spaceship.

Fallacy

Knowledge of causal mechanisms can also prevent us from falling into errors which Hume's observations on causality do not preclude. When Julius Caesar invaded Britain in 54 BC he was, apparently, horrified to find that the Ancient British Druids practised human sacrifice. Curiously, Caesar must have felt this was a different concept from that of public slaughter in the Roman amphitheatre. The sacrifices may have been intended, among other things, to persuade the sun to reverse its seeming winter decline into oblivion. The Druids left no written records and whether the story is true or not does not matter for the sake of the argument. Much later the Druids and their practices were wiped out by the Roman general Suetonius. If the Druids did write they might have presented their case to Suetonius as follows:

Stonehenge, AD58

Dear General Suetonius,

1. For some time we have observed a decline in the length of the day, with sunrise occurring later each morning. The direction of the sunrise has also steadily declined towards the south from its high point of midsummer in line with the Heel Stone. On 12 December (Julius gave us a copy of his new world-exclusive Calendar when he was here, which has an error of only one day in four years – a great improvement on the old) the position of the sunrise, when observed from the Western Station Stone, had reached a new low in line with the thirteenth stone (an ominous number we feel, and one which we would not like to see exceeded) of our latest fifty-six-stone 'X' circle computer. If this decline were to be allowed to continue, sunrise would eventually reach due south and disappear into its own sunset, thus leaving us in permanent darkness as, we are reliably informed, has occurred in certain unfortunate regions beneath the Pole Star. This would have the most severe consequences on the development of our crops and on the breeding of our animals, thus effecting negative growth in the employment situation.

2. Accordingly, on 13 December we were obliged to sacrifice a blonde-haired maiden on the Slaughter Stone in the accustomed manner of holding her head under water until no sign of life could be observed. We also sacrificed a small businessman in the usual way by stabbing him in the back and observing his convulsions, which obviously pained him greatly, from which we divine that the future, following the necessary sacrifice, will slowly improve.

3. With cautious optimism we can report that these drastic but time-honoured measures appear once again to have been effective. After seven days we observed that the time of sunrise had become earlier by two minutes, that is by point seven-nine of one per cent of one day, and had further moved a distance of two fingers towards the twelfth stone of the aforementioned stone 'X' circle computer, as observed from the

Western Station Stone. Accordingly we feel confident that sunrise will eventually regain its previous summer position, and that we shall soon see the green shoots of spring followed by long hot days.

4. We should like respectfully to point out that, according to our records, we have employed this same remedy at the same time each year, for some hundreds of years certainly, and it has *always* worked.

5. Accordingly *we conclude* that human sacrifice, carried out in the proper manner by ourselves, is both a necessary and sufficient condition or cause to effect a reversal of the sun's recession. We cannot too strongly recommend that this practice must be allowed to continue.

Yours obediently,
Chief Druid

A Celt of the first century would have been completely bowled over by this argument; it satisfies all three of Hume's criteria; in essence it would convince many people today. After all it did appear to work, which is more than some modern remedies do. But we know it is wrong. We are saved from a fallacious conclusion about cause and effect in this case only by common sense (modern common sense), by a knowledge of the solar system and by disbelief that such a causal mechanism (human sacrifice affecting the path of the sun) could operate. It is a rather different form of inductive argument than that used for the cholera outbreak; there new, different evidence was added; here the same evidence is merely repeated. In everyday life we all have to use this form of argument in gaining experience of the nature of the world, and it generally serves us well enough, as with the falling stone (Chapter Two). This simplest form of inductive thought is known as spontaneous induction. Young children and even animals have this capacity. But usually it is unsuitable – used alone – to determine cause and effect, and it is not sound logic. A common example might be the person who goes to Manchester twice, finds that it rained on both occasions and concludes that it will always rain when he goes to Manchester. Similar arguments in public affairs are possibly not so weak as they seem in that they may be supported by intuitive feelings and experience; or, rather, they are adduced in support of intuitive feelings. This more critical form of induction is arrived at by reflective common sense. The danger is that such argument can be used uncritically and selectively merely to *confirm* our prejudices or misconceptions. Student affairs for example usually are shown on the media only when students are being objectionable; hence the general public is confirmed in the (erroneous) view that students are always objectionable.

And what did the Druids think? Being extremely knowledgable about the movements of sun, moon and stars, they probably knew that the spring would return anyway. But they could conceal and use this knowledge to threaten and control their subjects.

The creative leap

Conversely, inductive argument can produce very creative results. When sufficient evidence has been accumulated in a creative mind an entirely new concept may be formed almost spontaneously but which cannot, however, be conclusively demonstrated at the time. This leads to the most advanced form of induction, arrived at through critical scientific study; the discoveries of genes, molecules, evolution and gravity have already been mentioned as examples. In the case of the carbon ring, a particularly stable yet interactive molecule of six carbon atoms which, in its almost infinite complexity, is practically synonymous with life itself, we have the discover's own account of its conception. The chemist Kekule, returning home on a bus after one of many days spent puzzling in his laboratory about the form of molecule which would explain his results, says that he fell into a trance or dream. Carbon atoms danced before his eyes like stars. Suddenly he saw them form themselves into the now famous hexagonal rings. It should be remembered that no one at that time had ever seen an atom in reality; it was entirely an abstract concept. But this form of molecule exactly explains the proportions in which carbon was found to combine with other elements in complex substances.

The problem of induction

Kekule's dream was, presumably, an example of a rational and informed mind working at a subconscious level. It is unlikely that anyone not already acquainted with the combining properties of carbon and other atoms could have conceived it. It is another example of serendipity, whereby a prepared mind discovers a happy cir-

cumstance, apparently by chance, but one which would have no significance to an uninformed mind. Nevertheless, induction is something of an embarrassment to scientific philosophers to the extent
that it is sometimes referred to as the Problem of Induction
(Popper, 1972 [1963]). Science, particularly as opposed to superstition or emotion, is to be seen as rational, deductive, logical, certain,
authoritative, objective. And yet scientific progress seems to depend
on processes which are imaginative, inductive, not entirely logical,
and provisional or tentative. Can these two aspects be resolved, and
if so, how?

Hypothetico-deductive method

A solution to the problem of induction is to use the strengths of
both deductive and inductive argument, the former entirely conclusive, but unimaginative, the second tentative, but creative. The two
are linked in a process of testing (Chapter Two). Induction provides
ideas, deduction is used to test and to confirm or reject ideas,
wholly or in part. The process is known as the hypothetico-deduc-
tive method and is practically synonymous today with the idea of
scientific method; it is essentially simple but rests on all the intellectual heritage already outlined and which is essential to its understanding. In the example described above, by *not* performing the
sacrifice one year, it would have been easy to test the inductive
argument that sacrifice caused the sun to return. This seems easy to
us because we know the sun will return anyway, but if we truly
believed in the inductive conclusion it would require some courage
to test the idea for the first time. Maybe some early Mill or Hume
suggested it. Probably the Druids bound him hand and foot and
chucked him in that peat bog where his body was found nearly two
thousand years later. Many people today are naturally afraid to test
their harmless superstitions by, for example, deliberately walking
under a ladder, or by changing the name of a boat, or even by relax-
ing exchange controls.

Confirmation and falsification

Testing can be carried out in two ways, one of which is of dubious
value and the other of which is rigorous. The Druids could claim

that they tested their system last year and it was working all right then. This form of so-called test is known as confirmation, but merely reinforces the inductive fallacy. What the man in the peat bog might have been asking for was falsification, trying to prove that the system was wrong or false. If the relationship fails this test then it is considered false and may be discounted unless we can think of sound reasons why it might have failed in this particular case. If the idea or notion survives the test of falsification this does not absolutely prove it is true, but it does increase the probability that it is so. If it survives repeated and diverse testing and if, in addition, it continues to provide a consistent explanation for all the events associated with it then we can accept it as effectively true for the time being. The idea is well on the way to being accepted as a *theory* in the strict sense, that is as a well-established explanatory principle. There is always the possibility that some future test may be failed, or that some event may be observed which cannot be explained by the relationship under examination. For example, Kekule knew that each carbon atom had four links which could join it to other atoms. But in some compounds he found that carbon atoms appeared to combine with less of other substances than would be expected from this and yet the compounds were very stable. In the carbon ring however each one of six atoms uses two or three links to join with its two neighbours, leaving only one or two links each for other substances. In this case knowledge became modified without rejecting what was already known.

Falsification, from its deductive nature, is a very powerful argument. Examples may equally be found in historical research or in law as well as in science. Take the case that a killing has taken place but that no one actually saw it. A suspect may be tried on circumstantial evidence as in this case:

1. The suspect was heard in front of several witnesses to threaten the victim.
2. The suspect's girl-friend had left him for the victim some time previously.
3. A knife, believed to be the murder weapon, was found bearing the suspect's finger prints.
4. Blood identified as similar to that of the victim was found on the suspect's clothing.

To argue from this that the accused is guilty is to use inductive argument. The conclusion is not 100 per cent certain; more evidence might increase or decrease our belief in the accused's guilt. The inductive conclusion can however be tested deductively *if* the evidence is available:

1. If the accused was not there he could not have carried out the killing.
2. At the estimated time of the killing he was playing darts in a Canterbury pub with the Archbishop and three Deacons all of whom are willing to testify.
3. Therefore the accused is innocent.

If the evidence is correct, this alibi or deductive argument is 100 per cent conclusive and outweighs any amount of circumstantial evidence or inductive argument.

Sir Karl Popper, the eminent contemporary scientific philosopher with whom the concept of falsification is particularly associated, has argued (1989 [1959]) that testing is not only a scientific procedure but represents an attitude of mind. We should not cling defensively to our ideas, selecting or twisting evidence only to confirm what we already believe. Rather we should be open to, even welcome, criticism: ready to question and test our own ideas in all possible ways, and to change them if persuaded. In this way, rather than stagnating, thought changes and develops.

To be open-minded is not always easy. For many years archaeologists believed that all Western civilization had diffused outwards from Ancient Egypt. Whole reputations were built on the inductive interpretation of squiggles on pots which clearly showed that the relationship between cultures supported this Diffusion Theory. When the deductive scientific process of carbon-dating was introduced, calculated on rates of isotopic change in carbon artifacts, this threw doubt on the idea of diffusion as then understood. But it was only when even more accurate carbon-dating was developed, calibrated on the growth rings and carbon dates of four-thousand-year-old Bristle-cone pines in California, that the accepted chronology had to be stood on its head and some supposedly derivative cultures were found to be older than Ancient Egypt itself (Renfrew, 1973). This evidence was, perhaps understandably, resisted by some traditional archaeologists.

Hypothesis testing

A hypothesis is a provisional statement put forward for the sake of argument, or for the purpose of being tested. We have seen that one and the same statement can have a different status according to its place in a developing argument. A hypothesis is not an assertion since no truth is even claimed for it at first, and it certainly is not a conclusion although linguistically the form of words used could be exactly the same for an assertion, a hypothesis or a conclusion. It is important to have an open-minded attitude to a hypothesis; it is not a belief to be obstinately defended or selectively supported. It should certainly never be the aim of a research project to 'prove' that some pre-conceived notion is true, though it may be acceptable to demonstrate that something would at least have been possible, such as Jason's mythical voyage to the Sea of Marmara (Severin, 1985). Nor, strictly speaking, is a hypothesis a theory (above), although the term is sometimes used in this sense.

By way of example we can continue to develop the illustration, introduced in a previous section, of human sacrifice. It is clear that not to have performed the sacrifice would have been a far more rigorous test than to continue performing it. This is not always so obvious or straightforward in the real-life examples which will be examined later. Usually it is not possible to test a hypothetical relationship directly; it is tested by the predicted consequences of it being true or false. Two deductive arguments can be employed, one of which is well known to logicians as being fallacious; it is called the method of *affirming the consequent*. The second method is that of *denying the consequent* and is a powerful and valid argument; it was traditionally known as the *modus tollens*, or the manner of removing or destroying. The first argument may be set out as follows:

Hypothesis – Human sacrifice causes spring to return.
Consequence – If a sacrifice is made spring will return.
Test – Carry out sacrifice.
Result – Spring returns.
Conclusion (fallacious) – The hypothesis is correct.

The consequent is confirmed, but today we know the hypothesis is in fact nonsense. But even if we did not know the truth in this case, logic tells us that the argument is not conclusive and is indeed fallacious: many other causes of which we know nothing could have produced the effect.

The correct and rigorous method of hypothesis testing is that of denying the consequent:

> Hypothesis – Human sacrifice causes spring to return.
> Consequence – If a sacrifice is *not* made spring will *not* return.
> Test – Do not perform sacrifice this year.
> Result – Spring returns.
> Conclusion (valid) – The hypothesis is *not* correct.

This test and its related argument are quite convincing that sacrifice is not necessary to achieve the return of spring. Furthermore, if spring had *not* returned this would suggest that sacrifice did have some connection with spring. In this case the consequence would have been confirmed of course and it should be noted that it is the method of setting up the experiment in such a way as to *attempt* to disprove or to falsify the consequence which is important for validity, not the actual outcome. In the event of the consequence then being confirmed the outcome is a much more convincing argument *for* the hypothesis than would have been the method of confirmation. The method of denial is the more versatile, more rigorous – and more challenging to established beliefs. Science accepts as knowledge those ideas which have survived various attempts at falsification. We do not in fact conclude simply that a hypothesis is correct on the result of one experiment, but say rather that the result tends to confirm the hypothesis, or lends support to it.

In the case of the cholera outbreak, above, it was clearly better, both morally and methodologically, to close down the suspect water source than to keep it open to show that even more people would die. But, as polluters still do today, the owners of the water supply would argue (incorrectly) that there was no evidence to suggest that the water was the cause of the disease and that there was no case for closing the supply. They could also argue (correctly) that there was no proof that the supply was the cause, or that the evidence was only circumstantial. In environmental management today this is a typical dilemma which becomes particularly acute when prevention of pollution or of other damage, such as decline in the whale population, can bring economic hardship to a community or to a culture.

Falsification, or the method of denying the consequent, has been seen by some thinkers and politicians such as Popper and Sir Keith

Joseph as almost synonymous with science. Joseph's criticism of the former Social Science Research Council was that it either could not or would not adopt a falsification approach to knowledge. It is clear from what has been said so far that in many cases social scientists could do this if they wished; in others it is at least controversial. If we think a particular drug may be keeping a patient alive do we stop giving it to test this? The tamoxifen experiment (Chapter Seven) is in effect, and controversially, doing just this. Having inferred inductively from experience that tamoxifen may arrest the development of breast cancer, medical researchers have identified a large group of women known, from various factors, to be at risk, and are treating half this group with the drug and the other half with a mere placebo. The principles of design of this experiment will be examined in more detail in Chapter Five, but the point here is that half the women are being denied a drug which might prevent a deadly disease. It could be argued that this drug should be tested by giving it to all the women at risk, the method of confirmation. Even though all the women are volunteers, and know and accept the conditions of the experiment, some people still find it disturbing.

Many British government policies of the 1980s could be seen as epic Popperian experiments to challenge accepted beliefs: that residential care is necessary for the welfare of the mentally disadvantaged; that state regulation is necessary for a good bus service; that exchange controls are necessary to keep money in the national economy, and so on. Unfortunately Popperian falsification is the only element of scientific rigour which most of these social experiments have displayed. They lack control (that is, in the experimental sense, see Chapter Five) and they lack agreed concepts and measurement. Also, they perhaps spring from normative rather than from positivist attitudes (below, p.70).

Nevertheless, correct logical testing of hypotheses, as part of a healthy scepticism about the truth of the hypothesis itself, is a valuable and often essential procedure in advancing knowledge and understanding. It occurs in a particularly formalized way in the concept of the *null hypothesis* which is used in statistical testing and which will be examined in Chapter Seven. First though it is necessary to look more closely at the nature of the hypothesis itself.

Formulating a hypothesis

Since a hypothesis is a statement made formally for the sole purpose of being tested, it should be in a form that can be tested. This is not so straightforward as it sounds. A good hypothesis is not just any old assertion which can form the basis of a good discussion, though the term is often used in this way. First, *a good hypothesis contains two concepts* and, second, *it proposes a relationship between the two*. A single concept can hardly be tested, or even described, except by relating other concepts to it. How can we test the concept of 'a swan'? We could however test the relationship of the concept of 'whiteness' to that of swans. 'All swans are white', states that whiteness is always, though not exclusively, associated with swans. This was the classic case used by Popper to illustrate the difference between confirmation and falsification. To see a million white swans can never prove or confirm conclusively that all swans are white – unless we are certain that we have seen all the swans in the world. But to see only *one* black swan, not known until Australia was discovered, conclusively disproves or falsifies the statement that 'all swans are white'. It may be useful to test the existence, if any, and, if so, the degree of all sorts of relationships: unemployment and crime, style and the artist, single parenthood and school records, and so on. Even without necessarily representing cause and effect, such relationships might allow predictions of a sort to be made. The relations are, however, essentially descriptive and, as explained in Chapter Two, knowledge of causal relationships is more powerful in terms of prediction and, especially, of control. For this reason the most useful and, usually, the most demanding research attempts to examine the cause and effect relation. In policy analysis for example the really interesting questions are, did the policy work effectively (did the cause have the desired effect)? If not, why not and what side-effects did it cause? Quite lengthy treatises on various aspects of policy are produced without even attempting these questions. It is very easy, also, in social and political enquiry, where both causes and effects are numerous and complex, to fall into the simple fallacy of affirming the consequent. The correct method is the *modus tollens*, above, though its application is often difficult in real-life situations (see p.69).

If a relationship is to be tested, obviously the concepts involved must be clear, identifiable and, preferably, measurable in degree so that variations of the relationship can also be tested. This usually means that the hypothesis has to be formulated at two levels, a *general hypothesis* which expresses the general ideas which are of interest, and the working or *experimental hypothesis* which contains more specific, but also limited, concepts or indicators which can be measured. The confirmation or falsification of the experimental hypothesis provides one more piece of evidence in the wider inductive argument for or against the general hypothesis. The process of refining a general hypothesis to a working hypothesis which can be tested is known as the *operationalization* of the hypothesis. A general hypothesis may have a large number of working hypotheses derived from it, any one of which can be the subject of a research project, and it is in this way that individual research projects can make contributions to general systems of knowledge, above (p.8).

Take the hypothesis that 'television causes violence'. This can be debated at length. Various bits of inductive argument and beliefs can be contributed to the discussion. But it cannot be tested as it stands. Presumably the statement implies that it is the watching of television that may cause violence, in the watchers. But what is watching? Which programmes, for how long, how often, at what age, under what conditions, how casually or intensively? Watching TV is a complex concept which cannot be adequately expressed in a single measure or even in many measures. If we try to reduce the complexity to manageable levels this raises problems too. Suppose we hypothesise only that watching *The A-Team* causes violence. The amount of this viewing can be measured, but what about the effects of all other viewing which will vary among individuals? These cannot be ignored. If watching is restricted exclusively to *The A-Team* alone this is clearly an artificial condition and may exaggerate any effect of this programme.

The other part of the relationship, violence or aggression, is also a complex concept. We cannot say simply, 'that is violence, this is not'. It is made up partly of what Locke called simple ideas which we can recognize from experience but which occur in various combinations; violent looks, violent speech, violence to inanimate things, violence to people or to animals, a liking for violent writing or activities, potential for violence, and so on. In combination, or alone even, any of these invoke the abstract concept of violence. Further, recognition of violence in others is relative to our own circumstances, experience, courage, sensibilities and so on. But we can only measure concrete things. Must we measure all the indicators of violence, or can we measure only some? Do we measure them only when they are expressed as criminal activity or can we measure suppressed or latent violence? If 95 per cent of people are unaffected and 'only' 5 or, even, 1 per cent become anti-social, is this result 'violence'? If we measure only some indicators we may not get the truth. Horrifically violent war criminals are known to have acted very kindly towards their families and pets. Child psychologists use as measures apparently innocuous behaviour indicators, such as how children complete a half-complete standard story, violently or happily, or how many violent words they use. Teachers observe play-ground behaviour that appears aggressive but may well be short of active bullying. How well these or other *indicators* might relate to actual violence is more than a research project in itself (Chapter Five).

When to all these complexities of measurement are added those of the conduct of the experiment, and the many other possible causes of violence in society, it is clear that there is great potential for contradiction, obfuscation, disagreement and special pleading over the results. None of this discussion is intended to argue that violent films do not cause violence; indeed there is evidence to suggest that they do, and good theoretical reason (that is reason based on established principles) to expect that they would. The point being made is that it would be difficult to demonstrate such a relationship conclusively.

The third requirement of a research hypothesis is that *the concepts used must be capable of being reduced to a level where they can be measured objectively, or at least recognized consistently.* A workable hypothesis might be that children aged seven to ten years who watch *The A-Team* regularly for more than six months will use significantly more violent words in their stories. (The use and significance of the word 'more' will be examined in Chapter Six where the need for comparative bases of measurement is examined.) Many social scientists do not like this sort of hypothesis. It seems too clinical, too reductionist, too trivial, too unexciting, does not treat violence as a total phenomenon; it does not deal directly with major issues of policy, it does not answer the big question and it has no theoretical content. Politicians always want quick answers to big questions.

Natural scientists know that big questions are rarely answered by a single research project, even a big one. And even with large budgets, research needs time in any case. And despite the criticisms of confirmation (above), natural science does proceed largely by repetition, although it is the repetition of testing rather than of confirming (Chapter Seven). Many research projects over many years will share more or less the same general hypothesis; this will be tested by use of diverse experimental hypotheses which are logical consequences of the general hypothesis. The general hypothesis will be confirmed (or rejected) under various conditions; it will explain (or not explain) a variety of observations. Gradually, opinion – inductive opinion – will be formed on the collective evidence and this will become the conventional scientific 'truth'. This is how the causal link between the smoking of tobacco and the development of lung cancer was conceived, and it is strange today to realize that even among objective opinion the conclusion was for many years finely balanced. A proposed similar relation between cholesterol in the diet and atherosclerosis is the subject of much conflicting evidence and debate today. In both cases there are interests which find difficulty in being open-minded; in the first, private commercial organizations and, in the second, professional state advisors and researchers. So a fourth requirement for a hypothesis is that *it should always, or nearly always, relate to an existing wider body of knowledge or theory*; or, as in the example given, to a more general hypothesis. In this way evidence relates to evidence, and knowledge accumulates iteratively and incrementally. In this process it is more useful to have relatively restricted hypotheses tested conclusively than broader hypotheses tested inconclusively. The terms theory and hypothesis are sometimes used as though they represent the same concept. There is no hard and fast rule, but the term theory is perhaps more usefully reserved to imply a substantial body of knowledge, such as the Theory of Evolution, which already has considerable support and to which individual hypotheses should usually relate.

Deterministic and probabilistic relationships

It is a common type of observation that 'old so-and-so smoked like a chimney and lived to ninety-three'. Many people see this as shedding doubt on the idea that smoking causes premature death. There is, no doubt, an element of subjective wishful thinking in this, but the logic of falsification seems at first sight to justify it. In fact, however, the falsification argument cannot be so simply applied to such *probabilistic relationships*.

A probabilistic cause and effect relationship is one where the cause is not inevitably followed by the effect *in any individual case*.

This may be compared to *deterministic relationships* where a cause invariably produces the corresponding effect. For example, if each of 100 persons swallows potassium cyanide, each will die, very quickly. If sixty people take cyanide and forty do not, those sixty will die and the forty will live. The effect is related inevitably and predictably (that is, deterministically) to the cause both in each case and for the group as a whole: all 60 per cent will die. We could test the effect of the poison in each or any individual case by withholding it or giving it (not of course that such an experiment would be conducted on humans, though it might on animals). If, on the other hand, the group of a hundred people had smoked heavily for many years we can predict *for the group* that 60 per cent (say) will die prematurely, though more slowly, but we cannot predict what will happen to any one individual except to say that the probability of him or her dying prematurely is 60 per cent. This is not always very meaningful to an individual who thinks of himself as dead or alive but not as probably dead.

Probability will be discussed in more detail in Chapter Seven but here it is sufficient to understand that we cannot falsify probabilistic relationships by tests on individual cases alone, but only by comparing group with group. Thus, whether we treat or do not treat an individual, we cannot test the result against an expected consequence since for any one individual we cannot predict even a hypothetical consequent. But if we withheld the cause for one whole group of 100 (that is if they did not smoke) and found that it made no difference (just as in the human sacrifice or the tamoxifen examples) but that they died at the same rate at the same age as those who did smoke, then this *would* tend to falsify the hypothesis that smoking increased the risk of lung cancer. This is greatly to oversimplify such an experiment, but for the time being it makes the point. The medical case against smoking is primarily statistical and probabilistic (Chapter Seven).

Positivism

Positivism has come to mean an attitude to knowledge which claims to see the world as it is, and hence to accept it as it is. The originator of the philosophy, Auguste Comte, was aware however that such knowledge is not absolute but relative since we can never be sure that we are seeing the world as it really is (Chapter One). It might be more correct to say that positivism tries to see the world as it is, not as we would like it to be, not through rose-tinted spectacles, nor as we think it ought to be. Positivism clearly has links with realism and empiricism, but acknowledges the philosophical gulf between what we see and what is, which is the concern of scientific philosophers. The natural sciences generally can be said to be positivist in their approach to knowledge, though this attitude may be weakened as science becomes more involved in environmental political issues. Social sciences on the other hand often adopt a *normative* approach, that is they start from a basis of how they think the world ought to be. The concept comes from that of a norm or standard, or example in the sense of ideal – as in 'to set an example'. Social science and applied social science such as town planning have a strong Utopian trait which looks to a better future. There can be no criticism of that in itself but there are grounds for dismay when this Utopianism is not grounded in the reality of the present and of human nature, nor of how we get from here to there, of the trauma involved in the transition, and of the Procrustean bed which we may find when we arrive.

Positivist work on the other hand is often seen by normative theorists as rather dull and unimaginative, as 'mere positivism'. Purely positivist approaches to gathering information have been associated, sometimes correctly, with an over-simple view of society, with reductionism, a naive understanding of social causes, and with perhaps a lack of social concern or 'commitment', a somewhat plodding and descriptive approach. In contrast, the theoretical analysis of policy issues against norms such as the idea of natural rights could be seen to display a much more imaginative and sophisticated (in the sense of worldly wise) social reality and sympathetic understanding of the complex nature of social systems. Such analysts would see themselves as concerned to comprehend innermost mechanisms rather than superficial manifestations, to understand causes rather than effects. Certainly positivist studies of such issues can often be criticized for providing inadequate afterthoughts by way of attempts to explain the causes of the effects which they have identified. When positivists do attempt to move into theoretical social analysis of results they may soon find themselves out of their depth. Conversely, positivists may see normative approaches as prone to the dangers of over-generalization from particular cases, to selective quotation from authorities as though their words were universal truths, as too concerned with big and complex causes rather than with effects, and whose measurements and concepts may lack empirical support and logical rigour. The young Thomas Hardy summed up the dilemma in his comments on J.H. Newman's *Apologia*: 'his logic is really human, based not on syllogisms but on converging probabilities. Only – and here comes the fatal catastrophe – there is no first link to his excellent chain of reasoning, and down you come headlong. . .'(Strong, 1951).

Can we, in any case, carry out meaningful research into what ought to be, as distinct from what is? We can investigate whether people are good, were good and, perhaps, whether they will be good; but can we investigate scientifically whether people ought to be good? (We can of course discover whether other people *think* that people should be good, but this is not quite the same thing.) A consultant's report or a political tract may properly argue inductively what ought to be, though both will inevitably display bias. But research is concerned first with understanding *what is* and from this may *predict* what could happen if various courses of action were to be taken. To decide, based on such knowledge and prediction, what course of action *ought* to be taken is then a human and a political decision. Any research based on pre-conceived theoretical norms is inherently suspect in terms of its objectivity, selectivity, logical use of confirmation or falsification, concepts, external validity and conclusions. In the cases, for example, of the archaeological Theory of Diffusion, Lysenko's work on genetics and Nazi racial theories, reality eventually overturned them.

It is very difficult to be objective. To take one example, in a number of countries Environmental Impact Statements have, by law, to be prepared for major development projects. These statements are intended to be a comprehensive and objective prediction of all the likely impacts (effects) of a proposed development (the causes) together with proposals to modify the effects where necessary. Impact Statements are, in effect, complex and sometimes large research projects, though usually of a particular rather than a general nature. They involve description, prediction and causal relationships. Developers who have to prepare these statements, or retain their own consultants to do so, thus have to produce evidence for and, it may be, *against* their own case. Many are almost incredulous at being asked to do such a thing, having, naturally, always presented their own case in the best possible light. The very idea of impartiality seems foreign. In the absence of a knowledgable and impartial arbitrating body, such as exists in the USA, these statements and their supporting investigations must inevitably at first sight be somewhat suspect.

Conclusions

This chapter has shown how knowledge, in the sense of understanding, is gained by the testing of ideas: that is, by experiment in the broad sense. Underlying all experiment is argument in the form of sets of related ideas, statements or evidence. Often these arguments are not made explicit and are logically weak or misleading. Sound research requires clear and logical argument. The essence of scientific method may be seen as the complementary and rigorous use of deductive and inductive argument in hypothesis formulation and testing and, in particular, in the practice of testing by falsification rather than by confirmation.

There are many forms of knowledge and understanding and many ways of acquiring these, all of which have their own value. What has been set out here are some of the criteria by which such activities might justify the name research. The application of these principles and some of the problems in their application, for example in experimental design and in statistical inference, are examined in the following chapters.

CHECKLIST : Chapter 3

You should know and understand:

- the nature of argument in logical discussion
- the components of argument:
    evidence
    conclusion
- the distinction between assertion and conclusion
- validity (valid argument) and the requirements for this
- fallacy (fallacious argument) and the reasons for this
- syllogism, requirements for a valid syllogistic argument
- the nature of deductive argument
- the nature of inductive argument
- the distinction between inductive and deductive argument and the strengths and weaknesses of each;

- the distinction between simple empirical evidence and the use of an understanding of causal mechanisms to reach conclusions
- the distinction between spontaneous induction and induction arrived at by scientific study
- the problem of induction
- hypothetico–deductive method
- the distinction between confirmation and falsification as means of investigation and the logical strengths of the latter
- the nature of circumstantial evidence and the use of the alibi;

- the term theory used in the strict sense

- procedures for hypothesis testing
- the argument of denying the consequent
  (*modus tollens*)
- the fallacy of affirming the consequent
- the requirements for and the formulation of a good
  hypothesis
- operationalization of a hypothesis and requirements
  of a good working hypothesis
- use of induction in research;

- difficulties of applying scientific method to social
  investigation
- distinction between deterministic and probabilistic
  relationships
- the problem of applying falsification to probabilistic
  relationships
- the distinctions between positivist and normative
  approaches to research
- institutional deterrents to objective investigation

Further reading

Copi, I.M., 1982, *Introduction to logic*, 6th edn, Macmillan, New York.

Eysenck, H.J., and Nias, D.K.B., 1978, *Sex, violence and the media*, Maurice Temple Smith, London.

Fearnside, W.W., and Holther, W.B., 1959, *Fallacy, the counterfeit of argument*, Prentice-Hall, Englewood Cliffs.

Field, G.C., 1949, *The philosophy of Plato*, Oxford University Press, London, pp. 28–65.

Hawkins, G.S., 1966, *Stonehenge decoded*, Souvenir Press, London.

Hodges, L., 1981, *Logic*, Penguin, Harmondsworth.

Popper, Sir K., 1982 [1959], *The logic of scientific discovery*, Hutchinson, London.

Renfrew, C., 1973, *Before civilisation: the radiocarbon revolution and prehistoric Europe*, Jonathan Cape, London.

Salmon, W.C., 1984 [1963], *Logic*, 3rd edn, Prentice-Hall, Englewood Cliffs.

Sutherland, S., 1993, *Irrationality; the enemy within*, Constable, London.

4

INFORMATION IN RESEARCH

'No, no, my man. You mustn't tell us what you *think*
you heard him say. It's not evidence.'

(W.S. Gilbert, *Iolanthe*)

Quality of information

Quality of information is one of the criteria by which a proposal for
a piece of research, and its product – whether as report, thesis or
dissertation – will be evaluated. It is important that an adequate
indication of material used is provided in the account of the
research: the purpose of this is to enable the quality of the information on which the work is based to be assessed.

Information is another word for knowledge, but it is unstructured
knowledge, raw information, not yet part of a system. It is perhaps
not knowledge in the sense of understanding. Information may, for
example, be laid before a magistrate, but the information does not
of itself constitute a verdict or a conclusion. First the information
must be evaluated or, in popular speech, 'sifted'. Some will be discarded; the rest will be organized in a rational way so that it
becomes evidence in an argument and may be tested logically
(Chapter Three). This process will often reveal a need for further
information before the argument can be completed. Only then can
an inductive conclusion be reached which in legal parlance is
'beyond reasonable doubt'.

Research proceeds in a similar way. Within an empirical system a structure of rational knowledge is built on raw knowledge or experience. Experience in the widest sense, including knowledge of previous research, may suggest that a pattern of events exists or might have existed. But to reach general or universal conclusions from a small number of particular cases is unsafe. More information is obtained. Gradually a general theory may be formed, based on many particular examples. However, a number of cautions must be applied to this simple outline.

1. Most individual pieces of research carried out by students are unlikely to involve information on more than a few particular cases or case-studies at most. While the results of such work may tend to confirm or reject more general ideas – and should be evaluated in that context – it is unlikely that sufficient information will be presented to enable generalizations to be made. (For further discussion of this point in relation to levels of degree see Chapter Eight.)

2. The information gained should not *only* (though it may to some extent) consist of repetition or confirmation of what is known already, but of testing in all possible ways, as outlined in Chapter Three.

3. Because of the enormous amount of information which is potentially available in relation to the limited resources for research, whether of personal time or financial support, new information should be sought within a system of existing theory and knowledge. This is one of the benefits of hypothesis formulation, that it can be used to examine a small and particular area of research that relates strategically to more general directions of thought and investigation.

4. Nevertheless, critical appraisal and re-appraisal of the theoretical aspects of the work should accompany the purely empirical and experimental stages.

5. It should be remembered that logic and rational argument are methods for testing and organizing ideas after they have been conceived. The conception of ideas is usually an inductive, intuitive, creative and imaginative process. Mature thought involves a balance between both processes and this may become so habitual that we cease to distinguish these two important phases of thinking.

6. Following from (5) above, it is often the case that a student, in

the early stages of planning a research proposal, is dismayed to find that completed theses, read as examples, display a clear logical and linear development of argument with a close relation between information, hypothesis and conclusions. This clarity of purpose and action can appear to contrast sadly with the student's own circuitous attempts to define a researchable problem with a relevant information base. However, it should be clearly understood that this initial confusion is a normal and possibly creative stage when beginning research. That clearly written thesis is likely to have started in the same confused way and, equally, the student's own thesis will appear much more rational when finally written up (Chapter Nine).

In previous chapters we have so far examined the problems of how experience is known to be genuine (which perhaps can never be known satisfactorily) and how experience or information is then assembled into rational and convincing arguments. It was stated that for a conclusion to be true two things are necessary: a valid or correct form of argument and true and sufficient evidence or information. In this chapter we will examine from a common-sense and logical point of view some of the requirements of research in relation to good information, leaving aside now the philosophical problems of the nature of reality.

As stated at the outset, quality of information is one of the criteria of good research. Without this, argument and conclusions will largely be valueless. Questions which a researcher might be expected to answer include: what information will be or has been gathered; how does this relate to the particular study, research question or working hypothesis; how does it relate to the wider theories within which the research is founded; is it new information; is it a new type of information; does it require or develop new techniques; what are the sources of information; will it be, or is it, reliable; will it be sufficient for the arguments employed?

All these questions have of course to be considered within the limitations of a researcher's expertise (or of expertise which can reasonably be acquired) and the time and money available. For an individual, when planning a thesis, these may be important constraints which, by restricting the quality of information which can be gathered, may in turn limit the nature of the research questions which can be addressed. Some of the more technical and, in particular, statistical requirements for information-gathering will be examined in Chapters Five and Six, but first the various types of information and their relation to the research argument will be outlined.

Primary and secondary sources

A distinction is commonly made between primary and secondary sources of information in research. This distinction is much more than just a classification of information sources but represents different types of information and arguments. Any serious research is expected (with a very few possible exceptions) to use primary sources; even junior school children are required now to find out for themselves. As with many distinctions, the extremes are clear but there is debate about the intermediate positions. The essence of a *primary source* of information is that it involves the researcher in direct experience and observation of the real world, in so far as that term has meaning. Thus possible distortions, deliberate or inadvertent, by other observers are avoided. A researcher assumes a personal responsibility for the reliability and authenticity of his or her information and must be prepared to answer for it: for example, by a spoken examination in the case of work for an academic degree.

In this sense, the emphasis on the use of primary sources is clearly in the empirical tradition. For many centuries scholars relied for their arguments and information, not on experience, but on the ancient writings of the so-called Authorities, in particular the works of Aristotle, which were then largely accepted unquestioningly. While there was much that was correct and scientific in these authorities, there was also much that was misleading. Not until the intellectual developments of the seventeenth century, which led in turn to the eighteenth-century Age of Reason, did scholars in general begin to test these things for themselves. Even Sir Isaac Newton, possessed perhaps with the most powerful mathematical brain which has ever existed, dabbled in mysticism in his later life. In modern times the writings of Lenin and Mao Tse-tung have been venerated as authorities. But in the natural sciences it is now the laboratory experiment, and in the social sciences the survey, interview, observation or collection of social and economic data, which are regarded as types of true primary sources. In archaeology or local history it would be the physical results (or artifacts) of human activity. This does not mean of course that primary information is necessarily sufficient or correct, but that a researcher should be personally acquainted with its nature and limitations.

Secondary sources, on the other hand are those where the information has already been sifted and structured by someone else, albeit for quite legitimate reasons. Though such information is likely to be true, it may not be the whole truth. Books and other writings prepared for publication are the most obvious examples here. It is a mistake to assume that what is in a book must be true, and in any case a good deal of selection is necessarily involved in preparing most books and reports. Some reports and academic papers may be considered to be exhaustive (that is, complete) treatments of limited topics but it remains a matter for a researcher's experience and judgement whether to accept that this is so in any particular case.

While primary information forms the substance of research, secondary sources are particularly useful in the earlier stages of definition of the research problem and its relation to existing work. Thus initial reading around the subject goes hand in hand with intuitive and inductive thought in a process which, as stated above, can at the same time be both frustrating and stimulating for a researcher. In addition to the refinement of the research question (Chapter Eight) the product of this stage of the work is, finally, incorporated into what is known as the *literature review* (see Chapter Nine) which, like the rest of the dissertation, usually appears much more structured and rational in its perfect form than at its inception.

An acceptable dissertation, then, is one which, among other requirements, makes good use of both primary sources (see Chapters Five and Six) and of secondary sources (Chapter Eight). Some sources or types of information do not fit neatly into either category. The important thing here is not to define some arbitrary classification but to be aware, (1) of the desirability of getting as close to understanding the original source as possible (with due precaution against bias) and, (2) to be aware of the exact nature of the information and its limitations.

Published statistics

Large amounts of descriptive statistics are published regularly by central government (the term statistics itself originally meant quan-

titative information published by the state) and by local government
and voluntary and private organizations. It is not intended, nor is it
possible, to describe these numerous and various sources here (see
the recommended reading at the end of this chapter), but rather to
explain in a general way how they should be interpreted for the purposes of research. For example, the results of the ten-yearly population census of the United Kingdom are published comprehensively
and in great detail. They are based on a well-organized empirical
and objective survey. The amount of information is far greater than
any one researcher could gather on his or her own. At the same
time many government statistics contain much more potential information than is ever extracted; there is a point of view that the great
cost of collecting the data is not justified by the use subsequently
made of them. Why should a student not use these or, indeed, other
statistics in effect as a primary source for his or her own research?

A case might be made for a student dissertation based on, say,
the United Kingdom inter-census 10 per cent sample population
survey of 1986, but three reservations would have to be made. First,
is the student sufficiently informed about matters such as the nature
of the questionnaire used, the sampling methods and any subsequent aggregation, or grouping, of data to understand the compro-
mises and limitations which inevitably are incurred? Second, do the
definitions, categories and catchment areas used in the survey
enable the data to be used to answer the questions which the student proposes to investigate? Third, since student dissertations are
primarily intended to be a training and experience in research,
might the student learn more from designing and carrying out his
or her own survey?

From what has been said it is clear that a student should not just
take the published results at face value but should go as far as possible back to an understanding of the original information-gathering
process. This should be true also of any research project or consultancy report which is based on such data; experienced researchers
will already have much of this background knowledge. A student
project might usefully combine analysis of the published statistics
for a particular area with a smaller *ad hoc* and more up-to-date
survey. It would be important then to know such things as what
precisely is the definition used of an 'economically active resident'
or a part-time worker, what age categories have been set, how are
particular occupation groups defined, what are the boundaries of
the areas used for tabulation of the results and have these bound-

aries changed since the last survey? Another important aspect concerning boundaries is the extent to which results from different
areas may have been aggregated, that is grouped together, partly for
convenience and partly, where personal records are involved, for
confidentiality. Conditions in a group of remote parishes, for example, may be obscured by being aggregated with all the parishes in a
district. Unless access is possible to the individual parish or ward
surveys (known as small area statistics) these differences will not
come to light. A researcher might wish to experiment with recombi-
nations of area data which are different from the published form in
order to see what patterns emerge. To do this it is useful to have
data in as disaggregated a form as possible.

National population data have been discussed here as one example of the need to understand published surveys as fully as possible
if they are to approximate to serving as primary sources of information for research. Analogous situations exist in all published statistics: journey-to-work statistics inevitably have somewhat arbitrary
boundaries, if these are changed comparison over time is made
more difficult; in the commercial world it requires much work by an
experienced accountant to see how company reports may have been
manipulated to disguise a serious financial situation; the definition
of unemployment has been changed considerably during the 1980s
in the United Kingdom. As long ago as 1846 social statisticians had
enumerated some of the ways in which statistics can be misused
(Easthorpe, 1974). These are: (1) having preconceived ideas about
the final result; (2) disregarding figures which contradict the result
one would like to see come about; (3) not fully enumerating all
causes; (4) attributing to a single cause the resultant of several
causes; (5) comparing data which are not comparable.

A researcher needs, then, first to be aware of the large amount of
statistical information which is available. Here a good library is
invaluable; it will not necessarily have all the statistics to hand but it
should have reference publications which show what is available and
where. Most researchers acknowledge their debt to a knowledgable
librarian. Second, a researcher should find out as much as possible
about the background and limitations of any statistics used (see, for
example, Dale and Marsh, 1993) and, third, where possible, any
one-off surveys which are specific to the research project should
relate to published statistics. In some cases the need to use published statistics may modify the form of research question itself.

Documentary sources

Documents are another type of information which in certain forms, original letters for example, appears close to being a primary source but whose nature cannot be taken at face-value by the researcher. Documents broadly include any papers, especially official ones, which provide more or less direct evidence of decisions, transactions, status, thoughts, debates or actions. In a sense all documents are historical in nature, a product of the past, even if only the recent past. Therefore, the methods and evidence of historical research are appropriate to them; an annual company report is in essence a historical account. A distinction could perhaps be made between documentary information which can be checked from original living memory and that which cannot. As with published statistics, there are a number of aspects of documentary information for the researcher to consider at an early stage. The outcome may well determine whether the proposed research is feasible at all. These considerations are: (1) availability, (2) relevance to the research question, (3) sufficiency, (4) authenticity, and (5) congruity (or fit) with the concepts to be used in the research.

Availability

Availability of documents is obviously the first consideration, not only in terms of physical existence, but of whether the researcher will be given access to the documents and, further, be allowed to quote from or copy them as necessary and, if so, under what limitations. As with statistical information, aggregation of information may be required in the case of modern documents to protect confidentiality of individual cases. This is no bad thing if a researcher is hoping in any case to reach generalized conclusions. Nevertheless, it may be desirable to see the original information in order to decide how best the aggregation should be done. Individual cases may sometimes be protected by the use of pseudonyms. Clearly there are issues of trust and responsibility here. It is well known that the UK Public Record Office only releases government files after a predetermined lapse of time and usually these have also been 'weeded', that is much controversial material will have been removed. Local government practice varies. For example, copies of planning decision notices, that is the written decision sent to applicants for planning permission, together with reasons and conditions, are by law available for public investigation. But the files on the case, which may include negotiations between developers and the authority and could shed interesting light on the detailed operation of policies, would normally not be made available to outside researchers.

Relevance

Whether or not the documentary information which may be available also has relevance to the research in question can, for a beginner in research, be determined only by preliminary investigation. This is obviously something of a circular process; the research question, the availability and the relevance of documentation must all be considered together. An experienced researcher will expect to acquire eventually a considerable knowledge of relevant sources and, again, this process, like experience in survey or experimental work, is part of research training. The beginner however may be in one of two extreme positions, either being largely unaware of the many documentary sources available or, on the other hand, having quite unrealistic expectations of the amount and nature of information which can be extracted from such sources or of the effort involved. It is often surprising how what one might expect to be fairly obvious information does not in fact exist. This should be seen not just as a problem for the researcher but as an opportunity.

Sufficiency

To answer the question whether or not the information is sufficient we have to ask, sufficient for what? What is the nature of the research argument? How important are the circumstances to which the results of the research might be applied? In the medieval Patent Roll of 1385 it is recorded, in Latin, that Richard II granted a licence to Edward Dalyngrigge, knight, of Bodyham in Sussex to crenellate his manor house and turn it into a defensible castle. This single document might be considered sufficient for a medievalist to infer the general conclusion that it was the practice of the king to control the building of castles by his potentially rebellious subjects (which is well-attested elsewhere). The information also suggests in particular that Dalyngrigge was seen at the time as a trusted and loyal knight. As another example, a single document might have shown, deductively, that Guy Fawkes was not, as claimed, the tool of reactionary Catholics but of a repressive Protestant secret service, and so have had considerable effect on the progress of Catholic emancipation in England. On the other hand, if we wish to know the success rate, believed to be low, of general medical practitioners in diagnosing skin cancer we are in the realms of statistical inference (Chapter Seven) and need a substantial number of documented case-studies to build up, in effect, our own statistics where none may be available.

A quantitative form of documentary analysis, known as *content analysis*, was pioneered in the early nineteenth century. Here the amount and frequency of references to specified topics are measured and used as possible indicators of importance or of attitudes (Ogburn, 1912). This is analagous to the quantitative analysis of children's essays or of literature (Chapter Three). Of more general importance was the realization that the selection and definition of categories for analysis not only gave emphasis to those categories at the expense of others but were themselves the outcome of pre-conceived ideas of what was important; that is, the selection of categories could pre-judge to some extent the results. Today, as for example in various forms of attitude measurement (Chapter Five), procedures have been developed which attempt to be more objective and to involve large groups of people in defining categories for analysis.

Congruence

In these various examples above, both the nature of the research arguments and their social significance to modern life are seen to vary. In some cases very large amounts of detailed information may be insufficient to answer important questions. For example, the Ministry of Agriculture's laboriously collected field-by-field crop returns have still left room for enormous debate about the extent of urbanization of rural land. The problem here is that, although the information is ostensibly about change of use of rural land, the information is not congruent with that needed to answer questions about urbanization.

Authenticity

Historical and political questions are, in fact, rarely solved by a single document; while one piece of documentary information may appear to suggest one conclusion, it may be contradicted by another. Since we assume logically that two contradictory conclusions cannot both be correct we are left with the more complex problem of deciding between them. Among other considerations which then arise is that of the authenticity of documents; we need to know whether or not they are authentic, or genuine. This requires, ideally, a reliable knowledge of the author or authors of a document, or at least of the organizations responsible for its creation, its date and, in most cases, status; what is the document's nature, or authority, who authorized it and when? We need also to assess the *truthfulness* of the document; it may be authentic but is the information exaggerated or played down, or is it deliberately or inadvertently untrue? For example, the duly recorded minutes of a certain County Council stated that the saving from closing a village primary school would be £40,000. Should the researcher take this as an authoritative figure? Further investigation showed this in fact to be a gross sum; it included the teacher's salary, which would still be paid elsewhere; it did not include the cost of building an extra classroom at another school to accommodate the children, nor the cost of transporting them there. The true net cost saved turned out to be £10,000.

In rare cases, as with the notorious so-called Hitler diaries, scientific tests may be performed on the ink and paper used. Generally, documentary evidence may be validated by things such as cross-reference, writing style, location, or by reference to other files in other places. The records of work on royal castles in medieval times, for example, are considered to be so thorough that the absence of a mention of work at any time is assumed to mean that none took place: a rather daring inductive inference. Working through a modern file of memoranda, agendas, minutes and notes, or other collections of documents, it is possible to build up a chronological picture of communications, influences and decisions. The process of investigation applies equally to a local case-study as to a major international event, though the latter will be more complex. But it could be a mistake to assume that because something was not recorded it did not happen. In recent years the use of word-processors, telephones, photocopiers and fax machines seems to have led to files being less informative. Until quite recently in modern times corrections and changes would be noted on original papers; letters and memoranda were annotated, circulated and initialled, and telephone messages were minuted. Official files generally were much more complete records of decision *processes*. Individual documents were naturally allocated more value, and more human interest, when they were so laborious to produce and to copy.

Summary

To summarize this section, it is clear that many forms of information are potentially available to a researcher in addition to the primary sources of direct observation of various sorts and secondary sources such as books. Of these intermediate types, the two most common are published statistics, which by definition comprise quantitative information, and the great variety of documentary sources. Other forms such as maps and, now, computer data-bases may, according to their nature, fit into either of these categories. A researcher should obviously, first, become acquainted with relevant information sources. A number of reference publications are useful here (see recommended reading), as are discussions with other workers, librarians, and staff in museums and record offices. Second, a researcher should be able to evaluate these information sources in terms of their nature and quality, as outlined above, and be prepared to support this evaluation.

Information for inductive argument

The conclusive or categorical nature of deductive argument has been shown above to be highly desirable. But it is often not attainable in social science argument and, perhaps, not as often in natural science as is sometimes claimed (see for example the argument by analogy, below). Simple refutation or falsification of a hypothesis is not in any case possible in probabilistic argument, as explained in Chapter Three. There the idea of simple deductive refutation was introduced to highlight the logical value of falsification as opposed to confirmation. Emphasis was given to the importance of the structure of argument. Here we look at the significance of the sufficiency of information or evidence contained in the argument.

Inductive argument has a simple and flexible structure, relying always to some extent on a creative or intuitive leap. Unlike a deductive argument, which if truly complete and valid is not changed by further information, the conclusion of an inductive argument can be either strengthened or weakened by further evidence. It is important therefore, in inductive argument, to obtain as much and as comprehensive information as possible since we do not know whether further information may tend to falsify or confirm the conclusion. If would clearly be intellectually dishonest to collect evidence for one side of the argument only.

Induction by enumeration

Suppose that a survey of 1,000 residents of a city produces the result that 100 are vegetarians and 900 are not. A simple inductive argument could be set out as follows:

> 90 per cent of the sample population were not vegetarian;
> Therefore 90 per cent of the total population are not vegetarian.

This is an example of what is known as induction by enumeration; the single premise or evidence is a statement about the preferences of an observed *sample population* (that is, a portion only of the total population, Chapter Seven) and an inductive conclusion or inference is made about the preferences of the *total population*. The proportion, in this case 90 per cent, could be anything from 0 to 100 per cent. Such inductive arguments (for the inference is not in fact categorically or certainly true) are extremely common in much research and survey work in both social and natural sciences, to the extent that they are often taken for granted. They are however subject to two defects in the basic information which may render the whole argument fallacious. First, if only a few people had been interviewed, instead of 1,000, we might feel that the sample, and hence the premise, was unconvincing; this is an example of the *fallacy of insufficient statistics*. Second, if, for example, the survey had been carried out at a time and place which would have largely excluded younger residents the information would have been unrepresentative, or biased, since it is known that vegetarianism is more popular among young people. This illustrates the *fallacy of biased statistics.* What constitutes sufficiency and the absence of bias will be examined in a more detailed quantitative way in Chapter Seven.

The conclusive deductive argument of the categorical syllogism has been discussed in Chapter Three. There is also an analogous inductive form known as the *statistical syllogism*:

> 90 per cent of residents are non-vegetarian; this customer is a resident;
> therefore this customer is a non-vegetarian.

In this case the conclusion could be incorrect even if the first premise (itself based on a previous inductive argument) is true. Nevertheless, the conclusion is the best 'odds-on' judgement we can make. If a restaurant manager sticks to this conclusion on all occasions he will be right nine times out of ten, and wrong in only 10 per cent of cases. The conclusion may be modified by the term 'probably' which indicates the uncertainty of the conclusion since it is the conclusion of an inductive argument. But any individual is either a vegetarian or not, and in many circumstances the best possible decision has to be taken on the evidence available. The strength of the conclusion depends very much on the value of the proportion given in the first premise. If the value is high, 90 per cent, we should be right most of the time; if the value is 50 per cent then there are equal chances of being right or wrong; if less than 50 per cent the conclusion will be more often wrong. These are examples of calculated *risks* where we know, and may accept or reject, the chances of a particular action being appropriate. This situation should be distinguished from *uncertainty* where the risks are not known or quantified. In Chapter Seven it will be seen that there is yet a further element of probability attached to the percentage figures themselves since these have been inferred from a sample only. The chance we are willing to accept of being right or wrong will depend on the importance to us of the conclusion being correct. Historical argument would not demand the same high degree of probability as studies of the health of workers in the nuclear industry.

It is clear also that, as with any inductive argument, the more information we have, the greater is the probability of our conclusion being correct. If, for example, we knew the differing proportion of vegetarians among the young and old members of the total population we could make more accurate conclusions, according to whether a particular customer was judged to be old or young.

Argument from authority

Two other inductive arguments depend particularly for their correctness on the quality of the information which they contain. These are the argument from authority and the argument from analogy. The first may be simply stated:

> Person x is an authority on this topic; x says y;
> therefore: y is true.

This is a form of argument which we are all inclined to accept every day, but to be correct the researcher needs to be satisfied on at least three points: (1) that x *is* an authority (and to know by what criteria); (2) that he or she is speaking within the scope of the relevant expertise (an expert in one topic may be quite mistaken on another); (3) that the expert is being truthful in this particular case and is not biased by some external objective.

Investigations of social questions, in social or political history for example, are frequently based on individual personal interviews or memoirs. Students often seem to feel that a few interviews with individuals in several organizations constitute research. It is very important, when using interviews, to apply rigorous criteria (Chapter Five) and to distinguish opinions from fact, for example on whether a particular policy is working or an objective achieved. Of course the opinion of a significant person may be of great interest, especially when it influences, or is influenced by, outside events or campaigns. In a sense opinion may be the raw material of research, and a legitimate and measurable objective of certain interest groups might be to change that opinion. But, as always, opinion should be tested against other opinions and preferably against more clearly objective information. Much of what has been said here applies also of course to views expressed indirectly in documents.

Induction by analogy

This form of argument is much more used than is generally realized. It is usual to explain or illustrate one system by comparing it with another: the flow systems of water and electricity, for example. Jaques Delors argued that the process of European union was like riding a bicycle and concluded that momentum was necessary to avoid a fall. Most people are aware that analogies must not be pushed too far, and that analogies might illustrate but do not prove. But similarities between two systems are often wrongly used as virtual proof in arguing from one system to another. Plato argued from an analogy between the conduct of the state and the individual. Biologists frequently assume that some higher mammals are sufficiently like humans for inferences about humans to be drawn from animal experiments. We all tend to assume that much of what is true for one human being is likely to be true for another. Sometimes the analogies are constructed artificially, as with mathematical modelling of physical or social-economic systems such as the UK Treasury model of the economy, or the type of model, outlined in Chapter Two, for predicting student grades. Argument by analogy should always be regarded as suspect. If anything more than illustration is to be attempted, two criteria are important in the use of the argument from analogy: (1) that similarities between the two systems should be present in as many aspects as possible and (2) that the analogy or model should be tested, calibrated and modified; that is it should be seen to have worked, at least experimentally, in the past. Delors' analogy of the bicycle is not very convincing, except perhaps rhetorically; animal experimentation, unfortunately, could be.

Conclusions

Emphasis in this chapter has been given to the importance of the general nature and quality of information in research rather than to particular techniques of information-gathering. Especially important are the criteria for assessing reliability of information. In the case of statistical or quantitative information it is necessary to know and to understand any sampling procedures, the types of question asked and definitions employed. The level of aggregation used may be crucial in teasing out conclusions. For all types of information, statistical, documentary and oral, it is necessary to be able to evaluate, preferably at the outset, availability, relevance, sufficiency, authenticity, congruity and the authority and truthfulness of the source. The information should be both sufficient to support the conclusions reached and demonstrably free from unconscious as well as conscious bias. In non-quantitative work the degree of sufficiency is a matter of judgement and inductive inference; this in fact is also true in quantitative work though the basis of judgement is there made more explicit (see Chapter Seven) and unconscious bias may be more clearly avoided.

Research which is to 'add to the sum of human knowledge' (Chapter One) clearly has to mine original or primary sources of information, though the idea for the research will, today, usually come from appraisal of secondary published sources. It is only at the doctoral level of student research however that work is expected to be substantially original. But even at an under-graduate level a student dissertation should display the ability to identify and work from original sources, although time constraints may result in the conclusion being indicative only rather than conclusive. Require-ments for different types of dissertation are examined further in Chapter Eight, but two points may be made here. First, not all orig-inal information is physical in the sense that scientific or archaeo-logical or even much sociological information is. If we were researching, for example, the history of scientific ideas then docu-ments and even published works would be primary sources since ideas do not grow on trees. Even so, in the pursuit of the original, the aim should be to find the earliest publications, to compare edi-tions, to look for the development of ideas in unpublished letters or papers, and not to be content with other researchers' commentaries but to read the originals – in the original language if possible since meanings cannot always be transferred in translation. The second point is that students do not always use primary information as much as they might. There seems to be a lingering attitude that authority is more significant than originality. But these must be kept in balance. Not only do students tend to think of authority first, in terms for example of interviews rather than original surveys, but may often spend a good deal of time and effort on a survey and then give little consideration or prominence to the results of this empirical work in their dissertation. Sometimes a survey which could form the whole basis of a dissertation may be relegated to a mere appendix while preference is given to secondary sources.

In the next chapter, drawing on the principles outlined here, pro-cedures for the collection of certain types of primary information will be examined in more detail.

CHECK LIST: Chapter 4

You should know and understand:

- the importance of correct and sufficient information on which to base research conclusions
- the need to give a correct and full account of information used in a research project
- how to identify and evaluate information which can be used to test the research question or hypothesis
- the nature and value of primary sources of information;
- the nature and use of secondary sources of information

- the precautions necessary when using published statistics
- the criteria of useful documentary information:
  availability
  relevance
  sufficiency
  congruence
  authenticity
  limitations of modern records in a computer age
- induction by enumeration:
  the fallacy of insufficient statistics
  the fallacy of biased statistics
  statistical syllogism
- the requirements for correct argument from authority
- the requirements for correct induction by analogy

Further reading

Central Statistical Office, 1976–, *Guide to official statistics*, HMSO, London.

Chapman, M., and Mahon, B., 1986, *Plain figures*, HMSO, London.

Dale, A., and Marsh, C., 1993, *The 1991 census user's guide*, HMSO, London.

Easthorpe, G., 1974, *A history of social research methods*, Longman, London.

Fenner, P., and Armstrong, M.C., 1981, *Research: a practical guide to finding information*, William Kaufman, Los Altos, CA.

Gash, S., 1989, *Effective literature searching for students*, Gower, Aldershot.

Hoskins, W.G., 1972 [1959], *Local history in England*, 2nd edn, Longman, London.

Irvine, J., et al. (eds.), 1979, *Demystifying social statistics*, Pluto Press, London.

Marwick, A., 1970, *Primary sources*, Humanities: a foundation course, Unit 6, introduction to history, part 2, Open University Press, Milton Keynes.

Mort, D., 1990, *Sources of unofficial UK statistics*, 2nd edn, Gower, Aldershot.

Nicholson, H., 1960, *The age of reason (1700–1789)*, Constable, London.

Ogburn, W.F., 1912, 'Progress and uniformity in child labour legislation', reproduced in Duncan, O., 1964, *On culture and social change*, University of Chicago Press, Chicago, pp. 110–30.

Quetelet, J.A.L., 1846, *Sur la theorie de probabilite appliquée aux sciences morales et politiques*, Hayez, Brussels.

Rhind, D., 1983, *A census user's handbook*, Methuen, London.

Scott, J., 1990, *A matter of record; documentary sources in social research*, Polity Press, Cambridge.

Wasserman, P. et al., 1980, *Statistical sources: a subject guide to data on industrial, business, social educational, financial and other topics for the United States and internationally*, 6th edn, Gale Research Company, Detroit.

5

METHODS OF PRIMARY INFORMATION COLLECTION

'If I had to say which was telling the truth about society,
a speech by a Minister of Housing or the actual buildings
put up in his time, I should believe the buildings.'
(Sir Kenneth Clark, *Civilisation*, 1969)

How does a researcher set about obtaining primary information in
an organized and objective way? A natural scientist has two main
methods, the *experiment*, whether in field or laboratory, and the
descriptive *survey* or record, which may be quantitative or qualitative, conducted in the field. Social science adds to these the methods of the historian, the so-called *comparative method* which is now
to some extent discredited since it was based on an idealized and
outmoded concept of inevitable and beneficial change in historical
development. Fourth, there are the methods of *participant observation* developed in anthropology and outlined briefly in Chapter Two.
As will be explained below, true experimentation is difficult in the
social sciences (see also the discussion in Chapter Two) except in
quasi-scientific disciplines such as psychology. Primary information
collection in social science work most commonly involves surveys of
various kinds, using the term in the widest sense to include surveys
of documents, literature and the use of interviews, as well as the
conventional social or economic survey. This chapter outlines some
of the principles involved in survey work.

Essentially, gathering information in the field may be seen as no
different from recording information in the course of a laboratory

experiment, though a number of experimental criteria (below) are more difficult to apply in field studies. Many students make the mistake of rushing out to do premature and ill-prepared surveys before the research question (see Chapter Eight) and the concepts involved have been properly defined. This is particularly unfortunate when the respondents are hard-pressed officials or business people and where much of the information might have been obtained from published documents. On the other hand, a student may become so involved in literature reviews, background studies, and largely descriptive case-studies that there is little time left for a survey which is then conducted as an afterthought because the student, or even the supervisor, has a vague idea that a survey ought to be done. For this reason quite useful surveys are sometimes not given their due weight in dissertations. *The main point to note here is that surveys do require careful thought, advice, discussion with more experienced researchers and time for preparation, and that the role of surveys within the organization of the research needs to be clearly defined.*

Experimental design

All research, as explained in Chapter Three, may be seen as attempts to relate two concepts. The relationship may be causal or it may simply be descriptive; for example, politicians (concept 1) may react in a defined way (concept 2) or, more particularly, Labour and Tory politicians may react in different ways or, specifically, Winston Churchill behaved in such-and-such a way. We may wish to know what the attitudes of farmers are to, say, wildlife conservationists, or of an ethnic minority to the police, or of the police to ethnic minorities. We may, further, wish to know what has caused these attitudes or whether, following a publicity campaign, they have changed. While perfect experimentation may not be possible, an understanding of experimental design is a useful start to designing rigorous and meaningful surveys.

Scientists use the concepts of independent and dependent variables which roughly coincide with the ideas of cause and effect respectively. A *variable* is some measure of a phenomenon which both varies and whose variation can be measured, or at least recorded in some way, even if only in terms of its presence or absence. An *independent variable* is a condition which, ideally, can be varied directly by an experimenter and, again loosely, may be thought of as a possible cause of some effect. A *dependent variable* is a condition which can only, if at all, be changed indirectly by the experimenter by way of the independent variable; the dependent variable may be thought of as an effect, or at least as a possible effect. By varying the independent variable a researcher hopes to find whether or not there is a relationship with the dependent variable, and, if so, what it is. If the independent variable cannot be made to vary, or at least observed to vary, experimentation is not possible. A simple illustration is provided by the degree of opening (independent variable) of a water tap and the rate (dependent variable) at which a bucket under the tap fills with water. More complex examples are the relation between drug dosage and recovery rate from a disease, or between time spent in higher education and attitudes to classical music. *Experimental design is concerned with a logical analysis of various procedures by which dependent and independent variables may be examined together.*

The one-shot case-study

Let us call the independent variable a treatment, T, and the dependent variable, whose value is unknown, X. The simplest relation between the two may be expressed as

$$T \rightarrow X$$

where the arrow indicates that condition X is observed to follow condition T where T may have been produced either inadvertently or experimentally. This sequence of observation, known as the one-shot case-study, is logically extremely weak. In the seventeenth century, however, it might have been sufficient to condemn a harmless old woman to an agonizing death; she was seen staring at the cattle, the cattle fell sick, therefore she must have cast a spell on the cattle, and so she is a witch. The argument is also known as the *post hoc ergo propter hoc* fallacy (after this, therefore because of this) or, more usually, simply as the *post hoc* argument. While we may tend to feel intellectually superior, in that we no longer believe in witches, this form of argument is still widely employed in public affairs; it is in fact quite useful in personal experience and can also be found in some less rigorous investigations.

The *post hoc* argument may in practice be more useful than it appears, but only because it is embedded in other implicit argument and experience of both causal mechanisms and of other similar events. For example:

Petrol was put in the petrol tank of the car → the car was then started.

A reasonable, but not categorical, conclusion appears to be that the car could be started because petrol had been put in the tank. However, there could be other reasons: perhaps we forgot to switch on the ignition the first time but did not notice this (it is obviously a classic car since the ignition and starter switches are separate), or perhaps during the time taken to get a can of petrol the flooded carburettor had time to dry. That is, other conditions may have changed quite coincidentally. But, above all, the argument as stated does not even say that the car refused to start before the petrol was put in, which renders the argument meaningless. There are thus two reasons for the dubious nature of the *post hoc* argument: (1) that it does not describe the situation before conditions were changed, or treatment applied (that is, it does not even show that a possible effect has taken place) and (2) that it does not exclude the possibility of other causes of which we know nothing. In everyday life, induction or experience may compensate to some extent, though not entirely, for these defects. The design also makes it difficult to exclude the effects of other possible causes, even when we do know about them. For example a change which we may wish to investigate in local economic conditions may be accompanied by coincidental changes in national or international economies. In its simplest form the *post hoc* argument does not distinguish the effects of such various influences (see, however, multiple correlation, Chapter Seven). The *post hoc* observation often provides of course a valuable starting point or hypothesis for research.

The one group pretest post-test design

The first criticism of the *post hoc* argument, above, as to whether change has in fact occurred, may be taken care of explicitly by the procedure known as the one group pre-test–post-test design. Here the conditions which exist before the application of treatment are also recorded or surveyed:

The car does not start (X_0) → petrol was put in the tank (T) → the car was then started (X_1).

This can be expressed generally as $X_0 \rightarrow T \rightarrow X_1$. A researcher who wishes to survey the effects (or rather the after-conditions, since cause and effect are not proved) of some change or event should if possible survey conditions before the event as well. This may not be possible if the event is unexpected or, as often happens, the research is an afterthought, in which case recourse may be had to existing records and surveys if these are available. Natural scientists continually monitor many aspects of the physical environment and while this may appear pedestrian it is in fact highly valuable in identifying change. Social statistics perform a similar role for the social sciences.

The static group comparison

Use of a pre-test, then, can show whether a change has occurred but does not in itself exclude the possibility of causes other than T, which was the second weakness of the *post hoc* argument. Thus an educational psychologist may attempt to evaluate the effectiveness of a new method of teaching decimal calculations by first testing the ability of a group of children, then teaching the programme, then re-testing. But what if most or all of the children have meanwhile seen a TV programme about decimals? This unforeseen and possibly unknown eventuality might be taken care of by another procedure, known as the static group comparison, of initially dividing the children into two groups and giving the special tuition to one group only:

$$(\text{group 1}) \; T_1 \rightarrow X_1;$$
$$(\text{group 2}) \; \underline{\quad} \rightarrow X_2.$$

It is assumed that any outside influences, such as a special TV programme, would affect both groups equally. Therefore if the score of results for group 1 is greater than that for group 2 $(X_1 > X_2)$ it seems likely that it is the treatment which has produced the effect; if X_1 is equal to X_2, it probably has not. Conceivably, if the teaching programme had been confusing, X_2 might be greater than X_1.

Experimental control

Group 2, above, is known as a *control group* and raises the very important principle of *control* in experimentation or survey work, or of the *controlled experiment*. It is only by the use of controlled experiments that arguments about cause and effect can be rigorously tested. The aim is two-fold: (1) to have two similar groups and (2) to treat each group in exactly the same manner except for the one particular treatment under test. This second requirement should apply not only to the conditions within the experiment, but also, it is hoped, to any external influences. These criteria are clearly much more easily met in the laboratory than in real life. In the case of the school children it is difficult to isolate them from all outside influences and the hope can only be that such influences will, by the laws of chance, affect each group similarly, thus cancelling out any effects on the results. If strict experimental control has not been, or cannot be, exercised then the researcher is in the position of the car mechanic who has put petrol in the tank *and* cleaned the spark plugs *and* cleaned the fuel filter; the effect may be to start the car, but the cause or causes remain uncertain (see, however, p.168 below).

While it is usually preferable to be able to investigate causal mechanisms directly, this is not always possible. Scientific theories sometimes survive for many years, based on circumstantial evidence alone, until techniques are developed which enable the mechanisms to be observed. As a simple illustration, consider the following analogy:

Hypothesis – Absence of petrol in the tank causes the car not to
   start.
Consequence – If petrol is put in the tank, the car will start.
Test – Put petrol in the tank.
Result – The car starts.
Conclusion – The hypothesis is correct.

Although the argument is strictly fallacious (as in the example on p.63) the conclusion is in fact very reasonable *if* we can be sure that nothing else has been done to the car meanwhile. In controlled laboratory experiment it is feasible often to exclude in this way all other possible causes except the one under test. But in social science investigation this condition is much more difficult to achieve. However, the main idea to note here is that, by testing the *consequence* of the hypothesis being true *under controlled conditions,* we can make reasonable inferences about it without ever looking in the tank or having any concept of how the petrol reaches and is used by the engine.

Randomization and matching

Similarity between two test groups, in everything but the treatment under investigation, may be attempted in two ways. First, the total group (in this case the class) may be randomly divided into two. In studies of larger populations two representative sample groups, the test and control groups, may be selected at random. In some cases (see below) more than two groups may be used. The assumption is that *two groups selected at random,* known as *randomized groups,* will each have an equal chance of incorporating any existing differences, such as in level of intelligence, or in home circumstances: for example, the possession of a TV set. In fact, in small groups, chance selection could still produce bias between the groups.

Randomization, it is to be hoped, should take care of *unknown influences,* distributing them equally between groups if the groups are large enough. *Known influences* however may be accounted for by a second procedure known as *matching groups.* Thus if parental income is believed to be a possible important influence on ability with decimal calculations, and if the facts on income are available, a similar profile of parental income could be ensured or matched in each group. Within the matching process individuals should be randomly selected as before: for example, if a number of individuals have similar parental incomes, those individuals should be equally *but randomly* distributed between the two groups.

The post-test only control group design

When the two groups in the static group comparison have been carefully randomized, and possibly matched, the resulting argument becomes much stronger. We may feel also that, inductively, there is an argument that a difference between X_1 and X_2 suggests that a change has occurred following treatment even though there is no pre-test. The procedure may be summarized as follows:

$$\text{Rm} \begin{cases} \text{(group 1) } T_1 \rightarrow X_1 \\ \text{(group 2) } \_\_ \rightarrow X_2 \end{cases}$$

This is the post-test only control-group design where Rm represents the very important randomization process. Students, and even some professional workers, often seem to regard randomization procedures as rather pedantic. In fact the general logic of the procedures and arguments involved in experimentation and survey design depend fundamentally on the assumptions of randomization, as also do the more specific processes of statistical analysis (Chapter Seven).

The pre-test post-test control group design

While each of the previous procedures overcomes specific problems it is only when they are combined that many researchers are prepared to accept that a true experimental system has been achieved. The *pre-test – post-test control group design* provides a test of whether a change has occurred and also provides a control group or groups as a check on possible other causes:

$$\text{Rm} \begin{cases} \text{(group 1) } X_1 \to T_1 \to X_2 \\ \text{(group 2) } X_3 \to \underline{} \to X_4 \end{cases}$$

It is interesting to examine both the advantages and the problems of applying this procedure to a real investigation. For example, agencies such as National Park authorities or the National Trust provide, at some expense, at attractive or sensitive sites, visitor information centres which are intended to improve visitors' knowledge, enjoyment and behaviour. How effective are such centres in achieving their intended purposes? Measures of 'success' such as numbers of people using the centres, or the amounts spent there, do not really answer this question.

Suppose for the moment that a questionnaire or survey could be devised which would measure the relevant knowledge or enjoyment of visitors (not in itself an easy thing to do). Presumably individuals should be interviewed before and after using the centre to see what changes the visit may have caused in these respects. The problem with this pre-test however is that the pre-test may influence the subject of the test; he or she may look more clearly at the information available *because* of the pre-test. This might be overcome by *randomly* allocating individuals into two categories and applying the pre-test to one group only, the assumption being that before the visit the two groups are similar in knowledge and that the aggregate knowledge of the one approximates to that of the other. This would give some indication of any effect of the pre-test. It would be a good idea to test also a group of individuals who had not used the centre. But how is this to be done in practice? One way might be to allocate individuals' results into groups following the post-test according to whether they said they had visited the centre or not. This is a common survey practice. But it could be that the people who have chosen to visit the centre are those more interested in knowledge and hence likely to be more knowledgable already. Alternatively, randomly selected individuals might be prevented from entering the centre; or the centre could be closed for a period. Clearly, these measures might be resented. It can be seen that an apparently straightforward investigation is difficult to carry out in a rigorous experimental manner. In fact the post-test only control group design is commonly used for this type of survey.

Apart from these difficulties of implementing the theoretical experimental design, how can any knowledge gained be measured? One way is that visitors leaving the centre might simply be asked if they felt they had learned anything. Here a researcher relies on the respondent's subjective and spur-of-the-moment *opinions* of his or her pre- and post-test states. Knowledge could be tested more systematically by a sort of mini-examination or quiz, but this might be rejected by some respondents. Or one could ask more objective questions about a subject's *behaviour*; did he or she even look at the information, for how long, and so on. Surveys of this type often reveal that most people only buy a drink and use the washroom.

Other experimental designs

There are a number of other experimental designs. Possible influences of a pre-test on treatment, as in the above case, can be identified by adding to the pre-test–post-test control group design two more experimental random groups, one which has the treatment but no pretest and one which has neither, thus making up the *Solomon Four Group design*. Another experimental procedure is to make a *series* of observations before and after treatment; this both establishes the average conditions before treatment and is a check on whether any change is merely temporary. This *time series* experiment may, for example, be used to monitor the effects of road layout changes on traffic flows, which normally vary over time; a control time series survey may be used at another location to check on general trends. Very few social science surveys attempt the higher levels of complexity outlined here, the post-test control group, and even the single-shot case-study, despite its logical weakness, are commonly used.

Internal and external validity

Meanwhile, our car mechanic has been busy, inductively formulating hypotheses based on his experience of cars, testing each idea in turn and effectively falsifying it as the car fails to start. Eventually he will find the correct hypothesis and the car will start. A car mechanic has to be a very logical person. The mechanic's problem is that with the next car he must start all over again. Having discovered what works for one car does not tell him what is wrong with the next (though it should be noted that in the process the mechanic will have increased his personal understanding, or insight, of cars). We say that his experiments have no external validity. External validity is that property of an investigation which enables its results to be applied outside of itself, or to be generalized. Internal validity is the property of an investigation which means that the conclusions are correct within that particular investigation or experiment. Internal validity is a necessary but not sufficient condition for external validity. Each is made up of a number of considerations. In the experiment on teaching method described earlier we saw that it was necessary to incorporate either a pre-test or a control group, or possibly both, if meaningful conclusions were to be reached. Further, if a control group is used it must be selected in such a way as to be *representative* of the test group (Chapter Six). If all these procedures are acceptable we may conclude that the results are true for that particular class of children, that is they are internally valid.

However, if the results are to be valid for all other school children not involved in the experiment, that is if the results are to be externally valid, then the children in the experimental class must be representative of all children. It is obvious that external validity may reasonably be restricted, in this case, say, to all other children of the same age and culture. But external validity cannot be achieved merely by retrospective restrictions of this type since the class chosen may not be representative even of its own age and culture.

This representativeness can only be obtained by random sampling (Chapter Six) across a number of classes, or schools or even, ideally, across a number of towns. But in research, as in all life, trade-offs are necessary. Increasing the range of population sampled will increase the *variability* of the results; that is, although the *average* results for the two groups may still clearly differ, the greater *range* of children's abilities in the wider sample may give a wider spread of individual results. This weakens the statistical argument (see Chapter Seven). The clearest test of methods of teaching decimal calculations would in fact be obtained from a group of children selected to have closely similar abilities; but this has to be traded off against more restricted external validity.

Asking questions

What sort of Information is being sought?

Many social science surveys, though by no means all, consist of asking questions of people; that is, the surveys use *questionnaires*. Most students, wrongly, begin a survey by writing out a list of questions to ask. So many questionnaires, good or bad, are encountered in modern living that to design a questionnaire seems an easy thing to do. It is not. Some of the pitfalls may become clear to a researcher as work progresses and information is found to be largely unusable; some may only be evident when a dissertation is expertly examined. At the centre of the process of questionnaire design is the question, 'what information do I need to obtain?' or, more rigorously, 'what hypotheses do I want to test?' Obviously, in a research project, information should not be sought merely to support a pre-determined point of view, but as a genuine attempt to increase knowledge. Then, when a question has been formulated to elicit the required information, the question itself must be re-examined for a number of general criteria (see below) and tested in a pilot survey to see if its answers will in practice provide the information sought.

A student preparing a questionnaire to discuss farmers' attitudes to a conservation plan might include the question, 'Is your farm small, medium or large?' Let us analyse this question, for it is not as simple as asking, 'Is your farming arable or dairy?' Is the question asking whether the farmer *thinks* his farm is small, relative say to his needs; is the answer a matter of fact or is it one of attitude? Even if the farmer treats the question factually, is his standard of 'small' the same as another's? A survey to discover the optimum size of gardens in housing estate design might be unwise to ask people how big an ideal garden would be: first, because it must be made clear that the question refers to the respondents' own gardens, requiring their own commitment of time and energy; second, because most people are vague about outdoor dimensions, tending to underestimate them. A professional survey in fact asked residents whether they felt that their own gardens were too big or too small and then measured the gardens. Thus residents' opinions could be related objectively to actual dimensions.

In the farm survey, if the information needed is the size of the farm this is better asked for directly. But farmers may not like to give precise information so the form of the question could be, 'Is your farm size less than 100 acres, 100–200 acres or greater than 200 acres?' A similar form of *banded* question is useful when asking about personal details such as income or a respondent's age. One problem with banding is that, at the outset of a survey, the natural or significant limits of the bands may not be known. Another is that by manipulating these limits or categories the significance of the results may be changed; for example the aggregate views of 'small' farmers may be biased by excluding or including the larger of the small farms. It is important to check whether other surveys or statistics or agencies have established standard size bands and to make the present survey congruent with theirs if possible. This increases the general interest and relevance of the survey. There is in the field of housing research, for example, a professionally designed standard questionnaire, the Housing Assessment Kit (HAK), developed by the Department of the Environment.

Formulating the question

In the example above we saw the importance of questions being quite specific in relation to the information needed, how it is usually easier for respondents to be precise about facts than about opinions and judgements, how attitudes may often be checked against quantitative information indirectly, how respondents should not be asked to make unnecessary and possibly unreliable judgements, and how banding may reduce the possible offensiveness of personal questions but can lead to bias and loss of information. There are a number of other characteristics which should be avoided when formulating questions. A question must be clear and, also, not ambiguous: that is, not have two apparently clear meanings which are contradictory. Questions should be as simple as possible; the answer to, 'Do you agree or not agree with proposal X?' might result in the answer 'yes'. This apparent perversity on the part of the respondent should be viewed in the light of a commonly used form of question, which though logical is confusing, such as, 'Are you either unemployed or retired?' to which the answer could be 'yes' without distinction between the two categories. Double negatives can be confusing and should be avoided: 'Do you think the Maastricht Treaty should not be ratified if the social chapter is not included?' Better to ask 'Do you agree with proposal X?' yes or no'; or, 'If the social chapter is not included in the Maastricht Treaty, do you think the treaty should be ratified?'

Even this last question is far from ideal however in two respects. First, for a number of reasons it is preferable not to include two ideas in one question. How is someone to answer it who thinks the treaty should not be ratified, but not for the reason given? To the researcher, would a negative answer indicate a concern for the social chapter or merely a strong opposition to the whole treaty? What interpretations might be placed on a positive answer? The question does not in fact produce clear information on what is presumably its main point of interest, the influence of attitudes to the social chapter on attitudes to the treaty itself. Second, there is the consideration of how much information should be given to respondents. Sometimes the giving of information may be necessary as part of the investigation. For example, visitors to the White Horse Hill Ancient Monument in Oxfordshire were asked what they thought of the fact that they were excluded from parts of the site. Half the respondents were told of the conservation reasons for the exclusion, the other half were not. The second group was resentful at being excluded, the first group largely accepted the situation. The aim here was to estimate the effect of information on attitudes; the information was given as part of a controlled experiment. But to give the social chapter as a reason for not ratifying the Maastricht Treaty may suggest, or at least crystallize, reasons that the respondent had not thought of until that moment. Opinions differ as to how gullible respondents might be, but generally the public is not only helpful to interviewers but likes to please, does not like to appear stupid or uninformed and may wish to give an impression of social or political correctness. If we really want to find out whether the social chapter is already in people's minds as a reason to reject the treaty then the social chapter is the last thing that should be mentioned if we truly wish to avoid bias. It is also unnecessary to ask the question in the confusing form, above. Two simple questions are sufficient at the outset 'Do you think the Maastricht Treaty should be ratified?' and, 'If not, why?' Particular attitudes could then be explored further with more questions.

Open and closed questions

Different types of question have their own problems of interpretation and analysis. As has been seen, requests for straightforward quantitative answers about personal details, such as income, can appear impertinent. Often a respondent may not know a precise answer to a question such as how much has been spent on a holiday. In both cases banding may be a solution. Questions about which places have been visited are straightforward, but it may be difficult to remember how many times one has, say, visited the countryside in the last year. 'Have you visited the countryside in the last month?' is easier to answer and can provide essentially the same information. Questions which seek information about attitudes or opinions are more dubious and are discussed further below. Questions may be put as either closed questions or open questions. The former give the respondent a limited number of options for reply, at its simplest yes or no; the latter allows any reply. 'Do you think smoking should be banned in public places?' is a closed question; 'Why do you think smoking should be banned in public places?' is open to a variety of replies. The open question clearly places less restriction on the expression of opinion but is more troublesome to analyse (Chapter Six). There could be as many answers as there are respondents, but in practice an attempt can be made to group the answers according to similarity into a manageable number of categories (Table 5.1) though this does raise both theoretical and practical difficulties. A researcher might try to anticipate these categories when designing a questionnaire, so producing a closed question from the outset, though this may bias the results; or a small initial or *pilot survey* can be carried out and the categories for use in the main survey defined from the open answers.

Table 5.1 shows the results from a pilot survey, where answers to an open question, '*Is there anything you particularly like about this place?*' have been recorded as expressed (right); the researcher has attempted to classify these answers (left). However, a good deal of work would be necessary to discover exactly what some respondents meant by their answers and whether these would have similar meanings for other people. The complexity and possible inaccuracies of attitude surveys may be compared with the much more straightforward behavioural survey shown in Figure 6.10 (p.153).

Table 5.1 Grouping of answers to an open question

Suggested groupings	*Answers given to question in pilot survey*
0 Nothing particularly liked	no answer
1 Countryside components	forest, woodland, trees, moorland, forestry, New Forest, whole area
2 Natural beauty	landscape, scenery, greenery, attractive surroundings, environment, picturesque countryside, nature
3 Peace and quiet	peaceful, tranquil, relaxed, away from traffic, quiet, safe, atmosphere
4 Lack of development	stays the same, not too much building, not built up, away from towns, no commercial tourism, uncommercialized, not too many people, no day-trippers, unspoilt, roads quieter, small
5 Open countryside	go where you like, non-conformist, space, open air, clean, fresh
6 Local interest	history, cottages, villages, farms, Island, animals, ponies, deer, wildlife
7 Seaside	beach, forest and beach close together, sea, near to coast, boats
8 Things to do	plenty to do, boat trips, agricultural show, butterfly farm, towns, shopping centres, food, places of interest, Beaulieu, inexpensive, good base, Black Gang Chine, Cowes Week

Suggested groupings	Answers given to question in pilot survey
9 Informal activities	good for cycling, walking, camp sites, horse riding, forest tracts, county parks, play areas, good for children, good for dogs, diving
10 Personal reasons	lived here, new area, different, change, friends, good for disabled, girls, holiday crowds, close to home, people friendly

The questionnaire

Questionnaires should be as short as possible, partly for ease of evaluation and analysis, but particularly to maintain the interest and cooperation of the respondents. It is very important to think carefully about what needs to be included by attempting to anticipate the sorts of relationship which may be of interest at the analysis stage; but it is also wise to ask if every question is really necessary and what for. Clear, short, well designed questionnaires with a purposeful appearance produce a good impression. Computer coding and analysis (see Chapter Six) can be considerably speeded up if questionnaires are designed with these operations in mind from the outset (Figure 6.10).

Summary

It is important when a questionnaire is being designed that a good deal of thought is given to the purpose of the survey and that the questions relate to that purpose, are clear, avoid jargon or technical terms, are unambiguous, as simple as possible, and do not suggest ideas to the respondent or lead him or her to a particular conclusion. A beginner in research should read a good introduction to questionnaire design (see further reading p.123). It is advisable to discuss the questions with a number of people – academic advisors, experienced researchers and, most important, some members of the general public who have to understand them. Ideally a questionnaire should be tested in a small pilot survey and modified if necessary before a large-scale and possibly expensive survey is attempted. A recent professional survey into physical fitness produced quite unbelievable results for the proportion of adults regularly engaging in 'vigorous exercise'. Subsequent investigation showed that many respondents had taken this to mean no more than walking the dog. Questionnaires used in less-advanced student dissertations, certainly below doctoral level, may legitimately be in effect only pilot surveys and an examiner might be as interested in what the student has learnt about questionnaires as in the wider application of the information acquired.

Attitude measurement?

Natural science developed as scholars began to separate the idea of fact from that of value. Science chose to study facts and became hugely successful within its own terms. Values were left to religion and politics. Early social reformers made their case by accumulation of the painful details of the life of the poor. But the growth of democracy, mass commerce, universal education and the humanistic study of psychology, as religion declined, all produced a need to measure objectively and quantitatively the values which individuals place on things such as ideas, policies, public figures, social groups, fashion or possessions. These values are rarely if at all expressed purely in money terms and, whether positive or negative, may be thought of as attitudes. While much social investigation is concerned with things which a natural scientist could accept as facts, such as income or material living standards, a good deal of research is devoted to attempts to measure attitudes, whether of individuals or of groups.

Opinion polling is now such a familiar activity that it is easy to forget the substantial reservations which exist concerning the nature of the information which is being collected. Indeed most criticisms of such polls are directed at their organization in terms of such things as sampling procedures or statistical analysis rather than at their inherent nature. While there are well established and accepted general procedures which purport to measure attitudes these should only be used with some understanding of the problems of attitude measurement (Summers, 1977). For attitudes cannot be measured directly. First, they are intangible, they can be discerned only by their outward effects, or indicators. Second, attitudes are multidimensional; an attitude cannot be measured by one indicator any more than physical volume can be measured along a single line. Third, attitudes may be changeable in an apparently idiosyncratic and irregular manner. Fourth, attempts to measure attitudes possibly violate an important tenet of science that the act of measurement should not change the thing being measured; it is not always clear whether this is true for attitude measurement and great care needs to be taken over this aspect. A fifth and most important question is whether the measurement of attitude is in any case useful. The aim as always is to establish relationships. One relationship which is of interest here is that which enables a knowledge of attitudes to be used to predict behaviour. The term is used in the widest sense: we do not necessarily wish to manipulate behaviour in an Orwellian sense but, it may be, to provide for a sense of well-being from our surroundings. Will people subsequently react in the ways which our apparent knowledge of their attitudes would lead us to predict?

These various reservations should be borne in mind when evaluating attitude measurement in practice. The most obvious indication of attitude might be thought to be a person's answer to a direct question. This is a common research assumption. In fact, for a number of reasons, not all reprehensible, people do not always tell the truth. Psychologists have discovered that people have a tendency to wish to appear to agree with propositions (or, less frequently, to disagree). Respondents may give the answer they think the researcher wants. For this reason it is unwise to do as some surveys do and to state the purpose of the survey at the outset of questioning. Many people, unless they feel particularly strongly about an issue, may tend to give what they feel are socially acceptable answers. In this respect it is interesting to note that a person's actions may indicate different attitudes, say to cultural groups, from those suggested by purely verbal responses. Some psychologists go so far as to suggest the existence of different types of attitudes, action and verbal. Action attitudes may further be influenced by the social setting, whether personal, communal or formal. Often people do not know themselves how they might react in the future to hypothetical situations.

It is for reasons such as these that many researchers are dubious about any attempt to measure attitudes which relies on self-reporting by the respondent and prefer instead to evaluate actions either in experimental or real-life settings. Further, whichever approach is adopted, a number (or battery) of indicators is preferred since a simple opinion expressed about a single topic or quality may not always be a good guide to a general and complex attitude about society or environment: an expressed preference for redheads does not mean that a man will not fall in love with a brunette. Another precaution is to vary the order in which questions, when used, are presented. The answer to, 'Do you think smoking should be banned in public places?' could be biased according to whether it was preceded by 'Do you know that passive smoking can harm unborn babies?' or, alternatively, 'Do you think the state should interfere in the private lives of citizens?' In fact either of these two questions, if used to preface the first, would be what lawyers know as a *leading question*, designed to influence the answer to a subsequent question, and should normally be avoided in such a context. Since opinions, which are indicators of attitudes, can be volatile it is usually best not to measure them immediately after exposure to a possible conditioning influence. Anonymity may be desirable, not just in the sense of not giving names, but because it may be difficult to express certain opinions face to face, even to a stranger.

'I'll put you down as pessimistic, then?'

One purpose of attitude measurement is to attempt to predict behaviour.
Cartoon: © The Telegraph plc, London, 1993

It can be argued convincingly that the use of indicators of attitudes may be less distorting than the asking of direct questions. The problem is that a good deal of preliminary research and experience is needed to find out which indicators are reliable guides to attitude and, ultimately, behaviour. But to solve this still requires of course some independent measure of attitude, which is a *Catch 22* situation. When natural scientists measure tangible phenomena by the use of tangible indicators these are used only for convenience, the relationship can be checked experimentally. The use of indicators to measure intangible phenomena which in a sense, perhaps, can never be measured directly is more dubious. From long experience psychiatrists have developed a battery of indicators, known as the *Beck Depression Inventory*, to measure the strength of mental depression and propensity to suicide. Professional opinion pollsters are careful to claim only that X per cent of people *said* they would do Y *if* Z occurred; no explicit claim is made about what people will do. It is important to remember, too, in the absence of experimental evidence, that the apparent meanings implicit in questions and

'I called you in to dampen any consumer confidence you may be feeling'

Opinion can be volatile and may be influenced by recent information.
Cartoon: © The Telegraph plc, London, 1993

answers may not be the same for researchers and respondents, nor, it may be, for different groups of respondents. Environmental planners see derelict land as bad and ugly; the public may see it as interesting and above all accessible where conventional scenery may be seen as private, exclusive and not accessible. A particular survey with the objective of identifying favoured sites included among other indicators the question, 'Is this a good picnic place?' The researcher assumed a positive answer would indicate a favourable response to location. But when the pattern of answers to this question turned out to be different from others it was discovered that many respondents perceived picnic places as being crowded, noisy and untidy.

Since attitudes, as distinct from expressed opinions, are complex, it can be misleading to evaluate partial attitudes. Social surveys of village residents may ask what extra social facilities they would like. Since we would all like more than we have, such surveys reveal a discrepancy between what residents appear to want and what they have; hence the attitude of the residents is assumed to be one of dissatisfaction. But when residents are asked if they would trade-off greatly increased development to justify new facilities they most often say that on balance they prefer things the way they are; indeed general expressions of satisfaction are often high. This illustrates also the pitfalls of normative research (Chapter Three), of trying to discover what ought to be, rather than what is. On the other hand there is clearly a need on occasion to discover what factors are limiting people's aspirations, attitudes or bargaining power, or to be aware that a sum of money has different values for different income groups.

In attitude measurement good experimental design, as discussed above, is important. Proper sampling procedures, the use of randomized control groups, and internal analysis of data, that is looking for differences in responses between identifiable sub-groups – which ideally have not been pre-determined – all help to reduce the possibility of incorrect conclusions.

Self-reporting by respondents and observations of respondents' actions in real life represent two extremes of attitude assessment. In between these are a number of other methods. These include (1) observation of overt behaviour in experimental settings such as in role-playing exercises or simulation; (2) assessment of respondents' reactions to partly structured, situations; for example the completion of incomplete stories or plays; (3) assessment of performances in apparently objective tasks, such as the memorizing of diverse material, and; (4) measurement of physiological reactions to material. The development and use of these methods are substantive topics in themselves for which there is not space here. On the whole they belong more to psychology and environmental psychology than to the social sciences generally where role-playing, for example, is used for training or to explain complex situations rather than for attitude measurement. Role-playing, combined with graphic presentation, has been used (rarely) to evaluate public attitudes to National Park planning. Behaviourial studies and, on the other hand, self-reporting of attitudes, particularly through questionnaires, are however both commonly used. A simple example of a behaviourial study is a survey of tourists which attempts to assess attitudes to various attractions, or to parts of attractions, by asking which of these have in fact been visited. Clearly such results are also affected by other attitudes, to value for money or to travel distance, for example, and by knowledge. These aspects might be investigated by further questions.

Open questions provide the simplest form of questionnaire; 'What do you think of this place (or person, or policy)?' The open question appears to minimize the possibility of bias in the way an investigator sets the question. But bias may occur when a researcher comes to analyse the question since, to do this, replies must be grouped, or summarized, or key words may selectively be isolated. Bias at this stage may be worse since it is not explicit whereas a poor question should be evident. Answers to open questions tell us what respondents feel to be important, to the extent that they are truthful, but they do not indicate the degree or strength of feelings in any consistent way. Particularly where attitudes of different groups are to be compared, some element of objective measurement is desirable. An *adjectival checklist* is one of the simplest measures. A list of words is presented to the respondents who are asked to mark those which best express their feelings. The number of words to be marked may be restricted or not. In another procedure, known as *ranking*, the respondent may be asked to mark the words in order of importance. It is the researcher, however, who selects the list and obviously its make-up may restrict or even bias the respondents' expressions of attitude. The method assumes also that the concept implied by a word is understood in common. One way of making up lists is, again, to select words from the replies to open questions in an initial pilot survey.

While the adjectival checklist provides some quantitative information, either by the *frequencies* with which words are selected or by their *order* or *ranking* if asked for, it does not provide a measure in the sense that this is popularly understood. To place things in order of perceived value, or of length, or speed, one–two–three, does not tell us whether number one is twice the value of number two, or ten times. To do this requires value to be *rated* on a scale, as on a ruler. A common form of scale used in attitude measurement is known as a *Likert Scale* or, more generally, as a *semantic differential*. This can take various forms (Figure 5.1), but although it looks like a ruler it is usually considered to fall short of being a true rating scale since it is not at all clear that the equal physical divisions or intervals represent in fact equal amounts of attitude or feeling.

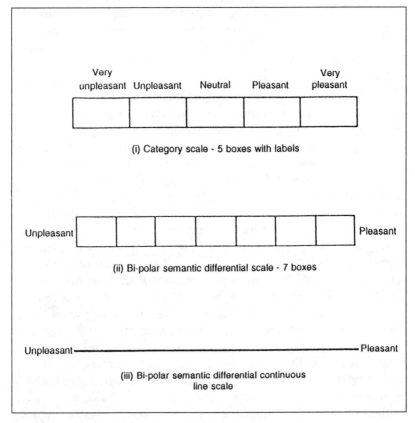

Figure 5.1 Various devices may be used in an attempt to scale or measure attitudes.

Detailed studies have been made of ranking and rating procedures in attitude measurement (Grigg, 1978). These studies have looked at comparative advantages, the degree of correspondence between results, and at the appropriate forms of statistical analysis (see Chapter Seven). A few points may be noted here. Ranking, putting in order, does force respondents to choose one attitude, or quality, or place, in preference to another; that is it is more decisive or categorical, but does not provide information on the degree of preference. Rating or scaling loses some decisiveness since all attributes might be rated equally, but the method does provide information on the degree of feeling or strength of attitude adopted. Increasing the number of boxes above nine (Figure 5.1) has been found not to lead to more discrimination or to more accurate results. Where every box is labelled, as in the category scale, more than five boxes makes the selection of meaningful labels difficult. Labelling the boxes probably increases the reliability of the scale. The linear scale possibly provides a true interval measurement scale but it is doubtful if respondents who are not familiar with the use of mathematical graphs could meaningfully use such a scale. Whatever type of scale is used it is best to provide several of them, a battery of scales, to test a variety of concepts, attributes, opinions or qualities since any single one could be misleading.

Perceptions of environmental quality

Environmental quality can be assessed in several ways, for example by the work of experts such as connoisseurs of architecture or of landscape, or by the scientific measurement of pollution. These topics are obviously beyond the scope of this book. Important measures or dimensions of environmental quality however are provided by the nature and strength of public attitudes to the environment, what is known as *perceived environmental quality*. Indeed it can be argued that this is the only possible measure of certain intangibles such as scenic beauty. The process is essentially that of attitude measurement as outlined above. Respondents may be asked to make open statements or to rank or to rate prepared words or statements, representations of the environment (in the form of photographs, slides or film) or locations in the real environment. In addition to the usual problems of attitude measurement, above, questions arise about the *presentation* of the environment to the respondents. Actual scenes cannot be compared directly but only from memory; evaluation *in situ* may be influenced by factors such as personal fatigue or weather.

Visual simulations can be compared more or less directly but how far do they represent the real environment? Method of presentation may affect the inferences made. The simulated presence of even a small modern building in a scene or its representation, such as a photograph, will normally reduce the evaluation of the scene compared with the untouched scene when respondents are asked to rate or rank these. This is so even where the comparison is made not directly (which is far too obvious) but indirectly by placing within a series of other scenes. Yet the great majority of visitors to the New Forest in Hampshire for example, when asked the open question 'Is there anything you dislike about the surroundings?' replied, 'nothing', even though a power station was in view.

Structured interviews

Interviewing is a technique peculiar to the social sciences and there is no analogy with the natural sciences. Nevertheless there is a need for an objective approach to interviewing technique. This in the broad sense should be scientific in requiring detachment, objectivity, uniform treatment and an awareness of possible influences arising from the subtlety of communication, not only of verbal inflection but of body language. Psychiatrists are often seen as cold personalities since they aim not to influence what their patients say. Interviews have the main functions of eliciting attitudes, information, or both of these. Interviews may be structured or unstructured. In the former, also known as *focused interviews*, a selection of carefully prepared questions or topics is used to make sure that the required ground is covered and that all interviewees are prompted equally. This is useful if the views or accounts of a number of persons or representative groups are to be compared, in which case the prepared questions should be carefully adhered to and not augmented. Alternatively it may be argued that a free-ranging account will give a better indication of a respondent's true attitudes. If this approach is taken then there should be no prompting, though the interviewer should have a check-list of points which he or she would expect to have come up. A combination of both techniques is possible, open self-reporting followed by prepared questions on topics omitted, or a structured session followed by open discussion to elaborate points.

Very little information will be obtained from a rushed, ill-prepared and unrecorded interview. Interviews can be recorded in note form or on tape and then transcribed to be read and studied at leisure. There should be a clear understanding about whether or not the interview, in whole or part, is 'on' the record', which has nothing to do with the tape recorder, but is journalists' jargon for information which can be attributed to the source and quoted. It is good manners to allow the interviewee to see and check any account which is to be made available to the public, as in a dissertation, since incorrect or even correct accounts may be damaging to the interviewee.

Conclusions

It is clear that this chapter can provide only an introduction to a large field of scholarship and experience. Even so, cognizance of what has been outlined here would improve many student dissertations immensely. Conduct of a survey or interview requires careful preparation, discussion, thought and reading. In particular it requires an understanding of the principles and details of experimental design and of obtaining responses which are meaningful and informative without having been manipulative or biased. Evaluation of the results of other researchers equally requires an informed and critical approach.

Checklist: Chapter 5

You should know and understand:

- the four methods of obtaining primary information:
    experiment
    survey
    comparative method
    participant observation
- the need for careful preparation of surveys
- the principles of experimental design
- the idea of a variable and of dependent and independent variables
- the fallacy of the *post hoc* argument;

- the principles of experimental control and use of control groups
- the importance of and reasons for the procedures of randomization and matching
- the commonly used experimental and quasi-experimental designs
- the requirements for internal and external validity in experiment;

- the process of formulating survey questions to elicit the type of information required (NB not preconceived answers)
- the criteria for a good survey question, and the danger of leading questions
- the distinction between open and closed questions, their uses and relation to possible bias

- common techniques of attitude measurement:
  adjectival checklist
  semantic differential
- alternatives to self-reporting in attitude measurement
- the objective conduct of interviews; structured and
  focused interviews

Further reading

Campbell, D.T., and Stanley, J.G., 1963, *Experimental and quasi-experimental designs for research*, Rand McNally, Chicago.

Drew, C.J., 1980, *Introduction to designing and conducting research*, C.V. Mosby, St Louis.

Festinger, L., *et al.*, 1950, *Social pressures in informal groups*, Harper & Row, London.

Grigg, A., 1978, *A review of techniques for scaling subjective judgments*, Supplementary Report 379, Transport and Road Research Laboratory, Crowthorne.

Kerlinger, F.N., 1973, *Foundations of behaviourial research*, Holt, Rinehart and Winston, London.

Leedy, P.D., 1980, *Practical research: planning and design*, 2nd edition Macmillan, New York, pp.166–80.

Oppenheim, A.N., 1969, *Questionnaire design and attitude measurement*, Heinemann, London.

Scottish Tourist Board, 1993, *Standardized Questions for Tourism Surveys*, STB, Edinburgh.

Social and Community Planning Research, 1972, *Questionnaire design manual*, SCPR, London.

Summers, G.F., 1977, *Attitude measurement*, Kershaw, London.

Van Dalen, D.B., 1979, *Understanding educational research*, McGraw-Hill, Maidenhead.

6
ORGANIZATION AND ANALYSIS OF SURVEYS

'It is a capital mistake to theorize before one has data.'
(Sir Arthur Conan-Doyle, *Scandal in Bohemia*)

Having decided what information is to be sought and, specifically, what questions are to be asked (Chapter Five), the next consideration is how to ask the questions. For interviews, or for documentary or statistical research, this is a matter of agreeing times and places and of deciding how best to sample and record information in an organized and retrievable manner. But for social surveys, with which this chapter is mainly concerned, a knowledge of special methods is required. Some of these, such as procedures for sampling and analysis, can also be useful in documentary and statistical research.

Location and conduct of survey

The location chosen for a survey must be considered in relation to other features of the survey such as the rigour with which sampling procedures can be followed and the length and detail of the questionnaire. Questionnaire surveys can be conducted in public or semi-public places such as in a street, beauty-spot or workplace, or privately in respondents' homes. Questionnaires may be presented to the respondents either directly by a surveyor or indirectly by post or by hand delivery. The questionnaire can be *self-administered*, that is filled in by the respondent, in which case it should be remembered that a substantial minority cannot read or write well if at all, and, in any case, the instructions must be very clear. If the completed questionnaires are to be collected by hand a few days later any problems of understanding may be cleared up then but it is important not to influence the answers in this way. If the forms are to be returned by post, a stamped addressed envelope should be provided. Alternatively the researcher, or in a large study his or her assistants, asks the questions and writes down the answers. *Household* or *work-place surveys*, especially where self-administered, generally allow longer and more detailed questionnaires but are more expensive and time consuming than *on-site* interviews. Response rates are often very low in postal surveys, as little as 20 per cent, which raises substantial doubts about representativeness. Student work usually has no authority to require response, and it may be unwise to base a dissertation on the uncertain response to a postal survey. A follow up reminder may increase response. Some commercial surveys now offer material inducements to participation; theoretically this should be acceptable if the inducement merely ensures response from a previously selected random sample, but the inducement should not itself be selective. Better response rates are achieved when the questionnaire is collected by hand.

Very high response rates, nearly one 100 per cent, can be obtained from on-site surveys but it is not reasonable to expect to detain respondents for long who are going about their daily business or enjoying themselves. A more serious reservation about this so-called *random approach interview* technique is that it is not random. During slack periods every visitor or passer-by can be interviewed; at busy times many will be missed. This produces a bias towards people who have leisure to shop or visit at off-peak times. If instructed to select one person in ten, the interviewer will be doing little at slack periods and unable to cope at others. Large surveys will draft in more assistants at busy times. Further, some potential respondents will tend to avoid the interviewer so creating a bias towards interviewing friendly approachable people.

Type of location may also have a distorting influence. While a country park is a reasonable location at which to investigate attitudes to that particular site, would the visitors represent a cross-section of the national population in terms of, say, attitudes to abortion or even to the countryside itself? Would we expect to get a representative political view if we interviewed outside an expensive London

store such as Harrod's? If, more likely, we interview outside a supermarket, it is probable that our sample will contain a high proportion
of supermarket users. Such people may not adequately represent the
views of those using small corner shops. These examples make the
point that just any old street is not necessarily typical. Although
interviewers are required to obtain a balance, or quota, of selected
characteristics, say of men and women or of age groups, this procedure of *quota sampling* leaves doubts about the randomness and
overall representativeness of the samples. The assumption is that
certain behaviour, such as voting patterns, is sufficiently explained
by the conventional sociological divisions of age, sex and class. If,
however, behaviour is explained by other factors, and these are neither sampled randomly nor represented in the quota, then the
survey may be misleading, as in the 1992 British general election.

On balance the directly administered household survey provides
the best combination of a good response with control in the selection of sample groups. A problem with household surveys is deciding which individual resident to interview. Conventionally this was
the head of the household, usually the predominant male wage-
earner. This concept is now often inapplicable. Household surveys
are most appropriate where information is sought on the whole
household, say leisure activities or travel to school and work.
Random on-site interviews, on the other hand, are the cheapest and
easiest, and for site-specific issues may be the most appropriate, but
the reservations expressed above should be borne in mind. Whatever the method, consistency of approach should be the aim whether,
as in much student work, the researcher is the only interviewer or
when assistants are employed and carefully briefed.

Sampling

So far the idea of a sample has been used here only in a general
way, as a portion of a population selected for study. It should be
noted that in research the term *population* does not refer to the population at large nor even necessarily to humans or indeed animate
objects at all. It refers to any whole group of subjects or things
which have the characteristics identified for research purposes.
Thus if we are interested in the educational needs of dyslexics, all
dyslexic people everywhere make up our research population. But
we may feel that such a large group is too variable and so choose to

limit our research to a particular culture and stage of education, say dyslexic British under-graduates. This group then constitutes the population for research. There is of course a problem of precisely how we define a dyslexic person, of what is our concept of dyslexia.

An ideal situation would be if the research population were small enough for us to study all of it. We could then make statements which describe the characteristics of the population, such as average examination performance, and these statements would require no statistical qualification since they would be true for the whole population. Usually, however, populations are too big, or resources too small, to study more than a selection of individuals. It is clear that this selected portion should have the same spread of characteristics as the total population that we claim to study, that is our sample population should be representative of the total population. Students often do not think in terms of a total population but select a sample in some way and assume the results will be true for the general population. Nevertheless, the sampling procedure does define a particular population. If we interview, say, every tenth household on

'Against, definitely against'

Care should be taken to ensure that a sample population is representative of the research population which is being investigated.

Cartoon: © The Telegraph plc, London, 1993

a large estate, the research population is the estate, not the town. If our aim is to study the population of the whole town it would be necessary to work from some device, called a *sampling frame*, such as the electoral register, which includes the whole town population, and which in this case of course happens to exclude non-voters. A different sampling frame would be needed to study the population of the county, region or nation, or for some definable group within these. It is important to decide what the sampling frame is to be and how it can be identified in practice. Differing definitions of dyslexia for example would produce different sampling frames and, quite possibly, different results. Students frequently ask if a certain percentage of the population (ten is a favourite number) will provide an adequate *sample size*. But in most circumstances it is the numerical size of a random sample rather than its proportion which determines the accuracy of estimates which can be inferred from the sample data. The question of sample size is examined further in Chapter Seven.

For a sample to be representative it must not be biased towards any sub-groups or characteristics. This lack of bias is normally achieved by random sampling, except when selected known attitudes are deliberately chosen in some way (Chapter Five). Biased sampling may occur even by chance but the probability of this is low and can be calculated (Chapter Seven). Random samples can be produced in two main ways. Completely *random sampling* is akin to drawing names or numbers out of a hat. In practice all individuals or locations are first allocated numbers; some populations may already have numbers, for example map grid references of locations. Then lists of random numbers, available as tables or generated by computer, are used to select the individuals which will make up the sample population. However, if the sample frame is considered to be already arranged randomly then *structured sampling*, that is selection at regular intervals, can be employed. This is usually less laborious. For example the names on electoral roles and in telephone directories are arranged alphabetically and are presumed to be random for all other characteristics; public records, such as registers of planning decisions, are often arranged in chronological order. Hence the selection of names or items at regular intervals from such sampling frames should produce a random and representative sample. Ethnic minority names, or decisions from extra busy periods, are likely to be represented approximately in proportion to their occurrence in the total population, though this may not be the case for very small groups. Note that it is important to sample across the whole of the chosen sample frame, not, for example, from one page only of a directory.

The sampling of locations or areas on the ground or on maps, *areal sampling*, can be treated in a manner which is analogous to the sampling of individuals. Here the grid of the map embraces the whole area and provides in fact a graphic analogy of the sample frame. Within this frame, point locations can be selected at random, or the selection can be structured at regular intervals. If, say, 25 per cent of the map is shown as forest then about 25 per cent of random points should fall on forest areas. This proportion thus provides an estimate of the forest area without the need for detailed measurement. The more points used, the more accurate will be the estimate (Chapter Seven). A structured or regular sample, above, appears to be less subject to any bias arising by chance from local random concentrations of sample points, especially when the sample is small, that is when only a small number of points is used. Thus *partially structured sampling* employs random sampling within a regular framework, say a random point in each grid square or a random name from every page of a telephone directory – the spatial sampling analogy can be useful when trying to visualize the sampling process generally. *Stratified sampling* is a particular form of structured sampling and is akin to matching. The sampling is controlled to ensure that the sample contains the correct proportional representation of selected characteristics whose proportions are already known in the total population. If for example 20 per cent of households were known to be tenanted and 80 per cent owner-occupied these proportions might not by chance occur in the sample. But if the two groups can be identified at the outset, and if the distinction is considered important, then an equivalent sample can be selected from each group or stratum.

A researcher should be clear about the definition of his or her research population, the sampling frames available and the sampling procedures which may be used either to obtain a sample population or to divide test and control groups where these are required (Chapter Five). Sampling is often one of the weaker features of student or, indeed, any work but statistical inferences drawn from work on sampling depend fundamentally on the assumption of randomization. Even where formal statistical analysis is not used the fallacies of insufficient and biased statistics should be borne in mind. This may be illustrated simply by the analogy of a commercial buyer of peanuts where the price varies according to quality. A buyer would clearly be foolish to offer a price based solely on inspection of nuts from the top of one sack, and would instead mix the nuts from the whole sack before taking a sample and inspect at least several sacks at random. This is common sense. If an emphasis on random sampling seems pedantic, remember the peanuts. Of course peanuts are not people; people are even more complex and variable.

Replication

In research terms *replication* means the repetition of observations, or in particular, of experimentation. It is not, however, simply an attempt at induction by confirmation (Chapter Three). It is, rather, a procedure to test observations or treatments over a range of unknown possible conditions. In this sense it is closely related to the ideas about sample size and representativeness discussed above.

A good deal of student work in the social sciences either takes replication for granted, as in the social survey, or ignores it, as in the one-shot case-study. A simple example will make the distinction. If we seek some measure of the physical height of a class of school children it would clearly be unwise to measure only one child who might by chance be the tallest in the group. The fact that he or she might be selected at random does nothing to improve the scientific rigour of the procedure; indeed it could be better to select by eye an average looking individual and measure him or her. What we need in order to describe the height of the class is an average, or *mean*, height and some idea of the range or *spread* of extreme values. These figures have an external reality. We can visually distinguish an under-thirteen football team from an over-eighteen one by our perception of the mean height. Further, if a member of the under-thirteens is six feet tall, outside our expected range, we may have doubts about his declared age.

Making observations on a number of individuals, as in a social survey, is in essence replication, though it is not always thought of as such; the observations are not repeated over time but all at once, but the effect is the same. To measure just one individual is like a single case-study of a town or an incident, and the logical weakness is clear. An election would not be forecast on the result of a sample poll of one constituency selected at random. This is not to say however that the single case-study is useless. Study of a single constituency may be valuable if it is known from experience of past results to be in some way typical, or if it reveals trends which can be applied to the wider electorate. Nevertheless, this is not so convincing as a replicated study over several constituencies.

Similarly, in a study of dyslexia the mean and spread of examination results for a sample of dyslexic students would give a picture of the group's ability, especially if compared with the mean and spread of results for a group of non-dyslexic students. But outstanding achievement by a single dyslexic student would show that dyslexia in itself does not necessarily lead to poorer performance. A detailed study of the individual might provide *insight* into the conditions contributing to his or her success. To generalize from this however would require a replicated survey or experiment on a group of individuals.

A researcher who is interested in differences between areas, say in terms of policy application or status, rather than between groups of individuals as such, should always consider the benefits of a replicated study. At the very least two areas should be compared. Replication in areal studies may involve more trouble and expense (though this is not necessarily so, as will be seen) but the results will be much more convincing. Even a survey of individuals may benefit from being replicated on different sites. It is useful therefore to have an understanding of the principles of true replication.

The experimental field plot analogy

Experimental design and statistical analysis grew largely out of developments in the scientific investigation of agricultural practice, particularly at Rothamstead in England. In the case of replication, the experimental field plot analogy is a useful one to pursue and it is interesting to see the extent to which the principles can be applied to other types of study. The difficulties of field experimentation have perhaps more in common with those of the social sciences than do those of laboratory work. The problem for agronomists (crop scientists) is that natural variations in intrinsic fertility of different fields, or between different parts of one field, will influence the results of experimentation with different treatments (or management policy) on the crops growing on them. The larger the area of the experiment then the larger is the problem since intrinsic variation is likely to be greater over distance. Thus, for example, to try to compare two management regimes (0) and (+) by applying (0) to field 1 and (+) to field 2 (or to the two halves or plots of one field respectively) would rightly be considered scientifically and logically unsound and meaningless and would justifiably attract no research funds. One plot might have been cultivated differently in the past and so have more or less fertility, or different drainage; these variations could either obscure or exaggerate any differences in the effects of experimental treatment (Figure 6.1). And yet this is the format for a number of so-called comparative studies in social research where different treatments have been investigated for what may be intrinsically different areas. Indeed, the problem of selecting similar subject areas for treatment, given the complexity of real-life situations, is one of the almost insurmountable difficulties of conducting rigorous comparative research in the social sciences. One option is to investigate the application of *one* policy regime to two different areas, which may at least throw useful light on characteristics of the two areas and how these might interact with the policy.

Agronomists and their statisticians have given much thought to these problems over the years. One solution is what is known as the *replicated experiment*. At this point it will be useful to set out the analogy in full. The crop grown on a small experimental plot is analogous

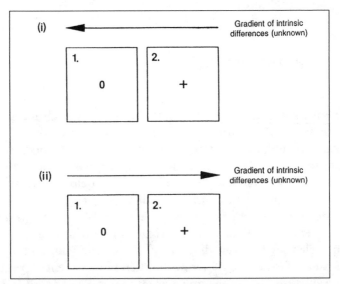

Figure 6.1 An unsatisfactory experimental design where intrinsic differences between the subject areas (plots) may: (i) nullify effects of policy application (treatment +); or (ii) who an effect where none exists.

to an individual person or town or area; the crops from all plots make up the sample population. The yield or performance of the crop, whether individually or collectively, may be thought of as the attribute we are researching, equivalent to, say, examination performance or social attitude. Crop treatment, for example fertilizer regime, corresponds to social treatments such as education method or welfare regime. Uncontrolled variations in the soil across the experimental plots correspond to unknown social influences outside experimental control. In practice the term plot usually has two meanings, either as a subdivision of the area of land on which the experiment is conducted or as the crop grown on that sub-division. Plot yield or plot treatment thus equates to crop yield or crop treatment.

A very simple replicated design is shown in Figure 6.2. Here the possible outcomes are both more complicated and more informative than in either Figure 6.1(i) or 6.1(ii). Suppose that there is an inherent variation in fertility from left to right. By further sub-dividing the plots in Figure 6.1(i) into four, and allocating treatments 0 and + in a diagonal fashion, the inherent variation may be inferred from the yields.

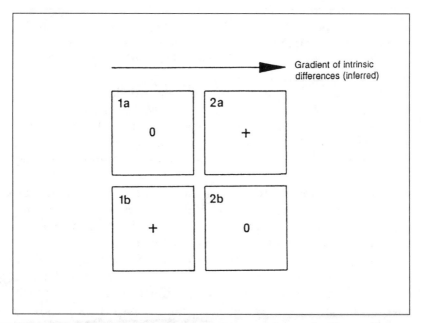

Figure 6.2 A simple replicated design where an inherent fertility gradient in the experimental area may be inferred from the results for individual experimental plots.

For example, suppose also that treatment + has in fact no beneficial effect on yield compared with treatment 0: the yield from plot 2a (treatment +) will nevertheless be greater than that from 1a (treatment 0) due to the inherent fertility differences. However, for the same reason, and because of the way the experiment has been designed, the yield from 1b (+) will be less than from 2b (0). Given the assumptions, above, the yield from 1a would equal that of 1b, that of 2a equal that of 2b, and the total yield of 2a + 1b (+) would equal that of 1a + 2b (0). A logical inference from this result is that the treatment has had no effect; note that this would be true whether the inherent conditions vary from left to right, top to bottom, or, in this case, even diagonally. Note also, however, that, if it is accepted that unknown inherent differences might exist, *no* logically valid conclusions can be drawn from the experimental design of either 6.1(i) or 6.1(ii) alone.

The reader may care to work out what the results might be for the layout in Figure 6.2 if the treatment (+) did have an effect, and if this was either more or less than the effect of the inherent differences – and, most important, whether the assumed conditions could be inferred back from the results. In fact, while this degree of replication represents some advance in logical rigour it could be said to be the minimum acceptable, and other problems remain, all of which have analogies in the social sciences. Inherent conditions – of which, like causes, there are many – rarely show uniform variation in either direction or magnitude; crop varieties themselves are not uniform but have an inherent variability also; nor is it possible to apply treatment uniformly in field conditions. In general the agronomist is aware that his subject plots are in effect only samples of all the similar experiments which could be performed, and that one or two plots, given the natural variability of living things, are not sufficiently representative. By the same reasoning, it may be questioned whether studies of one or two towns or locations are representative of the general state of things. Students sometimes claim to have picked a town 'at random', as though this admirable eschewing of personal bias were sufficient to overcome the likely experimental bias. In fact one or two locations picked at random are likely to be less representative than one or two which have been carefully matched to be 'average' for certain known characteristics.

Full replication is the solution which the scientist favours where possible. The experimental field will be divided into a large number of plots and the treatments allocated across the whole area at random (Figure 6.3). This (1) attempts to even out the possible distortions caused by unknown intrinsic gradients and (2) provides a large and representative number of sub-sample plots which can be used to gauge the natural variability of the sample crop. Sophisticated statistical techniques are available for these analyses.

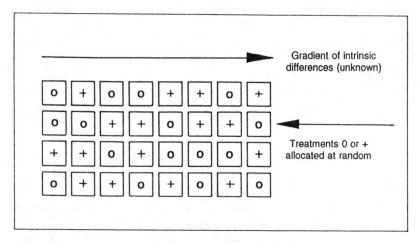

Figure 6.3 Diagrammatic representation of a fully replicated experiment: treatment plots and control plots are distributed randomly over the experimental area in an attempt to equalize and nullify any differential effects of inherent spatial variations in the characteristics of the area.

How far can social research pursue this analogy of full replication which appears to be the only logically rigorous approach? There are two main problems. The first is the political unacceptability of applying policy (treatment) at random to defined locations (plots). To some extent this can be overcome by randomly selecting locations which are already subject to different policies, that is to swop over the spatial and theoretical positions of inherent and applied differences in Figure 6.3, as in Figure 6.4. A second problem is that of the trade-off between using a large and representative sample number of locations and the desire to understand the sample locations in great detail. The agronomist requires simple information, basically yields or results; he does not necessarily wish to know the intrinsic characteristics of his substrate, except in so far as they may distort his results. At the same time, however, it must be recognized that other scientists will be investigating basic mechanisms in great detail, and will be using the same principles of replication and randomness.

What then should be the research strategy for the evaluation of area-based studies in social research? For instance, at a strategic level should an investigation into the socio-economic impacts of major construction projects be based on a detailed study of one or two project locations, or on an analysis of socio-economic conditions at a large and representative number of project locations *and* at similar control areas where no large-scale projects are in hand? The answer, surely, as above, is both. Detailed studies are necessary to understand the operation of causal mechanisms, while large-scale comparative studies will show to what extent the detailed studies are representative and how far external factors or pre-existing trends may be influencing the outcome. Policy analysts with a suspicion of number-crunching will opt for the former approach, and indeed if the number-crunching is not to be carried out on a rigorous basis they would be right. A compromise which may be used is the four-location analogy similar to Figure 6.2. Further, in the light of the many external causes of fluctuations in national and local economies, it would seem wise to have at least some experimental controls in the form of study locations where the causes being investigated are absent either spatially or, it should be emphasized, in time: that is, a *study of trends* for some years prior to the application of the policy treatments can be most illuminating, as will be seen below.

The concept of control (Chapter Five) deserves further emphasis here since it is bound up with the idea of replication. At its simplest it is the familiar idea that the presumed consequences of an action under investigation should be compared with the outcome in the absence of the action, thus avoiding the fallacious *post hoc* argument. This should always be borne in mind in social research, although it may be difficult to achieve rigorously in practice due to lack of comparable non-treated 'areas', as noted above. Control can be seen as the separating out of possible effects of *perceived* causes other than that directly under investigation by variously including or excluding these other causes in a systematic manner. Although not called control, replication and random allocation of treatment are attempts in effect to control also for *unperceived* possible causes in the hope that these will be equally distributed across the randomly selected groups or sub-groups. Given the potentially much greater range of possible unperceived causes in social investigation it would appear that randomness, which as explained above is meaningless without replication, should ideally be an important principle of such investigations as policy evaluation studies. Where this is not possible, because for example the policy 'treatment' is not under the investigator's control, then two criteria should be applied. First, the units of investigation should be as numerous as possible (or the data should be collected in as disaggregated a form as possible) so that various combinations can be analysed. The great increase in rigour in moving even from design 6.1 to 6.2 has been discussed above. Second, ancillary information should be available to form the basis of various different aggregations; these will allow *internal testing* of the data: that is, the subsequent testing of possible causes or relationships other than those of the original hypothesis. To some extent this will avoid the error of pre-determining results by the selection of categories used for the analysis. Collection of ancillary information needs to be done with some judgement, however, if excessive amounts of data are not to be collected.

All the decisions, of course, represent trade-offs against research resources and against each other. But, given some limit to resources for data collection and analysis, a typical choice when comparing two area-based policies might be between a comparison of five communities from each in full or of all the communities from both but using sample data only. Even given the limitations of sample data (and, after all, the whole study area is only an isolated sample of other such areas) it may be argued that the second option is the more logically rigorous because it approximates more closely to the pattern of 6.3 (in fact being 6.4). In this way, for example, in a development control study of conservation policies in an Area of Outstanding Natural Beauty (AONB) and an adjacent area, when it became suspected that settlement size and status might be as important, or more important, as a factor than AONB status itself in the pattern of development control, the effect of settlement size could be tested across data for forty-eight settlements rather than for a few possibly unrepresentative ones. In fact it was found for a range of settlement size that planning refusal rates varied inversely with size and that this variation according to size occurred equally inside and outside the AONB. These variations were sufficient to explain any differential treatment of the AONB itself since it intrinsically contained a much higher proportion of small settlements having low priority for development. And this had been true long before the implementation of AONB policies.

Thus, even where the nature of the research does not allow the laying out of experimental plots in a theoretically ideal manner, the

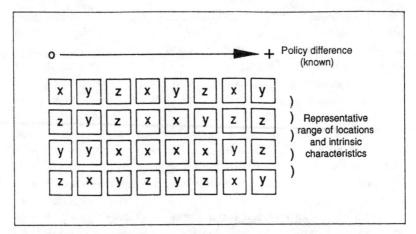

Figure 6.4 An alternative to Figure 6.3 for use where treatment has been pre-allocated: in real-life situations policy cannot be applied in the fragmentary experimental pattern of Figure 6.3, but a range of sample locations can be selected at random from both test and control areas.

collection of data in a disaggrated form may nevertheless provide some of the benefits of replication. It is therefore important to develop an understanding of the principles involved in replication. It should be made clear that replication essentially is a matter of applying a few treatments or policy differences to a large number of plots or localities in an organized way; it is not a case of applying a large number of treatments in a sort of blunderbuss approach hoping that something will work.

A comparative base

In the study of development control just outlined, the AONB conservation policy is analogous to treatment while the parishes are experimental plots. But the treatment does not appear to have been allocated randomly among the plots. It seems to have fallen more frequently on the smaller parishes and on the areas where these predominate: hence the use of internal analysis of data by population size to detect the bias caused by this non-randomness. An agronomist may do something similar by examining the range of yields for treatment and non-treatment for one section only of his field; if these are markedly different from other sections it suggests the section is inherently different. The situation may be anticipated at the outset by an experimental design which allocates equal numbers of treatment and non-treatment plots to each section. This helps to eliminate the sort of bias which could arise if, by chance, most non-treatment plots for example fell on the area of poorer fertility. Something analogous might have been used in the development control study by selecting two matched samples of equal number and size range from each policy area, a sort of replication by matching rather than by complete randomization. However, in the circumstances, above, this would have shown no difference between the two areas and a knowledge of the inherent characteristics of the total 'population' of parishes would still have been necessary for a complete picture.

Again, a social scientist has a problem not usually faced by an agronomist. For the social scientist it is rather as though the agronomist's plots were not all the same size and so he or she has to adjust or *weight* the yields to take account of this fact, to use yield per square metre rather than simple yield. Since areas which may be used in social investigation are seldom exactly equal in size, population or anything else these differences must be allowed for or weighted, per 1,000 population or per area or whatever seems relevant. This is true both for the individual area units or plots and for the total test and control areas: otherwise to say that some statistic about one area is more, or less, than the other is meaningless.

Differentiation over time

Another important basis for comparison is time. A mathematical treatment of trends would be out of place here but we may simply think of this as based on the replication of observations over time, thus indicating whether values of variables appear to be increasing, remaining steady, or decreasing. Some patience would be needed to do this for the future but records frequently allow it for the past. If we are interested in the effects of a policy, a simple test and control comparison in the present may suggest one thing: for example, that the test area is one of relative economic deprivation; a comparison of the way things have moved and are moving since the adoption of the policy may suggest something else: that the test area is nevertheless catching up with the control area in economic activity. Similarly, we may be interested not just in the quantity of pollution but whether it is increasing or decreasing at a significant rate. Most policies are attempts either to increase or decrease *differentiation* (or perceived differentiation) between two groups or areas or periods. This is the principal test of a policy's effectiveness, though its operation and side effects will also be of interest. It is useful to formulate a research hypothesis (Chapter Eight) based on this concept of differentiation, but careful thought is needed about measurement and about the possible fallacy of affirming the consequent (Chapters Three and Seven). Consider for example the following argument and compare it with that set out on p.63, above.

Hypothesis – conservation policies cause economic decline.

Consequence – if a conservation area is studied it will display a low rate of economic activity.

Test – study the economy of a conservation area.

Result – low economic activity is found.

Conclusion (fallacious) – the hypothesis is correct.

The fallacy here is that the design of the research does not take account of other possible causes of low economic activity: for example, intrinsic low activity in the area, due to things such as location, resources and physiography, probably accounted for its attractiveness and was a cause rather than an effect of the conservation status. Further, the results do not say whether economic activity is declining or increasing either absolutely or relatively. Clearly, the concept of differentiation only has meaning when related to the passage of time; a study of trends over relatively short periods and without a control area can be misleading (Figure 6.5).

Application of principles

Let us now consider how all these principles might be applied to the carrying out, or to the subsequent evaluation, of a survey into a particular social issue. The relative effectiveness of grammar schools and comprehensive schools is a matter which has affected millions of children and parents. In any investigation we have to allow for other possible factors besides any effect of the school system. It is believed that some homes are more conducive than others to the academic performance of children. If so, a comparative study of the two systems in, say, public examination performance would need to weight performance according to home background of pupils. But while examination performance may be seen as analogous to yield

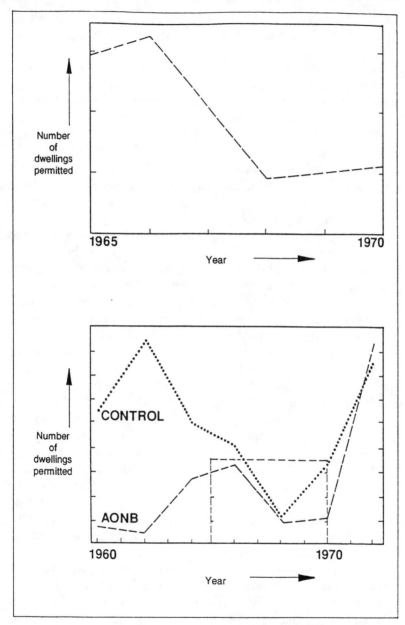

Figure 6.5 The importance of comparative studies. The graph (top) shows that permission for new dwellings in a landscape conservation area (AONB) fell dramatically after its designation; however, comparison with a control area and over a longer time scale (below) presents a broader picture and avoids the fallacy of concluding that designation was the cause of this decline.

(above), home background is a much more complex thing to conceive and measure than is plot area. Other things being equal, an increase in area leads to a simple increase in total yield, but this is by no means true necessarily of factors such as parental income, number of books in the home or ethnic background which might be thought to be influential. Clearly a comparison between the two systems is not meaningful unless previous work has been carried out *within* the systems to assess the differential effects of known factors within one regime. However, these may be outweighed by less tangible factors such as parental attitudes to education and the support which parents give to their children in this respect. But it has been seen above how difficult it is to measure attitudes in such a way as to predict outcomes effectively.

Three main approaches may be attempted. The first is to weight the results mathematically according to known factors before comparisons are made. This requires a quantitative knowledge of the relationships between these factors and performance. The relationship is unlikely to be a simple one, is subject to its own experimental error, probably only applies within certain limitations, and in any case it is unlikely we will have this knowledge for all known possible factors, let alone factors we may not even know about. It should be noted (and this applies also to the other approaches) that it is the individual children's results which should be weighted and not the total for the school. The individual child can be thought of as one of many experimental plots to which a treatment, grammar or comprehensive education, is applied. To compare two schools is like the very weak two-field experiment. A number of schools of each type could be used for comparison; that is, the school is seen as the individual plot, but the weight to be applied to each school's results would be more complex, less reliable and less direct than that applied to individual pupils. In either case, the weighting approach is far from providing a complete and satisfactory solution to the research problem.

A second approach is that of matching either individuals or whole schools. The advantage with matching is that we do not need to know the exact effect of various factors so long as these are likely to be equally represented in both test groups. Again, it will be less satisfactory to try to match the schools whose make-up is itself complex with their widely varying profiles of individuals. Put simply, is it possible to imagine that two schools can be exactly similar except for belonging to different systems, or even if they belong to the same system? Attempts are sometimes made to match two communities; a town which has only grammar schools may be compared with a similar town which has all comprehensive schools. In theory it would be best to avoid the dubious process of matching towns and to compare the two types of schools within one town (when they occur together), but it has to be recognized that in this case the grammar school, in practice, will by definition contain most of the academically more able children.

Even attempts at the 'four-field' experimental layout are far from rigorous. This is where two grammar schools, one from a 'rich' area and one from a 'poor' area are be matched and compared with two comprehensive schools similarly selected. The use of inverted commas highlights the relative crudity of this approach. Whatever procedure is used it is especially important, where only a few schools are assessed, to measure results over several years since any one school or subject department may have a difficult year and results could be influenced by even one teacher. It should also be remembered that only about 10 per cent of children were selected for grammar schools. Therefore it is only the performance of this 10 per cent whose achievements in comprehensive schools can meaningfully be compared with grammar schools generally. The other 90 per cent should strictly be compared with the former secondary modern schools; this cannot be done since they no longer exist. It is sometimes argued that since we are only measuring performance in external examinations, such as A-level, that these are the same 10 per cent or so of high achievers anyway but against this must be set an aim of comprehensive schools to enable pupils who would not otherwise have done so to take A-levels.

Replication and random sampling from the total research population is a third possible approach. The individual school as a unit is a distraction if we are comparing two systems, as opposed to simply finding the best school. Again, the individual child represents the sample plot. Since, for social reasons, treatment cannot be allocated to each plot at random as in a field-experiment, the best that can be done is to *select* at random, from the total population, plots which have received different treatment; that is to select from one 100 per cent grammar school areas and one 100 per cent comprehensive areas. The argument would have to assume, and the process as far as possible ensure, that the two sets of areas are alike in all but educational policy. The presence of private schools will complicate matters, as will the fact that there are no grammar schools in the most deprived areas. If this assumption were true no other information would be needed except the exam results (yield) and the treatment (education type). All other possible factors should be equated by randomization. In practice other characteristics would be recorded both as a check on the representativeness of the sub-samples and to allow internal analysis of data for effects of other possible factors. Relative effects of all factors can to some extent be compared by use of multiple correlation (Chapter Seven). To set up a nation-wide sampling frame of this sort and to gather personal background data on a large number of pupils across the country would of course be a much bigger and expensive undertaking than a local area study.

Yet another approach would be to interview experts in the field of education and also to try to assess the satisfaction, or attitudes, of the users, parents and pupils, always bearing in mind that any expert by definition usually has a vested interest and that users may not be fully informed. It can be argued that measurement of public attitudes, relying on the human mind inductively to synthesize situations which are difficult to analyse, represents perhaps the most important measure of success. Politically this may be true, but it is the answer to a different research question from that stated at the outset of this example.

As this brief account makes clear, social investigation, even of one measure only, is complex. It can be seen how easily numerous studies may lead to contradictory and contentious results so that each side can quote survey findings which appear to support its case. This arises in part because, for a number of reasons, many studies are too small and not conclusive (see, for example, the Tamoxifen experiment, Chapter Seven): research funds have to be divided up among a number of individuals and institutions, social scientists often have a predilection for the insight to be gained from individual case studies, and politicians and the public do not like conclusive findings since this would mean they have to make clear and rational choices.

Preparation of data for analysis

Replicated quantitative information, whether derived from questionnaires or from a researcher's own measurements or estimates, must be organized into lists and tables before it can be analysed and interpreted. Once this has been done, patterns and possible relationships may be discovered, either by eye or by statistical analysis. The process is made easier still if the data are displayed also in graphic form. For small sets of data this can be done by hand calculation but larger data sets are best analysed by computer. Since computing is so much part of modern academic activity a student may wish to demonstrate this expertise even when the data set is small enough to be analysed by hand. A computing component will increase the impression of competence made by the dissertation. However, an analysis by hand which displays understanding and familiarity with the data would be preferable to a half-understood computer analysis. Nevertheless, with the ready availability now of statistical packages (that is, complexes of computer routines) and of short training sessions, no student need be deterred from the use of quantitative research methods.

To acquire computing expertise takes time, though most students now have some computing ability. Even so, facility with taught exercises is not a complete preparation for designing and analysing a real-life investigation from scratch. In particular, many students find difficulty in making the link between designing their own survey and preparing the results in a form suitable for analysis. Adequate time must be allowed for the coding and entry of data (see below), for the elimination of errors and for delays arising from computer malfunction. Many professional researchers are over-optimistic in this respect. In essence computing is quick and easy but for beginners it can, in practice, produce delay and frustration and is a common cause for late submission of dissertations. On balance it is certainly preferable to include a computing component, and in many doctoral dissertations this would be essential, but a realistic appraisal of skills, experience and time is necessary. Many projects, both student and professional, will use the services of computer experts, at least in part, but, as in the case of statistical analysis, this is no excuse for not having an understanding of what is being done. It is usually more convenient and economical to design a survey with computer analysis in mind from the outset.

Statistical packages

Computer analysis of research data is normally performed using a form of computer program known as a statistical package. A number of such packages are available. The essential operations for any one package are standardized so that experience of using these is easily transferable from one institution to another. However, each computer system or personal computer will have its own local *operating system* procedure for gaining access to the package and for subsequent printing of output and this local system will need to be mastered also. Two common packages for example are MINITAB and SPSSX (Statistical Package for the Social Sciences). The first is relatively quick and easy to learn, the second is a powerful and versatile system used world-wide but requires a considerable investment of time in order to acquire proficiency.

Data sets are usually entered into the computer in numeric form. Although some packages, such as SPSSX but not MINITAB, do accept letters, words, and names (known collectively as *alphanumeric* characters) these clearly cannot be used in calculations, though they can be manipulated to some extent: for example, put in alphabetical order and compared with other similar lists. This may be useful for procedures such as logging the alphanumeric number-plates of cars as they enter and leave a site. Some data-files may consist entirely of names, addresses and other personal details, or of book titles and details. It is generally more convenient for the purposes of statistical analysis however to assign numbers, known as *codes*, to such things as places, names, objectives or opinions. The process of transforming completed questionnaires or other raw data into a computer *data-file* is known as *coding* and requires the preparation of a *coding schedule* (see below). Coding is at the same time both a tedious and important process where problems and errors are most likely to occur, especially with a large and complex survey. In large-scale surveys, coding is often performed by casual labour and requires careful organization, supervision and conscientious workers.

A knowledge of terminology is required here. Each individual set of information, such as *one* person's answers to a questionnaire, is known as a *case*. The details relating to one case, once they are in the computer, are also known as a *record*. A complete set of records is known as a data-file or data-base. Each category of information in the records or cases, for example the age of respondents, is known as a *variable*. Information in a data-file is commonly stored as a large rectangular block of figures (see Figure 6.6), known as a table or matrix, which consists of horizontal *rows* or lines and vertical *columns*. One record normally occupies one horizontal row or line exclusively. The

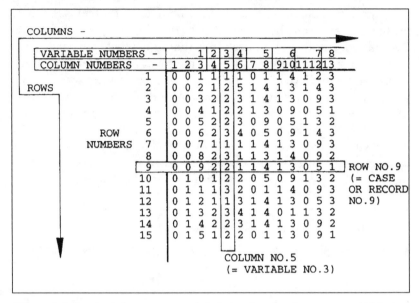

Figure 6.6 Portion of a computer data-base showing its structure. With the use of the relevant coding schedule this mass of figures can be read as follows; for example, row 9:

Variable 1 (columns 1–3): questionnaire number; value = 009 (no. 9)
Variable 2 (column 4): sex of respondent; value = 2 (male)
Variable 3 (column 5): age group of respondent; value = 2 (17–64 years)
Variable 4 (column 6): number in group; value = 1 (alone)
Variable 5 (columns 7–8): first choice of attribute; value = 14 (adjective 14)
Variable 6 (columns 9–10): second choice of attribute; value = 13
(adjective 13)
Variable 7 (columns 11–12): third choice of attribute; value = 05
(adjective 5)
etc.

particular quantity of any one variable for one record or case (such as the age of one respondent) is known as its *value*: for example, case no. 9, variable = *AGE*; value = 29. A vertical column, or set of columns, is devoted to each variable so that for all the cases the values of that variable appear vertically above each other.

Any particular value can be located and identified exclusively by its column and row numbers: for example, row (or case, or line) 10, columns 6 and 7. This format is frequently used when typing instructions to the computer such as when editing or correcting files. Some confusion may arise where, as with MINITAB, the programme automatically adds a first column containing the case or row identification numbers so that the variable entered in column 1, say, appears in column 2 and so on (Figure 6.7). Problems that may arise with rows are where a row has been mistakenly typed in twice, or omitted. Another complication is that individual cases or records often contain more information, in the form of numbers or letters, than can be displayed in a single line on the computer screen or on a printout. Since it is usually more convenient to be able to show the complete width of a data-file (though not its length) in one display, SPSSX, for example, has the facility to read groups of two or more successive lines of the data-file as single records. If this arrangement is used it must be incorporated into the coding schedule and the relevant instructions entered into the computer.

```
MTB > PRINT C1-C8

ROW   Q.NO.   SEX CODE   AGE CODE   PARTY NO   ATTR.1   ATTR.2   ATTR.3   ACCESS?
 1      1        1          1          1          1       14       12        3
 2      2        1          2          5         14       13       12        3
 3      3        2          2          3         14       13        9        3
 4      4        1          2          2         13        9        5        1
 5      5        2          2          3          9        5       13        2
 6      6        2          3          4          5        9       14        3
 7      7        1          1          1         14       13        9        3
 8      8        2          3          1         13       14        9        2
 9      9        2          2          1         14       13        5        1
10     10        1          2          2          5        9       13        2
11     11        1          3          2          1       14        9        3
12     12        1          1          3         14       13        5        3
13     13        2          3          4         14        1       13        2
14     14        2          2          3         14       13        9        2
15     15        1          2          2          1       13        9        1
```

Figure 6.7 The same data as that shown in Figure 6.6 but on a more 'user-friendly' package.

Principles of coding information

Before a coding schedule can be prepared it is necessary to consider some ways in which information can be represented by numbers. This in turn affects the type and convenience of analyses which can be performed. First, a respondent's age, for example, may be recorded as an actual *number*, say 29 years. In a survey of 100 persons, however, it might be found that any particular age between, say, 5 and 95 occurred only once or twice. If the computer is commanded to produce a *frequency table* of age, that is a list of all ages occurring in the survey together with the number of times each age occurred, the result may be a long thin table whose cells contain frequencies of only one or two. Such a table is not very meaningful and also presents problems for statistical analysis (Chapter Seven). An alternative is to *aggregate* or *band* the ages and to allocate a *code number* to each band, say: 5–16 years, code 1; 17–64, code 2; 65+, code 3–representing approximately school, employment and retirement ages. Only the codes are then entered into the data-file under variable *AGE* so that a value of 29 years for this variable becomes instead a code value of 2. This provides much smaller and more meaningful tables. But against this we can no longer calculate from the data such information as average age with the same accuracy as before. Clearly the bands can be formed according to what age groups are of interest or are found to correspond with noticeable differences in attitude or behaviour. However, these may not be known at the outset. One of the benefits of advanced statistical packages, such as SPSSX, is that they contain procedures to band the raw numbers after entry, giving the benefits of both methods. For example, 17–64 is a very wide age range and is likely to contain much variation within it; the more limited age group 17–25 typically has distinctive characteristics and the facility to select out the data for such a sub-group retrospectively is a very valuable one in the internal analysis of data (p.137).

A third way to express data is by a simple *code for presence or absence*. For example, to discover desirable attributes of a recreation site an adjectival checklist (Chapter Five) can be used having, say, fifteen adjectives, each adjective supposedly representing one attribute; one column in the data list can be allocated to each adjective, that is each adjective is a variable. Within each record the value for the variable could be, say, 1 or 0, corresponding with whether the individual respondent had selected that adjective or not. There are several problems with this method, especially where, as here, a number of similar variables occupy adjacent columns. Apart from using a lot of columns for what is in effect one question in the survey, it is very easy to place a 1 or 0 in the wrong column, both when coding or typing in data (coding sheets have very narrow columns, Figure 6.8). This sort of error is unlikely to be detected at later checking. Also, since one table can only show the relationship between two variables, it is not possible to summarize the answer to this question simply.

Most people in fact, when answering this sort of question, usually select only one or two adjectives out of the list. If, further, respondents are asked to place these in order of preference the

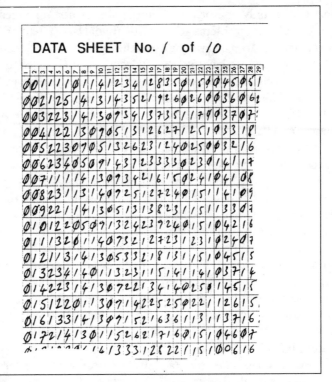

Figure 6.8 The data from Figure 6.6 shown coded onto a coding sheet before entry into the computer.

question can be coded differently. The variables are reduced to three: first choice, second choice and third choice. The values then become the code numbers of the fifteen adjectives: for example, variable name = *FIRST CHOICE OF ADJECTIVE;* value = 14 (that is adjective 14). The whole range of attributes in the first choice is now represented by the values of one variable in one double column (Figures 6.6, 6.7). As with age, a frequency table for that one variable will show the number of times each adjective was selected as first choice by respondents. Second and third choices are coded similarly.

Listings and cross-tabulations

Frequency tables are sometimes known as listings since, for any variable, they list in summary form all the values and their frequency of occurrence. The number of times any one value occurs may be shown either as a *count* or as a *percentage* of the total number of records or as both. A second type of table produced by computer statistical packages is the cross-tabulation. This shows the frequencies for values of one variable sub-divided by the frequencies for values of another. The table is divided into squares known as *cells* which are arranged in rows and columns. In this case the rows and columns do not represent different variables, as in the data-file, but the range of values within the two selected variables (Figure 6.9). In the example above there would be three rows for the three age groups (that is, the values of variable *AGE*) and up to fifteen columns for the fifteen adjectives (that is, the values of variable *FIRST CHOICE OF ADJECTIVE*, or attribute). In the cell of row 3 and column 14, for example, would be shown the number of individuals in the age group 65+ who had selected adjective 14 as their first choice. In practice if the frequencies for all values in any row or column are zero, then the packages usually omit any such rows or columns from the table format. Thus, in Figure 6.9, the MINITAB package has omitted columns for values where all the counts are zero (that is, for adjectives which no one has chosen) so that the counts for adjective 14 appear in fact in the fifth column of the cross-tabulation. Clearly, however, when writing up the survey it may be of interest to know which attributes have been rejected in this way.

```
MTB > TABLES C3 C5


ROWS: AGE CODE    COLUMNS: ATTR.1

           1        5        9       13       14      ALL

  1        1        0        0        0        2        3
  2        1        1        1        1        4        8
  3        1        1        0        1        1        4
ALL        3        2        1        2        7       15
```

Figure 6.9 A simple MINITAB cross-tabulation of the variables 3 (*AGE*) and 5 (*FIRST CHOICE OF ATTRIBUTE*) Figure 6.7, above. This sample is too small to have statistical significance (see Chapter Seven).

With advanced packages such as SPSSX the contents of each cell may be shown in a number of ways, as a count, as a percentage of the row total, as a percentage of the column total and as a percentage of the table total. The table shows at a glance the relative preferences for various attributes and how these preferences might vary between the different age groups. At the bottom of the table the column totals are in effect the frequency distribution for the top-variable in the table (in Figure 6.9, *FIRST CHOICE OF ADJECTIVE*); at the side, the row totals are the frequencies for the side-variable in the table (that is, *AGE* in Figure 6.9). Packages allow all combinations of variables to be compared in cross tabulations, though not all these comparisons will be meaningful. New variables can also be created by algebraic *transformations*, for example expressing one variable as the sum of two others, and the new *computed variable* can be displayed and used as any other in all procedures.

Coding schedules

With this outline knowledge it is now possible to prepare a *coding schedule*. A coding schedule shows all the data which are to be entered into the computer, whether as raw numbers, codes or letters. A schedule is essential for a large survey where several coding assistants are involved but is also advisable as a means of clarifying procedures and decisions when a researcher does his or her own coding. Typing raw data directly from questionnaires into the computer is a recipe for confusion and mistakes unless the data are very simple or the questionnaires have been carefully designed and pre-coded to this end, as in Figure 6.10. Even then the answer boxes will have to be checked and completed or corrected as necessary; answers to open questions (Chapter Five) can in any case only be coded after the survey has taken place. Ideally, data should be typed in from prepared coding sheets by people skilled in this work.

The stages in getting data from the questionnaires to the computer are discussed briefly below; they can be summarized as follows:

1. Sort questionnaires and number them (if not done previously).
2. Record all the various answers to open questions, aggregate these answers if necessary, and allocate code numbers to the aggregations.
3. Draw up a coding schedule.

1. WHEN DID YOU PURCHASE THIS PRODUCT.   PLEASE PUT
    ANY SINGLE NUMBERS IN THE RIGHT HAND BOXES.

    DAY [|]   MONTH [|]   YEAR [|]
        1   2   3   4   5   6

2. WHERE DID YOU PURCHASE THE PRODUCT?

    CHAIN-STORE (1) INDEPENDENT RETAILER (2) MAIL ORDER (3) [ ]
                                                               7

3. HOW DID YOU PAY FOR THE PRODUCT?

    CHEQUE (1)   CASH (2)   CREDIT-CARD (3) [ ]
                                               8

4. WHERE DO YOU LIVE?

    FLAT (1) TERRACED HOUSE (2) SEMI-DETACHED HOUSE (3)
    DETACHED HOUSE (4)   [ ]
                                                         9

5. HAVE YOU BOUGHT ANY OF THE FOLLOWING IN THE LAST 12
    MONTHS?

    CD PLAYER   [ ]10   COLOUR TV   [ ]13
    COMPUTER   [ ]11   VIDEO-PLAYER   [ ]14
    CAM-CORDER [ ]12   VIDEO-GAME   [ ]15

6. WHAT IS YOUR ANNUAL INCOME?

    LESS THAN £5,000 (1)   20,000 - 25,000   (5)
       5,000 - 10,000 (2)   25,000 - 30,000   (6)
      10,000 - 15,000 (3)   MORE THAN £30,000 (7)
      15,000 - 20,000 (4)   [ ]
                                                      16

7. HOW MANY CARS DO YOU OWN?

    ONE (1)   MORE THAN TWO (3)
    TWO (2)   NONE   (4)   [ ]
                                            17

8. WHICH SUNDAY NEWSPAPER DO YOU MOST ENJOY?

    SUNDAY TIMES   (1)   SUNDAY EXPRESS (5)
    SUNDAY TELEGRAPH   (2)   MAIL ON SUNDAY (6)
    INDEPENDENT ON SUNDAY   (3)   SUNDAY SPORT   (7)
    NEWS OF THE WORLD   (4)   SUNDAY MIRROR (8)
                                   NONE   (9) [ ]
                                                       18

please continue over page

Figure 6.10 Portion of a questionnaire designed to facilitate direct entry into a computer data-base. The survey is intended to build up customer profiles. All questions are factual and there are no open questions. Numbers beside boxes indicate the column for that entry: note that there is one box, and only one box, for each column.

4. Transfer data from questionnaires on to computer coding sheets in coded form.
5. Type (enter) data into computer.
6. Print out the data-file and list all variables to check for mistakes.

At stage 1 it is important to number questionnaires consecutively; the questionnaire numbers are entered as a variable (usually variable 1) which identifies each record so that the values in listings can be checked back to source if, for example, there appears to be an error. Other details such as location and interviewers' names can be added in if these have been omitted.

All answers to open questions must be written down at stage 2 from a visual inspection of the questionnaires; a simple example would be place of residence of correspondent which of course would be unknown in advance of an on-site survey and could have a large range of answers. It may be more convenient to place these in alphabetical order; each location is then given an individual number code and the list forms part of the coding schedule. Where open questions invite comment it is useful for the research principal to read and record pertinent comments verbatim since such information is concealed as these are aggregated and reduced to codes.

In the coding schedule itself, stage 3, will be shown, first of all, any general instructions for coders. For example, most packages allow for missing values in their statistical calculations; if a particular question is unanswered (which is not the same thing as a negative answer or an attribute not selected) this may require a specific missing value code. The schedule then lists for each question: (1) the question number; (2) the variable number(s) associated with that question (multiple choice and open questions may produce several variables, as seen above); (3) the value codes (if any) to be used for each answer; and (4) the column numbers assigned for the variables. Thus part of the questionnaire might look like this:

Q.7 Do you think the public should be excluded from the nature
reserve: all the year,
part of the year,
not at all?
Please tick one choice.

The relevant portion of the coding schedule would look like this:

Question No	Variable	Choice	Code	Line No	Column No
7	8	all year	1	1	13
		part year	2		
		not at all	3		

If, for example, questionnaire number 14 has the second choice ticked, and if each record only takes up one line, then the coder will enter a 2 in row 14 column 13 of the coding sheet (Figure 6.8). Unlike tables in books, where one column may contain several digits, a standard computer column, whether on the coding sheet or in the computer memory, is only the width of a single digit. For numbers greater than 9, two or more columns are needed and the coding schedule must allow for this. In this case it is essential to keep figures to the right of the columns since most packages, unless instructed otherwise, read blank spaces in a column as zero; if two columns, 9 and 10, are allocated to the variable AGE then a value for AGE of 8 years must be shown as 08 (or as blank 8) and not 80; 80 will read as eighty to the computer and to anyone typing in or coding data. However, simpler packages, such as MINITAB have multiple columns already set up which accommodate values of several digits each and the values are entered individually rather than as a row of numbers as with SPSSX. Therefore, it is helpful when coding for MINITAB to leave blank single columns between values. This package will automatically line up the numbers to the right. Blank columns between variables are not necessary for SPSSX, but an occasional blank column is an aid to location when coding, entering and editing data-files.

Typing, or entering, the data (stage 5) into the computer is best done by skilled personnel to minimize errors, but can be done by anyone. When the codes for a variable are 1, 2 and 3, an 8, say, will stand out when checking the listings (stage 6), but a 2 entered instead of a 3 will probably go undetected. It is because some errors are almost undetectable that care is needed throughout all stages. A common error, which the computer will highlight, is when an alphanumeric value is entered in place of a numeric one, say a letter O for a zero, or an I for 1. For important projects the data sets are entered twice, by two operators, and the two files compared by the computer as a cross-check against error. Specific procedures for entering data depend on the particular package and operating system being used; in some cases it is tiresome and inconvenient. It is wise at all stages to maintain a back-up (duplicate) data-file in case the working file is lost or altered inadvertently.

Conclusions

Once the data-file has been set up and edited it is possible to run the final results as frequencies or cross-tabulations, using transformation of data as necessary, as outlined above. It is important to realize, however, that even if the collection of data has been carried out rigorously and systematically, as outlined in the first part of this chapter, these initial computer printouts are still fairly raw data; they are results, but the strength of the inferences or conclusions, if any, which may reasonably be drawn from them depend, among other things, on their statistical analysis and validity. For quantitative data, such analysis is an important requirement for the *evaluation* of the results: some of the procedures involved are examined in the next chapter.

CHECKLIST: Chapter 6

You should know and understand:

- the choice of location for public surveys
- the methods of administering surveys
- the advantages and disadvantages of various locations and methods and possible related sources of bias;

- sampling procedures
- the meaning of research population
- the use of quota sampling and its limitations
- the use of the sampling frame and its relation to the research population
- the nature and appropriate use of random sampling, structured sampling and stratified sampling
- the procedure of areal sampling;

- the process of replication in research and the reasons for its use
- the field plot analogy in experimental design
- the design of a replicated experiment
- modification of the replicated experiment design for real-life situations
- internal testing of data
- the importance of comparative studies in research, over both time and place
- the concept and application of the weighting process
- the importance of the time-scale in studies of differentiation processes
- the problem of application of these principles to real-life situations;

- the preparation of raw data for analysis
- the nature of computer statistical packages
- a computer data-file
- methods of representing data in a computer data-file: real numbers, banding and coding, coding for presence or absence
- computer output as listing (frequency tables) and cross-tabulations
- the principles of coding information for entry into a data-file
- the preparation of a coding schedule
- the sources of error involved in the process of coding and entering data to a computer data-file
- the design of questionnaires to facilitate the coding and entering processes;

- the differences between results and conclusions (inferences).

Further reading

Dalton, R., *et al.*, 1975, *Sampling techniques in geography*, George Philip and Son, London.

de Vaus, D., 1992, *Surveys in social research*, 3rd edition UCL Press, London.

Hoinville, G., et al., 1978, *Survey research practice*, Heinemann Educational, London.

O'Brien, R.B., 1992. 'Was the voter soup stirred long enough?' *Daily Telegraph* (London), 3rd April.

Preece, R.A., 1990, 'Development control studies: scientific method and policy analysis', *Town Planning Review*, 61 (1), pp. 59-74.

Stevens, A., 1980, *Clever children in comprehensive schools*, Penguin, Harmondsworth.

Zeisel, J., 1984, *Inquiry by design: tools for environment-behaviour research*, Cambridge University Press, (originally published in 1981 by Wadsworth, Belmont, CA).

7
YOU CAN UNDERSTAND STATISTICS

'It is incident to physicians, I am afraid, beyond all other men, to mistake subsequence for consequence.'
(Samuel Johnson, 1736)

For any researcher the first rule of statistics is 'Always consult a qualified statistician'. The second rule is, 'Know enough about statistics to be able to view the advice critically'. Otherwise, abstruse statistics may obscure the original research question. This is not to say that analytical statistical techniques should be used in any other than a rigorous manner: quite the opposite. But statisticians may tend to overlook the more basic procedures which are often better suited to the sort of data used in the social sciences. These simple methods, although less discriminating, are in fact more robust since they require fewer assumptions about the nature of the data. It has been seen above that measurement in the social sciences is usually not so precise as in the natural sciences. There is, too, little point in evaluating very fine differences which often have no significance in social terms.

The contribution of statistical argument to the conclusions of a social research dissertation may in some cases be marginal or even nil. Whether such a work can be termed social *science* is questionable. Some quantitative component is usually desirable and in many doctoral dissertations the correctness of the statistical argument is essential to success. Students come to research with varying degrees of competence in statistics. This chapter is intended for virtual

beginners and for those increasing numbers who have some familiarity with statistical packages but may lack a critical understanding
of what is being done. Inevitably the account is much simplified.
More detailed explanation can be found in the books recommended
for further reading on p.185.

The nature of statistical science

At the heart of statistical science lies a simple idea: it is that the
chance or probability of various patterns of events can be predicted.
When we observe a particular pattern we can work out what the
chances of its occurrence would be, given our existing state of
knowledge or by making certain assumptions. If we observe something which is unlikely to have occurred by chance we can choose to
accept this occurrence as something new or different or significant,
or we can reject it as being due only to an unusual chance. This
argument should be carefully noted since all the statistical procedures outlined here are based on it.

An everyday example will make this clear. The chance of a tossed
coin coming down heads up is popularly referred to as 50/50 or 1 in
2 (50 per cent). The chance of two heads in succession is 1 in 4 (25
per cent); of three, 1 in 8 (12.5 per cent); of four, 1 in 16 (6.25 per
cent) and of ten, 1 in 1,024 (0.01 per cent). If we suspect someone
of cheating with a two-headed coin we might accept the chance of
three or even four heads in succession. Beyond that we would
become suspicious and at ten perhaps conclude the coin was significantly unusual or a fake. It is interesting to note that in much scientific work, and equally in the social sciences, results are considered
significant, that is unlikely to be due just to chance, if the probability of their otherwise occurring by chance is around 1 in 20. This is
equivalent only to between four and five heads in succession. But it
is by no means unthinkable that an event should occur which has a
probability of 1 in 1,000. If we observed such an event, say ten
heads in succession, we might replicate the experiment by taking a
further sample of ten tosses. The chance of these also being all
heads is less than 1 in 1,000,000. This is the order of chance given
against a nuclear power station blowing up, which may or may not
be a comforting observation.

The type of data involved and the method of sampling will affect
the general pattern of probabilities against which any particular

event should be tested. This pattern of probability is different for tossing a coin than it is for, say, the chance of random points on a graph falling on a straight line. Each statistical test is based on certain specific *assumptions* about a relevant pattern of probability. It is important that these assumptions are known and adhered to (below) when using any statistical techniques.

Description of relationships

Since the relationship between two variables or concepts is of fundamental interest in research it will be useful to start by examining some ways in which statistics deals with such relationships. Simple relationships can be conceived in visual terms. In the example in Figure 7.1 the bottom *horizontal* line shows distance in miles measured from left to right from a starting point marked zero. But we do not have to measure just along the line. If we imagine the left-hand *vertical* line to be the starting line for a race-track then we can measure the distance of any position from this starting line by reference to the bottom line. For example, any point on the vertical broken line is ten miles from the starting line.

If we now discard the analogy of the race-track and think of Figure 7.1 as what it is, a diagram on a piece of paper, then any point on the vertical broken line is a visual record or representation of a value of ten miles. Any value between 0 and 30 can be represented in this way by points at various locations on the figure.

Now imagine the bottom horizontal line as a start line. We can measure upwards in the same way. Any point on the horizontal broken line is a record or representation of two litres of fuel used. Most important though, one point can now represent two values; in Figure 7.1 the black point represents ten miles *and* two litres.

In fact this one point represents yet a third value which is an expression of the relationship between the first two. If we record that we have travelled ten miles and have used two litres of fuel then our fuel consumption is ten miles per two litres, or five miles per litre. If all relevant conditions remain constant this relationship would hold true no matter how many miles were travelled, but many relationships do not stay constant in this simple way. We could check in this case by recording fuel used and distance at regular intervals along our journey. The results could be *tabulated* as follows:

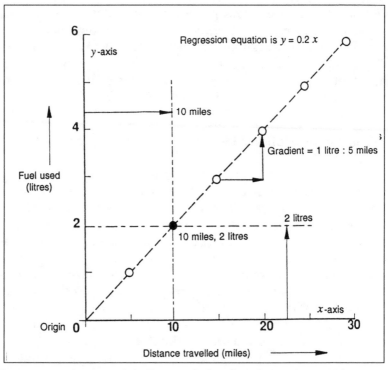

Figure 7.1 A simple straight-line graph describes the mathematical relationship between two variables: in this case distance travelled and fuel consumed.

Miles travelled	Litres used
5	1
10	2
15	3
20	4
25	5
30	6

These values are represented by the points shown on Figure 7.1. We see that they all lie on a straight line, that is the relationship is *rectilinear*, usually termed simply *linear*, over the *range* of the experiment. The relationship might vary over greater distances.

Figure 7.1 is a simple form of graph. The bottom horizontal line is called the *x axis* and the vertical line on the left the *y axis*. Values measured along the x axis are known as the *x coordinates*, and up the y axis as the *y coordinates*. The position of the solid point is thus defined as where x = 10 (miles) and y = 2 (litres), or simply as coordinates (10, 2); the value of x is always given first.

The regression equation

If the simple table above were entered into a computer data-file (Chapter Six) the computer might, if the particular statistical package had that facility, draw the graph as shown. However, the information can be represented or described in another way. We see that, numerically, fuel consumption is always one fifth of mileage; that is:

litres of fuel consumption = number of miles ÷ 5,
or, simply, $y = x/5$
or $y = 0.2x$

This last expression is a simple form of what is known as an equation; it expresses the relationship between x and y (representing in this case fuel and distance) in a mathematical form. In particular this linear equation, which expresses a linear relationship between x and y, is known as a *linear regression equation*. Any statistical package will produce this. It tells us all we need to know about the relationship: that y is always one fifth of x. From this we can calculate a value of y for any value of x (and vice versa). If we travel twelve and a half miles we will use $y = 0.2 \times 12.5 = 2.5$ litres of fuel.

The equation $y = 0.2x$ has two characteristics which enable us to draw the graph once we know the equation. First, if x is zero then, since 0.2 multiplied by nothing equals nothing, y is also zero; that is, the first point or *origin of the line* has the coordinates ($x = 0$, $y = 0$) in the lower left corner of the graph. Second, we know the angle or slope or *gradient of the line*. Gradients of hills are measured by how far we go along to go up one unit; 1 in 10 means that if we go along ten metres we go up one metre. So with the graph, if we trace along five miles, the line rises by one litre; the gradient is 1 in 5, or 1/5, or 0.2. This gradient is known as the *coefficient* of x.

Regression lines are seldom as simple as this, and in some cases can be misleading. It is always a good idea to examine visually the points plotted on a graph rather than to rely solely on a regression equation produced by a computer. Suppose for example that we fill up our vehicle but someone syphons out one litre while we have a last-minute cup of coffee. After five miles the vehicle will have consumed another litre, making two litres used up for five miles; the coordinates of this point are ($x = 5$, $y = 2$). After that the vehicle will consume one litre per five miles as before, producing coordinates of (10, 3), (15, 4) and so on. The points on the graph will now look like Figure 7.2. In this case the computer will recognize

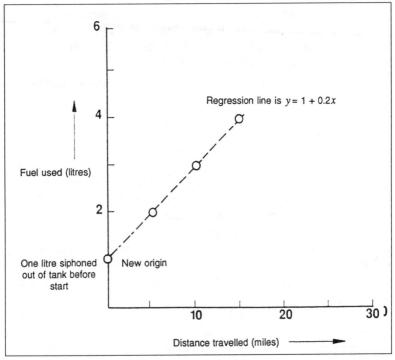

Figure 7.2 Essentially the same relationship as that shown in Figure 7.1 but with a different starting point or origin.

that when $x = 0$, y is already 1, that is the origin of the line is now at coordinates (0, 1). This is represented in the equation by the addition of a *constant c* (whose value in this case is 1) so that when $x = 0$, $y = 1$, thus:

$$y = c + 0.2x$$

or, in this case;

$$y = 1 + 0.2x$$

Suppose, however, at fifteen miles the vehicle hits a rock and the petrol tank begins to leak at a rate of one litre per five miles; we are now using and losing two litres per five miles. The relationship or gradient changes from 1/5 to 2/5 or 0.4. The new regression equation is thus $y = c + 0.4x$. The graph will now look like Figure 7.3. The origin for the new steeper line can be found, by extending the line downwards, to be where $x = 0$ and $y = -2$ (that is $c = -2$).

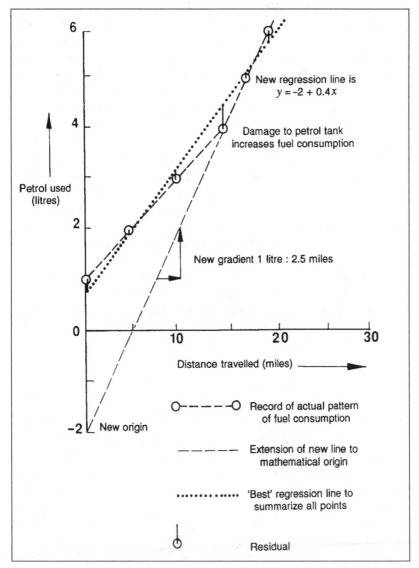

Figure 7.3 The relationship shown in Figure 7.2 between distance travelled and fuel consumed has been changed by an accident at fifteen miles.

Clearly this point has little basis in reality but is necessary to define mathematically the new position of the line as shown. It is also a caution against using a line to make predictions outside the range of values which were used to define the line in the first place.

The points on the graph now represent in fact two linear relationships having two different gradients which together accurately describe the pattern of fuel consumption for the journey. But if the computer is instructed to calculate one linear regression equation for all the points it will do this based on the best *approximate* line (shown dotted in Figure 7.3) and in this case the equation will not represent the complete truth. The computer package will however recognize that the line does not fit the points perfectly. In Figure 7.3 it can be seen that some points would have to be moved up or down some distance to fit on the line. These distances are called *residuals* since they are the distances remaining when the line has been fitted as closely as possible to the points. The computer calculates their size and number as a check on the reliability of the line. However, unreliability in linear statistical relationships does not usually arise from an accident happening during the experiment or survey. It may be rather that measuring devices are inaccurate or that unknown outside factors are influencing the results. Clearly these situations arise in the social sciences. Or it may be that the relationship is in fact *curvilinear*, that is the line is curved rather than straight. Try for example tabulating and plotting some values of x and y for the equation $y = x^2$. Most statistical packages have the facility to test for a variety of forms of mathematical relationship.

What a regression line means

Simple linear regression is one example of what is known as *correlation* which is a valuable statistical procedure. *It must be emphasized however that the fact that two sets of values appear to be related or correlated mathematically does not necessarily mean that they have any causal relationship in real life.* Also, while the computer will always produce a line of sorts, the reliability of this line must be tested. Visual inspection of the points on a *scattergraph* (Figure 7.4) is useful to see if there are changes in trend, as in the example above. If the points seem to be all over the place and do not even approximate to a line the correlation will be weak and unreliable. The computer summarizes the information from the residuals in a single figure, the *correlation coefficient* which can vary between +1 and −1. This is usually shown as r on the computer printout: values between about +0.5 and −0.5 are suspect since this means that the points are so scattered that no meaningful line can be drawn to represent them.

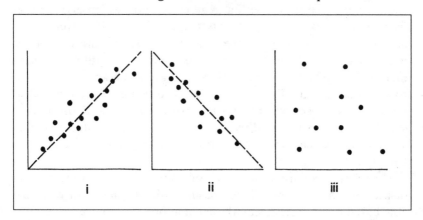

Figure 7.4 Visual inspection of the relationship between two variables when plotted on a graph shows whether the relationship is likely to be (i) positive or (ii) negative or (iii) non-existent.

Large values of r mean that the points do seem to cluster along a line. But this pattern could have been produced by chance. As with tossing the penny, above, the probability of a number of random points falling on or close to a line can be calculated. Two quite unrelated points can always be joined by a straight line and it is not unlikely that a third point will by chance fall on or close to the line. But it is unlikely that a large number of random points will fall on a line. Conversely, if a lot of points do fall on a line this is a pattern which is unlikely to have occurred by chance. These sorts of argument are employed in, for example, the debate about the reality of prehistoric 'ley-lines' supposedly linking ancient sites – what are the probabilities of ancient sites lying on a straight line by chance alone? Even a large correlation coefficient should be tested further by the simple t-test (see Appendix I) which takes into account the number of points in order to assess the probability of the r value having occurred by chance.

The graphs shown here are examples of *positive correlation*, that is as x changes positively (increases) so does y; hence the line on the graph rises from left to right. In some relationships y may decrease as x increases; for example, the incidence of some diseases may decrease as income increases. The graph will slope *down* from left to right. This form of relationship is known as a *negative correlation*. It takes the general form of $y = -x$; that is, it can be recognized by the fact that the coefficient of x is negative. A negative correlation should not be confused with a *weak* correlation which arises rather from a wide dispersion of points (Figure 7.4iii). Researchers are tempted sometimes to remove altogether certain values or points which are a long way from the line – some computer packages include a facility to do this – thus increasing the apparent significance of the results. But this should be done only if there is a clear reason why these extreme results are aberrant, and the reason should be stated in the dissertation. It should be noted also that some forms of data are not appropriate for regression analysis (see below).

Correlation equations are based on values obtained from samples of the total population. Therefore any estimates made of one variable based on another, using these equations, are approximate only; the reasons for this are explained on p.172. Thus values of y calculated from x, or vice versa, are expressed as a range rather than as a single value (see Appendix I).

Multiple correlation

It was pointed out in Chapter Six that it is possible to evaluate relationships between more than two variables. While this is not experimentally ideal it is inevitable where not all factors can be controlled, or where a number of social factors are being assessed for their possible influence on some measure of performance. We saw how the linear regression line could be thought of as a hill; as we go from left to right we go up (positive correlation) or down (negative correlation). If the line was horizontal we would go neither up nor down, the value of y is then unaffected by changes in x; the coefficient of x is zero. If the origin of this line was, say, at (0,2) the equation would simply be $y = 2$.

Imagine now that the hill is not represented by a line but by a surface extended behind the graph; Figure 7.5(top). We then have added a third axis, known as the z-axis. If x increases in figure 7.5(top) so still does y. But, in this example, movement along the slope from front to back, parallel to z, does not increase the height of y. If however the surface is tilted in both directions, Figure

7.5(bottom), then movement along either the x or z lines increases y. We thus have a relationship between all three variables which can be expressed as $y = c + a.x + b.z$ where c is some constant, as before, and a and b are the coefficients of x and z respectively. The relative sizes of a and b represent the sizes of the influences of x and z on y and it is possible, by further calculation of the value known as R^2, to make statements such as, 60 per cent of the variation in y

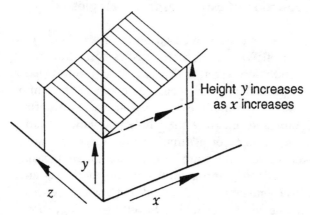

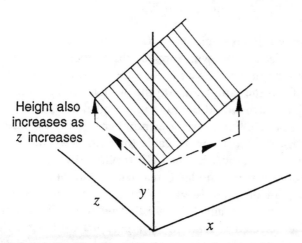

Figure 7.5 Relationships between three variables can be visualized as a sloping roof. Top: height y increases in direction x but not in direction z; bottom: y increases with both x and z.

is explained by variation in z. We cannot visualize more than three dimensions, but the computer can generate *multiple regression equations* containing several factors in addition to x and z which enable us to predict, within limits, the values of y under various combinations of conditions.

Production of estimates from samples

Statistics is a science based on the laws of chance or probability, as life itself. We need to use statistics every time we study a sample of a population. Even if the sample is randomized according to the best procedures, the measures made of the sample are by chance unlikely to reflect exactly what we would find if we had the resources to measure the whole population. Statistical science provides a means of estimating how close the sample measures are likely to be to the truth. When we compare measures from two samples, say a test and a control group, statistical analysis also enables us to calculate the probability that any differences might be real and not due to chance alone. Strictly speaking, though, statistics does not provide absolute truth or reality but rather a series of levels of probability which we can choose to accept or reject.

The theoretical population of samples

Let us return to the example, used in Chapter Four, of the proportion of vegetarians in a town. Suppose the proportion in fact is 10 per cent, though of course we do not know that; it is what we hope to estimate from the sample. To do this we have to imagine that we do something which would be quite impractical in real life; that we take not one sample but a very large number of samples. The whole population is assumed to be available for each new sample so that some people, by chance, might be interviewed more than once. This procedure can be simulated mathematically but early statisticians spent a lot of time testing this by putting numbers into hats and taking them out again. Suppose that we interview a sample of 100 residents selected at random. The proportion of vegetarians in the sample might be 18 per cent, though such a high proportion is unlikely. This number, eighteen, is called the sample value. A second sample is then selected and interviewed. This time the sample value might be two per cent. Further samples are taken. If, on a graph, a box is drawn for each sample the result will be something like Figure 7.6. The positions of the boxes along the bottom line indicate the various values found in different samples, eighteen per cent, 2 per cent and so on. When two or more samples have the same sample value the boxes are piled on top of each other. Thus three samples had values of 5 per cent. The number of samples in any one pile is shown by reference to the vertical axis on the left. It can be seen that most values cluster near to the true value of 10 per cent, though most samples will not have exactly this true value. Extreme values are rare, but they do, by chance, occur. The average, or mean, of all sample values is the true value.

Overall, this picture is quite clear. For example, a sample of value 12 per cent, represented by the black square, lies two percentage points to the right of the true value. The problem is that when we take *only one* sample, as is usual, *we do not have this overall picture ;*

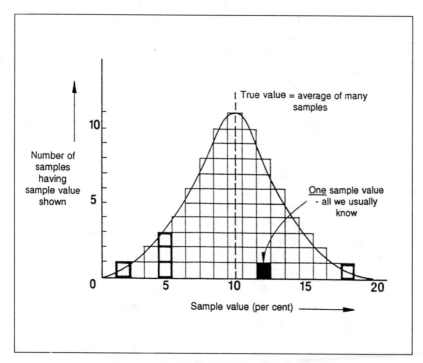

Figure 7.6 Theoretically, if a very large number of independent samples could be taken from a study population, the sample measurements for any characteristic would, by chance, cluster around the true value in this form.

we have only one isolated black square. We do not know how close this is to a true value, nor even on which side it is.

All the individual boxes taken together are known as the *population of samples*. This should be distinguished from the 100 individuals interviewed for any one box who, as seen already, are called a sample population. It is known that if a large number of samples were to be taken (many more than are shown here) then, by the laws of chance, the population of samples, that is all the boxes, will take the form shown in Figure 7.6 (a fact which has so far been taken for granted). This form is known as the *distribution* of the population of samples. The *distribution curve* which outlines the pile of boxes is not just any old curve. It can be described by a mathematical equation in a similar way to the regression lines described above.

The standard error of the sample

There are many variations of this distribution curve, above; the exact form which it takes is crucial to statistical theory generally and to the interpretation of any particular set of results. As stated above, the form can be worked out mathematically or by experiment. As with any mathematically defined curve it can be used to make predictions. An important characteristic of this curve or distribution is that 68 per cent of the boxes contained within the curve lie within a specific distance of the true mean or central value. Further, this distance can be calculated if we know the size of the sample and the sample value. The distance is known as the *standard error of the sample*. Then we can predict that for any one sample value, or box, there is a 68 per cent (roughly 2 to 1) chance that it is within one standard error of the true value. Putting it another way, there is a 2 to 1 chance that the true value is within one standard error of the sample value. But since we do not know whether the true value is on the high side or the low side of the sample value we say that statistically there is a probability of 68 per cent (p = 68% or p = 0.68) that the true value lies within a range of the sample value *plus or minus* one standard error of the sample.

The importance of sample size

A 2 to 1 chance of being correct with a piece of research is not very high. In fact it is known also that for this curve there is a 19 to 1 chance (95 per cent) that a box lies within a distance of *two* standard errors of the true value and a 99 to 1 chance (99 per cent) that it lies within three standard errors. Social scientists will usually accept a probability of 95 per cent or even of 90 per cent, but natural science may require a 99 per cent, 99.9 or even 99.99 per cent (1 in 10,000) probability of being correct. It is important to note that these inferences about the relation between sample values and true values, based on the theoretical distribution of a population of samples, depend on the assumption of a *minimum size of sample* (that is, a sample population) in each case of not fewer than thirty, and preferably of sixty. Even a perfectly random sample cannot be assumed to be representative of the whole population if the sample number or size is below this value. To take an extreme case, a random sample of one must be either 100 per cent or 0 per cent vegetarian; only as sample size increases does a sample value reliably approach a true value.

How then is a standard error calculated? The formula is based on complex mathematics but the end result is simple:

$$\text{standard error (s.e.)} = \sqrt{\frac{p \times q}{n}}$$

where   p = the sample value (expressed as a percentage)
       q = 100 minus the sample value
       n = number of individuals in the sample (sample size).

Thus in the example above, if the sample value is 12 per cent, and the sample size was 100, s.e. $= \sqrt{\frac{12 \times 88}{100}} = 3.2$. Therefore it is 95 per cent certain or, rather, probable that the true proportion of vegetarians in the town lies in the range 12 +/- (2 × 3.2), that is somewhere between 9.6 and 18.4 per cent. There is no way of knowing which value is the more correct; clearly the true number of vegetarians could be over-estimated by nearly 100 per cent. One way to be more exact is to take a bigger sample. Since sample size, *n*, divides the formula, then the bigger *n* becomes the smaller is the standard error. A sample size of 1,000 instead of 100 produces a standard error of $\sqrt{\frac{12 \times 88}{1,000}} = 1.03$.

The best estimate is then that the true value lies between the limits of 12 +/- (2 × 1.03), or roughly between 10 and 14 per cent, which is a much smaller range. Sometimes the attributes of one group within a sample, that is a *sub-sample* or sub-group, are analysed separately: for example, the views of women may be analysed separately from those of the men in the sample. In this case it is important to note that the value of n used for calculating the relevant standard error is the size of the sub-sample only, which here would be the number of women, and to bear in mind that the requirement for minimum sample size (above) also applies to sub-samples. Election opinion polls normally use a sample of 1,000 or more electors, which is perfectly adequate for the degree of accuracy required. But with over 600 constituencies in Britain the sub-sample for any one is too small for reliable prediction at that level. Even though not all constituencies are sampled, the sub-samples are sometimes as small as ten and have to be selected with great care to be representative.

There is always a chance that an extreme sample value will produce an estimated range which does not include the true value; this chance is 5 per cent if the range of plus or minus two standard errors is used. That is, if there is a 95 per cent chance of the true value lying within the calculated range there remains a 5 per cent chance of it being outside. Using the formula above, for a sample size of 1,000, a sample value of 13 per cent would produce a range of 13 +/- 2.12 per cent, or between 10.88 and 15.12 per cent. If the sample size had been 100 the resulting range of 6.3 to 19.3 would of course have included the true value of 10, but in fact the narrower range of the larger sample is still closer to the truth.

All this should produce a critical but not destructive attitude to estimates based on samples. Suppose we are told that a sample shows that 55 per cent of people are in favour of some policy. We might start by asking whether the sample is truly random; was it conducted in the street outside the Rotary Club, or the Working Men's Club? If we discover that the sample size was 100 (such information is often not provided) we can quickly calculate that the lower estimate of the true value is 45; that, is there might be no majority at all. A sample size of 1,000 or even 2,000 would be more convincing.

Overview technique

A particularly interesting example of the importance of sample size is shown by the so-called overview technique developed in medical research, especially in connection with the use of the drug tamoxifen for treatment of breast cancer. A large number of trials worldwide has produced not entirely convincing results because in each case the sample has been too small for benefits to show up clearly. For a few cases the results have been negative. A team at Oxford University has combined all these disparate findings to produce in effect one large experiment. Obviously there are reservations; each individual trial must have been properly conducted; negative results, which perhaps were not published, must not be ignored. The result has been to give a much clearer picture of the beneficial effect of treatment and this is now largely accepted in clinical practice. The overview technique could also be seen as an illustration of replication. With data based on just one or two trials it is possible that, because of chance factors, one trial will show no benefits from the drug. In 100 or more trials it is very unlikely that the effects of chance would obscure an overall trend. (Compare, for example, the field plot analogy in Chapter Six.)

Estimation and comparison of population values

Estimation of population means

So far the illustration used has involved a very simple measure of a characteristic of a population: are you a vegetarian, yes or no? This provides a single measure of, say, 10 per cent for the population. A measure which is used in this way to describe and define a population for research purposes is often called a *parameter*. However, as was seen in the example of the football team (Chapter Six), some other measures, or parameters, of a population, such as height, are more complex and variable, and the calculation of the standard error of the sample in these cases is different. One measure of the height of a total population is the average or mean height. This may be estimated, within limits, from the mean height of a sample population using the appropriate standard error in the way described above; that is, there is a 68 per cent chance that the true mean lies within the range of sample mean plus or minus one standard error, and similarly for other ranges. The *standard error of the mean of a sample* is calculated as shown below. Statistical packages will calculate this instantly for a variable but it is useful to see how both the size of sample and the variability of the data around the mean value affect the precision and significance of the results.

The standard error of a sample mean $= \sqrt{\frac{\Sigma (x - \bar{x})^2}{n}}$

The calculation is as follows:

1. Calculate the mean height of the sample, $\bar{x}$.
2. Find the difference between the average height $\bar{x}$ and the height of each individual $(x - \bar{x})$.
3. Square each difference $(x - \bar{x})^2$
4. Add all the squares (Σ represents the process of addition) $\Sigma(x - \bar{x})^2$.
5. Divide by n (sample size).
6. Find the square root as above.

The formula shows again how a larger sample size decreases the standard error. As before, if a characteristic of a sub-sample is to be analysed separately (such as height of females only) then the value used for n is the number in the sub-sample. It also shows that if a lot of the individual values of x differ greatly from the mean value, $\bar{x}$, that is if the population is very variable, the standard error will be greater and the estimate of the true value is less accurate or precise.

Comparison of two populations: the statistical argument

It has been seen (Chapter Five) how the use of control groups in research, and of some common base of comparison, avoids certain fallacies such as the fallacy of affirming the consequent, or of finding what we expect or want to find. To make a comparison between two groups we have to estimate, not just what the true value of a characteristic is for one population (above), but whether this estimate differs significantly from that for another population. That is, we have to judge whether the difference could have occurred just by the chance involved in the sampling of two populations, or whether the difference between the two samples is so large that it is probably real and exists in the total population. In fact there is no absolute level or borderline below which we can say the results are due merely to the chance processes of sampling, and above which the difference is real. Rather, as with tossing the coin, there is a whole range of possible results and each result has an associated probability of happening. We decide, preferably before the experiment, what probability we are going to accept as the borderline, whether it is in effect, say, five consecutive tosses or ten or even twenty. We decide this according to the degree of our own suspicious natures and according to the importance of the question. A farmer must decide, based on the crop-scientist's results, whether buying a more expensive variety of seed is likely to be paid back by increased yield: a doctor whether the chances of a cure outweigh the possibility of harmful side-effects of a new drug.

The null hypothesis

A discerning reader may observe that this process of choosing a probability level veers towards the fallacy of affirming the consequent, of choosing the probability level that enables us to accept the sample results as 'true' if we want to. Certainly a student whose results just fail to be statistically significant or 'true' at the 95 per cent level (a commonly adopted criterion) may feel inclined to argue that they really are true and in any case are more likely to be true than not. This latter argument is also put forward by some statisticians. It is unlikely however that we would accept the argument at this level of probability if it was the safety of a nuclear power station that was at stake. The conventional attitude of statisticians is that of structured and explicit scepticism which is related to the testing and questioning attitudes outlined in Chapter Two. A statistician argues as follows, by a process of falsification. First, it is hypothesized that there is *no* difference between two populations as a result of treatment, policy or whatever. This is known accordingly as the *null hypothesis*. The *consequence* of this, it is argued, is that any differences between samples of the two populations will be of such a size that they could easily have occurred by chance. The consequences are *tested* by the taking and measuring of samples. If the differences are easily explained by chance then this tends to *confirm* the null hypothesis that there is no difference or effect. If the results are such that they are unlikely to have occurred by chance then this tends to *falsify* the hypothesis, that is it suggests that there *is* a difference. Note how the process conforms to the logical argument of *denying the consequent* (Chapter Three) though this denial is probabilistic rather than categorical.

It is important also to be clear that if the null hypothesis has to be accepted this does not necessarily prove that there is no real difference, merely that it would be unsound to argue that there is. This is the reason that we say the results *tend* to confirm (or reject) rather than prove or disprove the hypothesis. A larger sample, or more accurate measurement, may yet show a difference, as seen in the use of overview statistics in the tamoxifen experiment, above. In situations of environmental risk, for example, there is a distinction between saying that no risk has been demonstrated and saying that it has been demonstrated that there is no risk. In the first case a sample difference has failed to reach an acceptable level of statistical significance. In the second case a sample difference would have to be so small that we could say, if we hypothesize that there *is* a true difference, that such a small sample difference would be very unlikely to occur by chance. That is, we reject the hypothesis, judging that the true difference is so small as to be negligible. Clearly in some areas of work it may be as interesting to demonstrate the probable absence of an effect as to demonstrate an effect.

Science places great emphasis on the repeatability of experiments or surveys. An observed difference which has only a 19 out of 20 chance of being true (or a 1 in 20 chance of being wrong) is not entirely convincing. But if this difference is always, or nearly always, found when the experiment is repeated many times, perhaps under various conditions, then it becomes much more persuasive. Remember that the pattern of ten heads in a row has a 1 in 1,024 chance of occurring; the odds against this pattern being repeated by chance alone in several consecutive tests run into millions of millions. Since, as has been seen, hypothesis testing is normally based on the argument of denying the consequent, replication in science should not be seen as mere confirmation but consists rather of repeated attempts at falsification. The criteria for falsification, in terms of probability levels, are thus made explicit for the researcher and also should be set out in the report or dissertation so that a reader or assessor can apply his or her own judgement.

Comparison of two populations: chi-squared test

A simple comparison of two populations can be made by means of a table. Suppose we wish to compare the types of work done by men and women. A sample of 200 each of men and women might produce these results:

Occupation	Men	Women	Total
Professional	40	20	60
Skilled	100	80	180
Unskilled	60	100	160
Total	200	200	400

Even if, in the total population, the proportions of men and women engaged in the different types of employment were exactly the same we might still experience some differences between the samples due solely to the chances of sampling. The question is, are the differences shown here, with men predominantly in professional jobs and women in unskilled jobs, sufficiently large for us to conclude that they did not occur by chance but reflect real differences? If the proportions were in fact equal in the total population, and if the sample repeated this exactly, the proportions in the two columns of figures would be the same. Since, in this example, there are equal numbers of men and women in the survey we would expect the sample numbers of each in each class of occupation to be equal, being half the total for that class. The figures in the professional row for example, from the table above, would be $(40 + 20)/2 = 30$. The table would become:

Occupation	Men	Women	Total
Professional	30	30	60
Skilled	90	90	180
Unskilled	80	80	160
Total	200	200	400

The values of the first table are called the *observed values*, those in the second the *expected values*. Note that the totals for the two tables are the same. The probability of the observed values deviating from the expected values by the amounts shown, or by any other, can be calculated.

The calculation is analogous to that for the regression line, above. There the distances of all the points from a straight line were incorporated in a calculation which produced a test statistic known as *r*. The probability of the particular value of *r* occurring purely by chance could then be tested using the *t*-test which takes into account the number of points involved. But, in the case of the two tables, above, another form of test statistic is calculated based on the differences between observed and expected values; it is known as *chi-squared* or χ^2. Its probability can also be tested using, not the *t*-test, but special χ^2 tables (see Appendix I) which take into account the number of items, or cells, in the table, excluding the totals. Once again, as with the tossed coin, we observe a pattern of events and we estimate the probability of this pattern occurring by chance by reference to existing theoretical statistical calculations (in this case the χ^2 tables). In the light of this we can judge whether to accept or reject the pattern as being significant.

A statistical package will compute χ^2 for a table, or cross-tabulation, of almost any size, but certain *assumptions* must be complied with. First, the numbers in the tables to be analysed must be absolute numbers, that is counts, and not percentage values. The figures can of course be expressed as percentages after analysis, for the purposes of discussion, and the arguments about significance would still apply. Second, not more than 20 per cent, 1 in 5, of the cells should contain values of less than 5. Computer packages usually draw attention to this second condition. It may be necessary to aggregate rows or columns to achieve this requirement; for example, in the table shown, had it been necessary, skilled and unskilled could be aggregated to form one category of non-professionals. The chi-squared procedure can be seen as a form of correlation, in this case relating gender differences to differences in occupation. As with other forms of correlation it does not prove any cause and effect mechanism; this would have to be sought by other, possibly non-quantitative, means of investigation. Chi-squared can also be used to test the distribution of a single variable, in which case the expected frequencies are calculated according to some known outside factor which is not strictly part of the experiment or survey, such as the proportions of men and women in the population at large.

Comparison of two population means

Chi-squared is useful as a test where the information analysed is in the form of counts; that is, it has been produced by counting numbers of individuals and their characteristics. Where a wider and continuous measure, such as height, is employed a different method is used to compare populations. In the discussion on the estimation of true values based on sample means, above, it was shown that the estimate is not a single figure but a range. If we find that the mean value of one sample population, say of a test group, is larger than that of a sample control group, what is the probability that this difference is or would be true for the total population? We know that the true values may lie some way either side of the sample means. If these ranges overlap to some extent it could even be that the control group has a larger true value than the test group, or at the least that there is no difference.

Comparison of two sample means is dealt with in a way very similar to the process of estimation from one sample. If, theoretically, we take a great many pairs of samples from both a test and a control population the values of the differences between the sample means would vary around a true value in a way similar to that shown in Figure 7.6. The probability of the true difference being within a set range of any one sample difference can be calculated. The range is based on yet another type of standard error, the *standard error of the difference of the means* (see Appendix I). There is then a 95 per cent probability that the true difference lies within the range given by: (difference between sample means) +/- (2 × standard error of difference between sample means), and so on for other levels of probability as before. Further statistical tests can be applied which need not concern us here.

Types of data and methods of analysis

It has been seen how the nature of the data affects the type of analysis which can be used; standard errors are calculated differently for counts and for measures such as height; the χ^2 test is based on the assumption that data are in the form of counts and not percentages. The linear regression coefficient r is based on data such as height which are continuously variable. If we wish to compare or correlate two data sets which have been produced by a ranking process, for example where two sets of people have been asked to put environmental preferences of some sort into order, a different form of correlation must be used known as a *rank correlation*. This is similar to linear regression but is based on different assumptions. It will show whether the orders chosen by the two groups, the group preferences, are significantly different or not.

Type of data, method of sampling, and in some cases the size of sample all affect the theoretical distribution or pattern against which the probability of any particular result is estimated and so determine the type of test to be used. This is an area where, if there is any doubt, the advice of a statistician is essential. There are three types of data; their characteristics have already been introduced (Chapter Five). *Nominal data* are those where particular attributes, identified by name – hence nominal, are simply counted, for example 'professionally qualified', 'unemployed', 'do not agree', and so on. These counts can be converted into percentages after analysis but their original nature should not be ignored. Second, *ordinal data* are those produced by putting things in some order; the data are known as ranks. Third, *cardinal or interval data* are produced by what we normally think of as true measurement (though all data are measures of a sort) where the figures can vary continuously, not in discrete steps as with ranks, and where the difference or interval between two values has meaning and is itself a measure.

Methods of statistical analysis fall into two groups. The simple more robust methods, such as chi-squared, are known as *non-parametric*. They do not discriminate between very small differences but are appropriate for the simpler forms of data, the nominal and the ordinal. Indeed *non-parametric methods are the only ones which should be used for these data*. *Parametric* methods are appropriate for cardinal data and require more assumptions about the quality of the data. Computer packages will not distinguish between the types of data. If percentages are used in chi-squared analysis, or rank values in linear regression, the computer will generate what appears to be normal output but the results will be largely meaningless. It is important therefore that a computer is instructed to perform only those calculations which are known to be appropriate to the variables used.

Conclusions

This chapter has covered, in outline only, the statistical techniques of linear and multiple regression, the estimation of population frequencies and means from samples, the concept, calculation and use of standard errors in setting probability limits to such estimates, the importance of sample size, the comparisons of population frequencies and of means, and the evaluation of differences between population means and between population frequencies. None of these techniques should be used uncritically. The nature of the data used and the assumptions on which each technique is based must be appropriate to the technique. These criteria are given in most statistics textbooks but the particular nature of any research is best discussed, or at least checked, with a statistician. Statistics is similar to life itself. We assess, usually intuitively, the probability of certain events, and then act on this, whether we decide to cross the road or to live beside a nuclear power station. Statistics regularizes and standardizes this process for certain types of event in certain situations which can be relatively controlled. Statistical analysis is particularly useful for supporting generalized statements about populations and for attaching probabilities to predictions of events. It does not in itself identify causal mechanisms nor produce insight or understanding of situations. It should be viewed rather as a series of techniques which where possible are used to complement and test the arguments of the main methods of research. These, as outlined in previous chapters, are experiment, interview, observation, documentary research, and the detailed case-study which uses a variety of methods. The next chapter will examine how those methods may be combined in the formulation of a research proposal.

CHECK LIST: Chapter Seven

You should know and understand:

- the essential principles of statistical analysis;

- the modelling of a simple linear relationship both graphically and mathematically
- the meaning of (a) the origin, (b) the gradient, (c) the constant, (d) the coefficient in a linear regression equation
- the idea of the residual when a straight line is fitted to a set of points
- that correlation does not necessarily indicate a cause and effect relationship

- how to interpret a scattergraph
- the meaning and significance of the correlation coefficient
- the principle of multiple correlation;

- the theoretical distribution (curve) of a population of many samples
- the meaning of the standard error of a single sample for data produced by counting (nominal data)
- the importance of size of sample for the estimation of true values from sample values
- the importance of variability in the population and sample data for estimation of true values from sample values
- the standard error of a single sample mean when measurement is on the cardinal or interval scale
- the standard error of the difference between two sample means when measurement is on the cardinal scale
- the argument of the null hypothesis and its relation to the argument of denying the consequent
- the chi-squared test for data produced by counting (nominal data)
- types of data: nominal, ordinal and cardinal (interval) and the appropriate types of analysis for each;

- that statistical estimates are neither precise nor certain but consist of ranges of values to which can be attributed appropriate probabilities that a true value lies within (or without) the range

Further reading

Brown, P., 1992, 'Breast cancer: turning facts into figures', *New Scientist*, 18 Jan., pp. 16–17.

Gregory, S., 1963, *Statistical methods and the geographer*, Oxford University Press, Oxford.

Henckel, R.E., 1976, *Tests of significance*, Sage, Beverley Hills.

Norcliffe, G.B., 1982, *Inferential statistics for geographers*, 2nd edn, Hutchinson, London.

Rowntree, D., 1991 [1981], *Statistics without tears: a primer for non-mathematicians*, 2nd edn, Penguin, Harmondsworth.

Siegel, S., 1956, *Non-parametric statistics for the behaviourial sciences*, International Student edn, McGraw-Hill/Kogakusha, Tokyo.

Yeomans, K.A., 1968, *Statistics for the social scientist 1: introducing statistics*, Penguin, Harmondsworth.

8
THE RESEARCH QUESTION

'In the same way Byzantine men of letters passed from the study of classical Greek historians to imitations of their methods and style. Side by side with the Chronicle, which was concerned essentially with recording events in order, we begin to find a new interest in the character of participants in those events, their motives and their understanding of what they are doing. The important is distinguished from the trivial, and the causes and effects of events were explored.'

(Robert Browning, *The Byzantine Empire*, 1980)

For many students the two most difficult stages of research occur at the beginning and the end; they are the choice of topic at the outset and the final writing of the dissertation. This chapter is concerned with how to define a research topic or, more precisely, a research question; Chapter Nine will deal with the many considerations involved in the production of the final account of an academic research project. While the time allocated for the preparation of a research dissertation may seem long, up to three years full-time in the case of a doctoral thesis, excessive delay in defining a topic in the early stages may lead to a failure to submit an adequate dissertation on time. This is not to say that the choice of a topic needs any other than careful consideration. Indeed the initial reading around the subject area, which is part of the process, is an important and enjoyable stage of the research. But, particularly as academic institutions are under pressure to improve submission rates of dissertations, this first stage needs to be well organized and carried out with a clear idea of what is being sought in terms of a research question.

The structure of research

A dissertation is a substantial and complex piece of writing but a good dissertation can be seen to be constructed from a few essential and distinct parts.

1. *Justification* – why the research question is important and should be investigated; limitations of the research due to constraints of time, resources or information.
2. *Background* (literature review) – what is known about the topic so far; in particular, what other relevant research has been carried out.
3. *Introduction to the empirical work* – why the particular experiments, surveys or case-studies have been identified as relevant to the topic.
4. *Design of the empirical work* – how the empirical work has been designed in detail to relate to the topic (for example, methods of measurement used).
5. *Results of the empirical work* – description, tabulation, analysis and critique of the empirical work.
6. *Inferences* – use of the results and other evidence to make rational conclusions about the topic.
7. *Discussion* – a review of methods, results and inferences; any limitations to the applicability of the results due to, for example, lack of resources or variables not investigated; some speculation about relationships involving the topic; possible future work.

Running through each stage, except stage 5, is the motif of the research question; it is the touchstone against which the relevance of every point and sentence of the dissertation is judged. The term 'research question' could be substituted for the word 'topic' in every stage. This does not mean that every statement and argument is directly related to the research question. The research question, sometimes called the research problem (problem in the sense of a thing to be answered rather than an obstacle), will generate subsidiary questions and problems which will need to be answered before the main question can be tackled. A series of questions might be as follows:

Research question: Has policy A been effective?

This leads to a main subsidiary question.

Subsidiary question: 1. What is meant by effective?

One answer to this question might be: Effective in producing the results intended by the policy makers. Further related questions follow.

Related questions:
1(a) What effects were intended?
1(b) Where are these stated?

The statements of intent will involve certain concepts such as, for example: improved education, increased fairness, more efficient administration. These concepts need to be operationalized, that is, put into a form in which they can be subject to testing by experiment or survey.

Operational questions:
1(c) What interpretation should be placed on the
      stated concepts?
1(d) How can these concepts be measured?
1(e) How might the effects of the policy be
      distinguished from other coincidental effects?

Each of these stages is a small research project in itself, for example 1(a), 1(c) and 1(d). A researcher must decide whether to carry out such projects anew or whether to accept interpretations or measures developed by previous workers. In either case the decisions must be justified by argument. Other subsidiary questions may be considered such as: 2, how has the effectiveness of the policy been influenced by its administration? or, 3, have there been important side-effects of the policy? or, 4, is the public aware of the effects of the policy? These might in themselves be suitable topics for separate dissertations. It can be seen how a question which can be simply stated can result in a complex research project. Some of the ancillary questions are related only indirectly to the main questions, but those relationships must be there and be made explicit if the research and its account is to be coherent. It is quite usual to find that the original question is far too broad to be investigated with the required rigour and depth; it is then necessary to *narrow the research question*, or to select a new, narrower, question altogether.

It is unlikely that at the outset these stages 1 to 7 will be conceived so clearly and distinctly as they have been set out here. It is extremely helpful however to have the stages clearly in mind as an ideal towards which the whole work is being progressed. Intellectually it is essential that the stages of results, inferences and discussion are kept separate: if not in different chapters then in distinct paragraphs or sections. Note that stage 5, results, is the only one which does not refer to the research topic or question; once the survey or experiment has been set up the results should not be allowed to become biased by what the researcher hopes to find. It is rather like a horse race where, once the training and betting have taken place, the race itself should be run without fear, favour or influence. When the results are known these can be analysed and discussed.

It is important to distinguish clearly between results and conclusions. Results are the raw information from the survey or experiment; conclusions or inferences are what can reasonably and logically be deduced and inferred and argued from these results (Chapter Three). Discussion can include speculation about reasons or causes which may lie outside the present research, and perhaps about associated ethical or political issues. This section will usually demonstrate the mental process of *conceptualisation* whereby the specific phenomena or events encountered in the research are seen to relate to wider more abstract concepts. But while it is important for a researcher to see his or her own work in the context of wider theory and practice, this should be done critically. The logical errors of drawing general conclusions from particular cases and of forcing results to fit pre-conceived patterns must be borne in mind. The most important criteria of success in a dissertation are the quality of rational argument from results to inference, stage 6 above, and the light this sheds on the original research question. Much of the content of Chapters One to Seven has been devoted to introducing and explaining the nature of such argument. When selecting a research question it is important to be sure that it can be treated rigorously in this way within the limits of available resources.

Levels of dissertation

Since the requirements for a good research proposal depend to some extent on the type and academic level of the proposed dissertation it is necessary to consider these aspects. There are four levels of dissertation, school (A-level), bachelors, masters (either taught or by research) and doctoral. At the lower levels these may overlap in terms of standards. A good A-level study might, in some cases, be equal to a bachelors dissertation (first degree) – and a good bachelors to a taught masters. The standards in each case are distinguishable, rather, by the minimum acceptable, which naturally increases with level. What they all have in common, and what distinguishes them from being just a very long essay, is that they all contain original or empirical material, that is *original information* obtained from primary sources (Chapter Five). The student is not content only to read what others have written; he or she sets out to check this against the real world, if only in a small way, in the empirical tradition of first-hand experience through observation or experiment.

Originality is an important but elusive concept in research. Essentially, something which is original is new in itself, not copied from something else. Doctoral dissertations or theses have traditionally been expected to make a substantial and, in particular, original contribution to knowledge. A distinction has been made in previous chapters between information and knowledge, the latter being seen as a generalizable system of ideas. A kernel of a freshly cracked nut is in one sense original; it has never been seen before (and if promptly eaten will never be seen again). But, even if carefully observed and described, it adds nothing to the concept of what a nut is nor gives any insight into the complex relationships of its existence. This latter sort of knowledge could only be obtained from a sample of nuts which were the outcome of some experiment or the subject of systematic observation. Observation of the single nut might of course trigger intuitively some research question or hypothesis in an informed mind. It is also conceivable that an artist of genius might illustrate the simple nut in such a way as to say something universal, as did Van Gogh with his chair or sunflowers, but this lies outside the scope of science.

Dissertations are evaluated, according to their level, in part by their degree of originality, and dissertation proposals by their potential for originality. What in them is original? An A-level student may carry out an excellent survey of the pattern of employment in local business. As in the case of the nut, the survey is in a sense original; it contains information which is unique in its detail, which may not have been gathered before. It may be relevant to some local issue.

The student will have gained useful experience and insight and displayed intelligence and organization. But a thousand similar studies could be carried out through the country, and probably have been. The sample is likely to be too small to allow, on its own, generalization to a wider system of knowledge of commercial activity, even though some degree of conceptualization may be evident in the discussion.

An A-level or bachelors dissertation is normally only a part of a course of study which is also formally examined by written papers. The dissertation allows a student to display a range of talent and thought outside the more formal feats of memory, rapid organization and expression otherwise required. A similar balance exists in the case of taught masters courses. Distinctions between bachelors and taught masters dissertations are not absolute. Clearly the minimum acceptable standards of writing, expression, methods and rational argument are higher for the masters. The empirical content of either might not be unlike that for A-level work, but a deeper and more realistic understanding of the context of the investigation would be expected. In a purely academic work this context would be provided by the existing writings or literature on the topic; in applied subjects the real-life context could be equally important. More attention to relationships rather than just to information would be expected.

Thus in the case of the employment survey above, the information should be related to an analysis of such things as local policies for the promotion or control of employment, or for environmental conservation. This would require further empirical work with documents and interviews. Where possible, explanations should be sought to questions such as: Why does a certain pattern of employment or development exist (that is, what are the causes)? How has it come about (what are the causal mechanisms)? How successful have been the relevant policies? There is thus a range of questions from the descriptive but useful 'what' and 'when' to the more interesting but difficult to answer 'how' of causal mechanisms and the 'why' of cause, purpose and intent. Depending on the present level of knowledge of a topic the higher level of study will tend to concentrate on how and why, though clearly what and when have first to be answered. Strange as it may seem some studies, in policy analysis for example, do attempt to answer why and how without establishing what exactly has happened.

Doctoral degrees and masters degrees by research, unlike taught masters, are normally based entirely on an evaluation, including live discussion and questioning, of a written thesis. Masters degrees by research differ from other types of dissertation in that this degree can be seen essentially as a preparation for a doctoral study. Most students today aim to pass to the doctoral stage of study without formal completion of the masters (or, at Oxford, B.Litt.) stage. For this reason a masters dissertation by research, even where formally completed, is principally a substantial and exhaustive background study of a topic which should lead to the identification of a research question which would be appropriate for empirical investigation at a subsequent doctoral stage. Originality here lies in the amount and scope of literature brought together on the topic, and in the quality and authority of the conclusions and relationships which may be inferred. Clearly the topic should be one which previously has not been treated in this way. The writer, in effect, becomes the world expert on the literature of the topic with an exhaustive knowledge of the relevant secondary sources. This is not as unlikely as it may sound provided the topic or question is carefully chosen to be original and suitably restricted. A masters dissertation by research is thus essentially stages 1 and 2, above. Some empirical work may be included but the results might be indicative rather than categorical. In practice the masters level work is usually incorporated into, and becomes, stage 2 of a doctoral dissertation.

Higher level and better quality dissertations need to display more understanding of background and context, more explanation and conceptualization, and more rigorous use of research methods. They will contain original material or information; they may, especially in the case of the research masters, contain an original and unique combination of existing information which may suggest new relationships or explanations. Such work, ideally, will define original questions, or at least questions which have not yet been answered. A doctoral dissertation must go further still and produce a categorical answer to an original question. This answer must be based on a range of empirical material which is substantial enough and comprehensive enough for the conclusion to be accepted as a contribution to the system of knowledge. If, say, a masters level dissertation did achieve this it would merit the award of a doctorate, as has occasionally happened.

Many bachelors and taught masters dissertations appear to be based on questions similar to ones which would merit a doctoral level and depth of study. But in the former case there are seldom time and resources to acquire more than an adequate background knowledge or to carry out sufficient field-work to produce answers which might have a general application. For example, in the 1980s a number of local authorities adopted a policy for building conservation which involved a concentration of care on those historic buildings which had been identified by a number of criteria as being most at risk. These buildings were recorded on so-called 'buildings at risk' registers. Like many other policies and management systems, the register appeared at a first consideration to be a 'good thing', and it satisfied a need for something to be seen to be done. Here was a new practice, with potentially important effects on the national heritage. Was it effective? Would more buildings be saved than without the policy? No one knew for certain. A bachelor or masters level dissertation which attempted to investigate this topic might be based on case-studies of a few buildings in one local authority area. This would be interesting and provide useful insights and experience. But too many unknown variables are involved for such a small sample to provide conclusive results of general value. A doctoral study however could systematically cover perhaps thirty local authorities, with several building case-studies in each, and also develop a more thorough understanding of the processes and relationships involved. Conclusions from such a study could be both original and significant, and might well influence future practice. The amounts of work, ability and time involved in designing and carrying out a study of this sort satisfactorily are much more substantial than might appear from this brief outline.

The main points to note, in conclusion, are the distinctions between simply, on the one hand, original material and, on the other, the original ideas and knowledge, based on sufficient information and systematic investigation, which are required in a doctoral dissertation.

The research question

It is helpful to make a distinction between research areas, research topics and research questions as representing progressive refinements of the aims of research. A student in the field of rural geography, for example, might wish to do work in the area of rural recreation; this means, not a physical area, but the area of ideas which relate to the subject. He or she might choose the particular topic of recreation in forests, or even more specifically in either state or private forests. Many students have difficulty in defining their research more precisely than this. There are two reasons. First, students are often afraid that they will not have enough to write about if their topic is too narrow. This is hardly ever the case; rather, too broad a topic will not allow a student to display any depth of thought and will result in a superficial and apparently unoriginal dissertation. It will be found that to attempt to answer categorically even the smallest research question involves considerable work; in the end the experience of most students is that they have difficulty in restricting the length of their dissertation to required limits.

A second reason for difficulty in defining a specific research question is that many students start research with only a superficial knowledge of their chosen topic area and of available research methods. A good deal of background reading is necessary before gaps in existing knowledge can be identified and questions formulated. For dissertations associated with taught courses this period for reading is quite short. It is advantageous to start thinking about dissertation topics as early as possible. Ideas can sometimes be generated inductively by a type of personal brainstorming, noting down freely all sorts of concepts and relationships which might be investigated in the topic area. The act of then writing out these ideas, in correct grammatical form, will help to expose any which are nonsense; resource constraints will eliminate many more. For research degrees the masters stage is the period in which this necessary development of knowledge, maturation and definition should take place but there is now increasing pressure formally to define the research at an early stage. The advice of an experienced tutor is invaluable during this period, though ideally the final choice of topic should be left to the student if he or she is to feel motivated by the research.

Suppose then that a student proceeds on the basis of a topic area only. In the example given above an interesting account of forest recreation may result, possibly illustrated with some descriptive case studies. But the reader, and especially an examiner, will wish to ask questions. Why did this happen, would it have been better if . . ., how can this be controlled, is the Forest Authority the best provider of this form of recreation, are grants effective for their purpose, what does the public want, does recreation interfere with economic production, with wildlife, and so on. If the student is lucky there

will be an opportunity to answer such questions in a spoken examination, if indeed he or she can answer them. Or there may not. It is
far better if a student displays the awareness to identify these questions in the dissertation itself. If there are too many questions, then
the scope of the study might need to be restricted as work proceeds;
as has been seen, subsidiary questions will in any case arise. This
process of defining and then attempting to answer questions will
require a student to think about the concepts involved, to identify
issues and questions, to test relationships, to face the problems of
measurement and argument, to face the problem of knowledge
itself. This is far advanced from mere description and story-telling.
It is unlikely in any event that a student dissertation could contain a
definitive and exhaustive account of forest recreation. What is
expected is that a student can identify within a topic area a particular issue or question and investigate this empirically in a local case.
The research, it is to be hoped, will be conclusive, though probably
for that restricted example only. More work, perhaps at doctoral
level, would be needed for generalizations to be made. But, *by starting with a question*, the student will have demonstrated a potential to
think critically and deeply and to gain original knowledge.

Hypotheses

Research questions are often reformulated as hypotheses; at the
more advanced and critical levels of research this should be regarded as a requirement. It is sometimes a little too easy, in response to
a question, to say, 'yes', or even, 'I would like to think the answer is
yes', and selectively to produce evidence in support. Barzun and
Graff's aphorism should be borne in mind: an objective judgement
is one produced by *testing in all possible ways* one's subjective impression (Barzun and Graff, 1985, pp. 164–8). The procedures and
arguments related to hypothesis formulation and testing have been
described above (see Chapters Three and Seven). They need not be
repeated except to say again that a hypothesis provisionally states a
relationship between two concepts in such a way that the various
consequences of the statement being true can be tested.

Two examples will illustrate how questions can become hypotheses. Although the examples are, naturally, specific, they clearly have
analogies in many aspects of life. A student might put forward as a
proposal the rather journalistic question, 'Is a design-guide for farm

buildings needed in the XYZ National Park?' This question could be debated at length in political, social and cultural terms. It is ultimately not a scientifically researchable question, being of a normative nature. However, research can usefully inform the debate. For example, the question can be rephrased as, 'Would a design-guide improve the design of farm buildings in XYZ National Park?' (since presumably that is why one might be needed), and then as a hypothetical statement: 'A design-guide would increase the quality of design of farm buildings in XYZ National Park'. Here are two concepts, a design-guide and the visual or aesthetic quality of a type of building. Design-guides, as their name suggests, are documents in which a local authority sets out guidance or requirements for developers, in this case farmers, to follow when designing new buildings. The hypothetical relationship, one of effect or influence on quality, needs to be tested. If the hypothesis were true then use of a design-guide would improve the quality of design. Does it?

Since, by implication, a design-guide for the area does not exist, it has to be made. This involves acquaintance with the principles of other design-guides and experience of examples. It also requires knowledge of the XYZ National Park environment and of the vernacular architecture since design-guides are usually specific to local character. The potential effects can be tested by evaluating recent buildings to test whether, if the design- guide had been followed, they would have been designed differently, and if so whether this alternative would have been aesthetically more acceptable. This assessment may be carried out by the researcher, using accepted design criteria, or by experts or by the public, as outlined above (Chapter Five). If the design-guide is found to be effective this does not quite answer the original question; rather it says that *if* improved design is desirable then the design-guide is a way to achieve this. Whether better design is desirable or necessary is another question which can be answered in a number of ways. There are of course several other aspects of the original question which could be investigated;, these include cost, value for money, equity, political and public attitudes, bureaucratic objectives, and so on. It is only by breaking the original question down in this way that it can be properly answered. Whether in real life the issue would merit this amount of research is another question in itself.

A second more straightforward example concerns the relationship between social deprivation and village life. There exists a considerable literature on the social and economic problems – for certain groups – of living in modern villages with poor transport and services and often low wages. There is undoubtedly some justification for this view of village life. There exists also a number of groups in whose interest it is to exaggerate these problems. In part the picture may have been produced by over-simple attitude surveys (Chapter Five). Residents are asked what facilities they would like in their village. Of course everyone would like things which he or she does not have. Since many of the facilities mentioned are not present it is possible to make statements such as, 80 per cent of villagers want X. The assumption is that therefore residents must be dissatisfied with their social and economic conditions. From this sort of background reading various hypotheses can be formed and their consequences tested by surveys of village residents' conditions and attitudes. The more thoughtful surveys will not be based on deterministic assumptions about attitudes such as dissatisfaction but will attempt to measure things such as perceived levels of satisfaction, the nature of the trade-offs villagers make in terms of environmental quality and ability to choose, and the ways in which apparent problems such as access to services are overcome. A detailed survey of one village would provide an adequate empirical content for a bachelors or taught masters dissertation and would indicate that the student was capable of questioning and then testing by experience the conventional wisdom as expressed in the literature. A much larger sample would be necessary for a research degree.

The process of background reading for a research project is likely to expose many unsupported statements or assumptions and to raise various questions in a reader's mind, all of which provide material for questions and hypotheses for empirical research. The extent to which a student recognizes and deals logically with these questions is a good measure of a critical and questioning quality of mind.

Background reading

It can be seen that background reading, leading to a sound knowledge of the research area, is an essential stage in the final selection of a research question or hypothesis. The exact situation, however, varies widely. In the natural sciences a doctoral student may be expected to start more or less immediately on empirical work or on a question which has already been defined by, and forms part of, a wider programme of research by the supervisor. In the humanities on the other hand a research student might initially submit only a couple of well-written pages outlining the area of research. It is expected that a research question will emerge following a prolonged period of substantial reading when a formal research proposal can be made. This produces a more scholarly approach but, as indicated above, can lead to delayed submission. In other cases a student may be contracted to carry out research in a particular area but the precise question is left open at first. Students on taught courses are normally expected to choose their own topic for dissertation, based largely on what they have learned so far; time for deep reading is limited.

As early as possible during background reading it is important to discover whether the proposed research has been done before. In taught courses it may be sufficient to check whether a student in the same institution has dealt with the topic recently. Even so replication or, if the work was poorly done, repetition may be acceptable. In the case of doctoral work the research must be internationally original. To this end, reference books listing past and current research, including research dissertations, are available (see recommended reading on p.207).

There is a somewhat perplexing chicken-and-egg situation about this process. A research question cannot be finally chosen without an acquaintance with the background of relevant knowledge, yet some idea of the research question is needed to direct the reading and keep it within reasonable bounds. Sometimes a student will have a particular question or case-study in mind at the outset. Reading is then necessary to check what is already known or what concepts and issues might be related to the case-study so that it does not become a mere account. In other cases a student may read widely with no clear concept emerging and perhaps feel frustrated at an apparent lack of progress; this is a quite normal stage and does no harm so long as it does not become prolonged. As possible research questions begin to take shape, relevant items encountered during reading or even in the daily news, or in conversation, will suddenly appear interesting and important. The research project is then beginning to acquire its own momentum. These items must be followed back to their sources. Later in the research, too, need will arise for specific information, such as how certain qualities might be measured. This must be sought out. Advice at this stage is also useful.

Use of libraries

Since, in the academic world, nearly everything that is written has references to other literature appended to it, the number of items available to read grows rapidly. Some system is needed both to find and to record this information. The use of reference libraries is an art and a science which researchers need to acquire in the same way as skills are needed in other activities. Each library has its own idiosyncrasies and there are usually leaflets available in which these are explained and which merit careful study. Librarians are almost invariably helpful and professional people but they are increasingly busy. There is much more to research than looking at the books on an appropriate section of the library shelves. Library catalogues must also be searched, under subject and author headings. Various organizations, such as government departments, publish reference volumes which systematically list their publications. Bibliographies on selected topics are produced by libraries and other organizations. National catalogues are available on computer disk or on microfilm. Particularly useful are the various abstract publications in which are regularly published, under selected topic headings, short summaries or abstracts of articles in journals and papers. If a required book or journal is not on the shelves it may be on loan, being rebound, or being borrowed; items can usually be reserved. There will be a list available of journals held by other libraries; these can be consulted there (an appointment may be necessary for small semi-private libraries) or alternatively photocopies of papers may be obtained on the inter-library loan service for a small fee. Books and other dissertations may be borrowed from other libraries by the same service. If the full details of a book are not known it may often be found under either author or title alone in catalogues of books in print: if out of print it may be found in earlier volumes.

Recording information

Having acquired an item, how should it be read and recorded? First, it is very important that full reference details (see Chapter

Nine) of the book or journal (or broadcast programme) are record-ed at the time it is consulted. This practice will save much otherwise unnecessary effort at a later stage when these details have to be included in the dissertation. Clearly, some record of the contents is necessary also. There is in fact no set way of making this and it can be annoying to try to use someone else's system which has been put forward as the correct method. The only requirements are that a researcher feels comfortable with his or her system, that informa-tion is recorded accurately, and that it is retrievable by the researcher him- or herself for use in later stages of the research. The procedure does not have to be as complex as that of a public library since retrievability will rely to a great extent on the researcher's knowledge of the material. It is useful to record the bibliographical details of references, as in the library catalogue, on small index cards since these can be arranged in alphabetical order by author and added to or discarded as necessary.

Many students attempt to make detailed summaries or précis of other writings; this is laborious, slow, boring and nearly always unnecessary. In the rare event that this level of recording is neces-sary, or for tables or diagrams, modern researchers are fortunate in having the use of photocopiers. Usually a paragraph, page, paper, chapter or even a whole book will make one main point (or at most a few), supported perhaps by a few items of evidence. If it does not do this it is probably not worth reading, for research purposes anyway. A reader should be able to discern and record these points and, preferably, to summarize the reading in his or her own words; the short abstracts in the better abstract journals are good examples of this where lengthy papers are reduced to short synoptic para-graphs. To rephrase ideas in one's own words indicates and requires greater understanding than mere copying; of course the meaning must not be distorted and occasionally a verbatim quotation may be desirable.

It is not always necessary, and may be disheartening, to attempt to read all papers, books and reports exhaustively. Sometimes, for example, all that is required is to know what author A says about subject B. There may be no need to read the whole of A's book to do this. Or a writer's main argument may be summed up in his or her introduction or conclusion, or in a short passage. A book may be read through, or even skimmed, quite rapidly, not for the pur-pose of taking notes, but to gain acquaintance with what is there for future reference; sometimes, or in parts, knowledge of chapter headings may be sufficient. It is indeed often more efficient to take notes at a second reading of a passage once a general understanding has been acquired. The ability to assess a book and its contents quite quickly is essential if a large amount of reading is to be accomplished. Clearly, though, some portions and some books, particularly those which are technical or authoritative, or provide an overview of a topic or are central to the study, will need to be read and studied in detail if deep knowledge is to be achieved. It is up to the reader to be satisfied, in any particular case where use is to be made of information from another source, that the information has been understood and evaluated and can be supported by argument if questioned.

Valuable points should be noted with page numbers; slips of paper as bookmarks are useful reminders. It is very inconsiderate to mark physically the books of others or from libraries; it is a matter of choice and taste whether to mark one's own. Excessive underlining is usually a lazy substitute for proper reading and understanding. Light marginal marks of a few main points can be useful for future reference.

Some workers like to record points on cards. Again, the importance of proper referencing (Chapter Nine) should be remembered. Ideally one idea only should be on a card; the cards can then be read and re-ordered and used as notes for writing up. Others find this far too mechanical, preferring to record ideas and summaries on paper; these, together with any photocopies, can be filed, annotated, indexed, queried, points highlighted in colour, and numbered. The ultimate aim in either case is for the information to become part of the researcher's own knowledge and understanding. Then an account can be written up on any particular point of the topic area, using the researcher's own words and drawing on the references for support and illustration as necessary.

The research proposal

From what has been said so far the main elements of a research proposal should now be clear. These are: a *title*; the *aim* of the research; a *research question* (or more formally a *hypothesis*); evidence of *background reading* which should include a *justification* of the research; some idea of the *possible outcome*; and an *outline of methods*.

If an outline of the dissertation is required, that shown at the beginning of this chapter provides a useful model.

The actual form of the proposal varies between institutions and with the level of the dissertation which is proposed. In some cases a detailed form has to be completed: in others a student is required to provide in effect a short essay. In either case particular care should be given to succinctness, that is brevity and relevance, and to clarity and accuracy. The preparation of a proposal is not some arbitrary task imposed by authority; it is in a student's interest to be as clear as possible about what he or she is going to do. A proposal should be the result of careful thought, and several drafts should be prepared and discussed before the final product is submitted. Admittedly, dissertation proposals for taught courses are often prepared in the midst of pressures from other work, but the sooner some idea is formed, around which other ideas can crystallize and grow, the better. It is rarely possible to sit down the night before the proposal is due and to think up a sound idea in a few hours. Research masters and doctoral students have several months in which to prepare proposals, but given the depth of reading and originality required, and any new techniques which may need to be studied, this is seldom too long.

For dissertations on taught courses the exact *title* is not of great importance and a final title may not be decided until the dissertation has been written. A change of topic may even be allowed, subject to concern only about its suitability and the student's capacity to cope with the change. But the quality of the title is very important; it provides the first, perhaps the only, impression of the quality and nature of the dissertation. A title should not be a question; it should not be excessively lengthy; it should not be grammatically incorrect; it should not be some attention-grabbing but uninformative journalism. Unfortunately all these characteristics do occur. Essentially the title should be informative, giving a clear idea to a potential reader of the subject of the research covered, and in good style.

In the case of research masters and doctoral dissertations, the exact title is itself important; it forms the basis of a sort of contract between the student and the validatory body. In some institutions, once approved, it can be changed only by agreement, and at a late stage sometimes not at all. It is common, though not essential, for the form of the title to express the conventional research process whereby general ideas are tested by particular cases. Thus, *Problems of inner-city housing: a case-study of the Isle of Dogs,* usefully indicates the general area of interest, inner-city housing, and suggests that the case-study will contribute in some way to this area of knowledge, that common concepts will be used in the work and that the study contains a review of inner-city housing issues generally. The title is doubly informative to other researchers. The relevance of *A study of housing in the Isle of Dogs* is less clear. A title such as *The role of the Forest Authority in rural recreation, with particular reference to the New Forest* has an almost syllogistic form, progressing from the general to the particular. *A study of the New Forest with reference to the role of the Forest Authority* suggests a work of less systematic interest and has a vaguely illogical form.

Frequently the *research question* is stated in the *aim of the research*; the aim is to answer the question, to discover what, who, how, why, to compare, or to test a *hypothesis. It should be possible to state the aim of a research project in a single sentence,* or at most two. If not, then the project has not been thought out sufficiently. An aim should never be expressed as an intention to prove something; this suggests a mind already made up and an intention to use evidence partially.

For a proposal, the *background to the research* need only be brief. It should be a reasoned account of the context in which is argued the *justification* for the research, supported by a few appropriate and authoritative references. It should not be a lengthy summary of everything the student has read to date. In a purely academic discipline the need for the research will be related to the state of knowledge in that discipline; in an applied vocational subject the possible value of the outcome to the theory or practice, or both, of the profession should be argued also. For example, research into aspects of recreation provision by the Forest Authority could be justified simply as follows:

The Forest Authority owns extensive areas of land on which it has for some years provided professional recreation services. The role of the Authority is changing and land is being sold off to private owners. At the same time informal rural recreation is a major and possibly growing activity among the public. It is not known what general recreation provision will be made on the newly acquired private land; there is some indication that access is being restricted. It is necessary therefore to evaluate and compare current levels of informal recreation in public and private forests in the light of demand, to attempt to forecast future trends, and to consider what measures may be necessary and desirable, nationally and locally, to ensure the future of such provision. No study has been made of this to date.

Clearly some considerable reading will be necessary before this last statement can be made with confidence. It would be sufficient to support each statement in this argument by one or two authoritative and up-to-date references. The whole thing need occupy only about half a page. It is the clarity and soundness of the argument and the conclusion, not the detail, which are important at this stage.

There are two exceptions to this last statement. In the first case, an initial proposal for masters work which is intended to progress to a doctoral stage would need to be argued a little further. The proposal would be expected to show a *potential for doctoral work*, that is the possibility of leading to a question or hypothesis of sufficient importance, scope and originality to justify its study at doctoral level. Even though this does not commit a student to investigate the particular question on reaching the doctoral stage, it is nonetheless a difficult thing for an inexperienced research student to foresee when only two or three months into his or her studies. In the example given, above, the doctoral work might be a substantial comparative study, related to an appropriate hypothesis, of a representative number of forest areas which had been recently privatized. The masters work might include a pilot study to this end. Any or all of a number of aspects could be put forward for possible investigation, such as type of recreation offered, charging, type of client, effect on various aspects of the environment, and so on. In the second case, a fresh appreciation of the research is usually necessary when a student applies to transfer from the probationary masters (or B.Litt.) stage to the doctoral level. This application normally has to be supported by a substantial background report, or literature review, of several thousand words, though it may be sufficient for the supervisor to confirm that this, the masters stage, has effectively been completed.

There are only a few general *methods of research* (as distinct from techniques, which are numerous), all of which have been discussed in previous chapters. These are: the literature review; analysis of primary source documents; analysis of semi-primary documents, such as policy statements, which may have a limited circulation; the social survey; physical and visual surveys; field or community observation; structured interviews; and experiment. The case-study is a complex research activity which may combine a number of general methods, though if case-studies are proposed they would be listed in the methods section. Study of documents, whether primary or secondary, is often referred to as the desk-study stage; empirical survey work is known as field-study. While the actual planning of say, a social survey, may be complex (Chapters Five and Six), there is no need to go into detail at the proposal stage, except possibly at the transfer to doctoral level. The balance of methods used in research for a dissertation may vary from consisting largely of a literature review to being mainly experimental supported by a small, but sound, background argument. A literature review would have to be exhaustive for it to be considered more than a long essay, and some empirical content is nearly always desirable.

Conclusions

Preparation of a good research proposal demands considerable intelligence, thought and imagination, especially from a student doing this for the first time. Consultation with a supervisor or with someone more experienced is essential. While the principles have been outlined here, different disciplines and institutions will have their own emphasis and these should be taken into account. Preparation of a proposal is also good practice for later life when such proposals have to compete with others for funding in the academic world or in consultancy.

CHECKLIST: Chapter 8

You should know and understand:

- the nature of and distinction between the various components of a research dissertation
- the need for sub-questions and operational questions in a research project
- the need to choose a relatively narrow and manageable research question;

- the requirements for various levels of dissertation
- the requirement for an original contribution to knowledge in higher research degrees
- the difference between original information and original knowledge
- the difference between the questions what, when, how and why;

- the distinctions between research field, research area, research topic, research question and research hypothesis
- the need for background reading when defining a research question
- how to begin a literature search and how to record the information obtained
- how research questions can be reformulated into hypotheses which can be tested
- the difference between a hypothesis and a theory in the strict sense

- how to prepare a research proposal and its main components
- how to design an informative title for your research
- what is meant by 'potential for doctoral work'

Further reading

Bulmer, M. (ed.), 1984 [1977], *Sociological research methods: an introduction*, 2nd edn, Macmillan, Basingstoke.

Dixon, B.R., et al., 1987, *A handbook of social science research: a comprehensive and practical guide for students*, Oxford University Press, Oxford.

Dominowski, R.L., 1980, *Research methods*, Prentice-Hall, Englewood Cliffs.

Gash, S., 1989, *Effective literature searching for students*, Gower, Aldershot.

Howard, K., and Sharp, R.A., 1983, *The management of a student research project*, Gower, Aldershot.

Leedy, P.D., 1980, *Practical research: planning and design*, 2nd edn, Macmillan, New York, pp. 41–180.

Locke, L.F., 1987, *Proposals that work: a guide for planning dissertations and grant proposals*, 2nd edn, Sage, Newbury Park.

Phipps, R., 1983, *The successful student's handbook: a step by step guide to study, reading and thinking skills*, University of Washington Press, Seattle.

Reference works and journals

(This is only a small selection of the many available reference works.)

American book publishing record cumulative 1876–1949, 1950–1977, 1980–1984, R.R. Bowker, New York (published annually).

Books in print, 1948– , R.R. Bowker, New York (published annually; formerly *Publisher's trade list annual*).

British books in print, 1874– , J. Whitaker and Sons, London (published annually; formerly *The reference catalogue of current literature*.

British humanities index, 1962– , Bowker-Sauer, London (published quarterly; formerly *The subject index of periodicals*, 1915–1961).

Current research in Britain, 1985– , Longman, Harlow (published annually; formerly *Research in British universities and polytechnics and colleges*, 4 sections including humanities and social sciences).

Dissertation abstracts international: A; the humanities and social sciences, University Microfilms International, Godstone.

Index to theses with abstracts accepted for higher degrees in the Universities of Great Britain and Ireland and the Council for National Academic Awards, ASLIB and Expert Systems, London (published quarterly).

Woodrow, M. (ed.), 1975, Clover Information Index, Clover Publications, Bigglesworth (published quarterly).

Woodrow, M. (ed.), 1985, Clover Newspaper Index, Clover Publications, Bigglesworth (published weekly).

9
THE RESEARCH DISSERTATION

'In September 1939 the Prime Minister, Neville Chamberlain, announced the declaration of the Second World War in a café in Charing Cross Road. I have that curious piece of information on the authority of the late Kenneth Clark, Lord Clark of Saltwood, who writes: "I heard Mr Chamberlain's tired old voice announcing the declaration of war in a café in Charing Cross Road". But perhaps I misunderstood, and Lord Clark meant the Prime Minister was announcing the declaration of a war that was shortly to be waged in a café in Charing Cross Road. With the death of Lord Clark perhaps I shall never know for certain, but I have little doubt that a war did in fact take place.'

(Eric Hebborn, *Master Faker*, 1991)

Communication is a subtle thing. The droll teasing, above, by an excellent writer, shows how the casual arrangement of the parts of a sentence can produce at least two meanings other than the one which appears to be intended. The assumption about what is true in this case can of course only be made on previous knowledge of the relative scales of wars and cafés or about where Prime Ministers make important public statements. A similar statement: 'I heard local radio report a riot in the Bluebird Café,' is totally ambiguous. Writing a dissertation, however, involves much more than clear sentences and should communicate more than chronological facts. Not only the structure of the sentences but the structure of the whole dissertation, the sequence of its parts and the ways in which they are shown to be related are important. In addition to presenting facts it is necessary to explain arguments and relationships, and ultimately to communicate the best possible impression of the quality of thought of the author. But linguistic expression is more than just communication; it is an integral part of the nature and process of thinking itself. Without language, it may be argued, what we have is not thought, only feelings. Language is intimately related to meaning: confused thought cannot be expressed in clear language and thought is only clear when it is clearly expressed.

This chapter will outline the process of dissertation writing; the principal aspects covered are: the structure of the dissertation, the conventions of presentation, and common stylistic problems and errors. The account is based on questions which students most commonly ask when seeking guidance on writing their dissertations. It begins with what might loosely be termed psychological problems.

Psychological problems: starting to write

Even a short dissertation is several times longer than any essay or report that a student is likely to have undertaken previously. One common reaction is that the student becomes overwhelmed, not to say mentally paralysed, by the seemingly daunting prospect of writing so many words. This can lead to dangerous delay in starting to write; however, it is this type of student who is likely to end up wanting to write too much and wishing he or she had started earlier. Validating institutions wisely specify maximum rather than minimum lengths for dissertations. At the other extreme is the student who calculates that a small dissertation is only three or four times the length of the essays which he or she has been used to scribbling in a weekend. This is an even more dangerous delusion; not only does it also result in delay, but the student has underestimated the task involved. This attitude is likely to produce an insubstantial dissertation. It should be understood that the complexity of a work develops proportionately much more than the increase in length, and that a dissertation is a more rigorous, complex, exact and original piece of work than is a student essay. In some cases, particularly in the case of higher levels of dissertation where there is no absolute deadline for submission, a student may become obsessed with the idea that just a bit more information is needed, or by a wish to include the absolutely latest publications, and so feel unable to finalize the dissertation. Here a tutor's advice is invaluable. Later developments or publications can always be dealt with if necessary in a spoken examination. Indeed, a student should make a point of keeping up to date with the dissertation topic in the interval between submission and the spoken examination.

All this rationalization of delay is largely a reflection of a reluctance to commit the first step of a journey whose length is unfamiliar and destination unknown. Students should feel encouraged by the fact that it is a task which many have undertaken previously; that if a reasonably capable student works with reasonable application, experience shows that the result will be successful. Lewis Carroll's advice on where to start, 'Start at the beginning and keep going until you get to the end,' is not as facetious as it sounds. In the case of dissertations it could be said: 'start anywhere – but start'. Writing feeds on writing; it helps to make ideas clear, or to show where they are not clear. Some writing shown at an early stage to a tutor will enable him or her to assess a student's strengths, weaknesses, style, grasp of concepts, quality of argument and whether the research appears to be progressing in a promising direction. It is easier to write up, even if roughly, each stage of the work as it occurs, when ideas are fresh. Clearly this must not be allowed to bring to a stop other parts of the overall investigation. The writing will need to be modified in the later stages but the final preparation will then be a less enormous task. When a few sections have been written in this way the whole project will begin to be seen in proportion.

An academic institution may suggest or even require that a student give open seminars or talks on the progress of his or her work. While this may appear tiresome or inconvenient it is in fact a valuable opportunity and motivation to a student to sort out what are often rather vague ideas. It is worth doing well since these seminars often become, with some modification, chapters of the dissertation.

It is particularly helpful to read one or two examples of previous dissertations, not so much for any relevant information which they might contain, but to gain a feel for their length and substance and a concept of what is being attempted. In the same way a high-jumper examines a cross-bar closely and wills him- or herself to get over it. Another way of coming to terms with the apparent enormity of the task is to have a clear idea of the stages and structure of what is proposed (for example, see p.187 above). It would be helpful to read Chapter Eight through again before beginning to write. The prospect of producing an apparently undifferentiated mass of 20,000 or more words may appear forbidding, but a student can happily accept the idea of writing 2,000 words on this or that aspect. These will soon add up.

While each individual has a work pattern and schedule which suits his or her temperament, there are clear advantages in producing at least some writing at an early stage, especially for discussion with a supervisor or others. Writing in stages, rather than all at the end, will boost confidence and allow progress to be monitored, and will reduce the bulk of the task, thus allowing more time for the important stage of reflection and amendment.

Organizing the dissertation

A dissertation's structure is rather like the plan of a building, or the building itself, a static thing. Organization may be thought of as the process of building, the order of doing things and the ways in which the parts are joined together. The final structure is of course a reflection of the organizing process. Organizing the dissertation is distinct also from the organization of the whole research project, that is the allocation of periods of time to reading, designing the empirical stages, making arrangements in good time for field-work, meeting any intermediate deadlines, and allowing adequate time (usually more than might be supposed) for analysis of results and for writing up. But the organization of the dissertation is a reflection of the organization of the research itself and should continually be in mind from the outset.

Writing to length

Each validating institution has its own requirements for dissertations; these requirements should be read carefully at an early stage and consulted periodically. A basic requirement is that for the maximum number of words. This allowance varies but on average is in the order of 12,000 words for a bachelors dissertation, 20,000 for a taught masters, 50,000 for a research masters and 75,000 for a doctoral thesis. As the research progresses, ideas for chapter headings will become clear, and since, depending on the level of work, a chapter should not be less than about 1,500 words, and perhaps not more than 4,000, it will soon become clear how many aspects of the topic can be accommodated. Some aspects might be expanded to two chapters, others be cut to a half or reduced to only a mention as the research becomes more concentrated. In some cases what is cut out may have been merely a lengthy, though interesting, diversion; in others hard choices may need to be made about the direction of the research, preferably before too much time has been expended on an alternative. It is far better to keep a reasonable check on length as work proceeds than to have to cut large amounts of material at a later stage. Although students, indeed most writers, are reluctant to admit it, it is surprising how much pruning is possible to almost any writing; but it is discouraging work and hard to do well.

Organizing the time

Adequate time must be allowed for the final writing. While thousands of words can be written in a day, it is unlikely that a relatively inexperienced writer would produce work to dissertation standard at this rate. Even experienced writers mostly reckon to do at most 800–1,000 words per day; this is properly written finished material which has been re-written perhaps several times and checked. Admittedly it does not sound much, just a few pages. Probably twice as much time is required in addition for the checking of calculations, production of figures, tidying up reference lists and so on. When planning the final writing, arrangements must be made in advance for typing, and for the re-typing of corrections; a realistic time should be calculated for this, and also for binding if required. Many otherwise good dissertations are marred by an appearance of having been rushed in the final stages, not just in physical presentation but, more importantly, in style and organization.

Continuing for the moment with the analogy of the dissertation as a building, what has been done so far is to select the number, size and functions of the rooms, or chapters, to be appropriate to the function of the whole structure. The next requirement is to ensure that the rooms relate to each other in a rational manner, that the transition from one to another is reasonably smooth, that there are no long passages which lead nowhere, no doors inviting the reader to step into blank space, that the contents of each are appropriate to its use – not a bath in the living room, or the kitchen sink in a bedroom – and that there are windows which allow the orientation of the whole to the outside world to be perceived.

Setting the scene

The *introduction* is usually the first substantial section of a finished dissertation, but it is not the beginning; an introduction is rather like a guide to the finished structure and for this reason is commonly the last part to be written. The aim of the research and the research question should be stated quite early on, possibly in the first sentence, followed by a brief justification along the lines of the example on p.203. An introduction is not the same thing as the background to the research, though clearly the justification will make brief reference to the subject matter of the background. The detailed account of the background reading will be a substantial section in its own right, normally consisting of at least one chapter and possibly more. When the dissertation is short, or the background slight in relation to the empirical work, an introduction and the background could be the first and second parts of a first chapter. Alternatively, and more commonly, an introduction is a short initial section in chapter format followed by the proper first chapter comprising the background alone.

A dissertation is not a mystery novel and care should be taken to guide a reader through the argument, or plot, as clearly as possible. It is usual in the introduction to summarize in turn the purpose and content of each chapter briefly. A diagram which shows the relationships of the principal phases of the research and the form of the main argument can be useful to map out the territory and the route before the reader begins. A dissertation is one of the rare occasions where a student has the opportunity to specify his or her own task. However, it is important at the outset that this task be clearly set out for the assessor or examiner. One of the criteria for success is the relationship between a student's ability to define a research question and then to answer it. The findings at the end may be useful and well-supported, but if they do not answer the question which the examiner thought was being taken on at the beginning, if he or she has been abandoned at some stage up a blind alley, then the quality of the guide may not be rated highly. As has been seen in the previous chapter, a dissertation can tackle only a small aspect of a large topic. While it is important that a student displays an awareness of issues in the whole topic area, this must not be allowed to become confused with the usually much narrower research question. This broader awareness is best expressed in the form of discussion and of statements about relationships rather than as questions; generally it is best not to pose questions in the introduction which are not answered in the dissertation. It should be made quite clear both what the dissertation is about and, where any misunderstanding could arise, what it is not. The introduction – the first paragraph even – is thus very important in determining the interest, expectation and initial judgement of an assessor.

Structure

In the account of the background reading, usually called the *literature review*, a student must tread a fine line between displaying a good knowledge of the context and not losing the interest of the assessor to whom of course much of the information should be familiar. This interest will be better maintained if the account does not consist merely of a chronicle of the student's reading but compares, contrasts, questions and hints at relevance to the empirical work to come. The practice of cross-referencing to other parts of the dissertation, below, makes it easier to be brief in communicating these relationships. It is essential that full and proper references are given, as explained below, for any other works discussed or mentioned.

Both the length and the intensity of a dissertation produce a complexity which is more difficult to handle than that of an essay. A dissertation is sometimes likened to a tree in the way that consideration of sub-topics or sub-questions requires a branching away from the main theme. The account is not merely linear in form, one topic does not simply follow another. A writer may have to choose between two or three possible routes at some stage. But in fact the analogy of a tree is not a good one since these diversions must not end blindly but be brought back into the main pattern at some stage so that a synthesis can be achieved at the end. There are two rules for dealing with this complexity: first, keep the reader informed about what is going on and, second, always be clear about which branch is being followed at any time.

Cross-referencing

It may become obvious that a topic has, for example, three main aspects which need to be considered in depth before further progress can be made. When reading an essay a reader may carry these ideas in mind as each one is treated in a separate paragraph. If, however, the first topic is dealt with at the length of a chapter the reader may begin to wonder if the author has forgotten about the other two. A student, aware of this problem, may attempt to keep all these topics going at the same time and so produce a very confused account. The problem can be avoided by the practice of cross-referencing. This uses a simple form of words such as: 'This topic has three main areas which need to be considered. The present chapter will deal with A; B and C will be discussed in Chapters N and M respectively'. It is helpful also to remind a reader of what already has been covered, for example: 'It will be remembered that topic B was discussed in Chapter N; it can now be seen how this relates to C'. Used sparingly, such orientating devices in the text can be helpful both to a reader and in clearing the mind of the writer to concentrate on the topic at hand. It should be remembered that although the writer has an overview of the dissertation and knows what is coming, the reader or assessor does not. As stated above, the dissertation is not a mystery novel, which is not to say that it should not be interesting. But the interest lies in the quality of the argument rather than in confusion.

Numbering paragraphs

A structuring device which allows very precise cross-referencing is the numbered paragraph. The use of numbered paragraphs in dissertations is optional; it can help a writer to keep control of large amounts of material but some writers dislike the rather bureaucratic appearance. A general rule in any writing is that each paragraph should deal only with one topic or aspect of a topic; a new paragraph is started for a new topic or aspect. Related paragraphs may usefully be grouped under sub-headings within chapters. The numbered paragraph system, used for much professional and consultancy work, emphasizes the basic paragraph arrangement by numbering individual paragraphs, or groups of paragraphs, with consecutive decimal numbers. Thus paragraphs one and two in

Chapter One would be numbered 1.01, 1.02, and so on up to 1.99 if required. Minor sub-divisions, such as lists, can be shown as, say, 1.09.1, 1.09.2. There are variations. For example, 1.09.1, could be used to represent Chapter One, sub-section nine, paragraph one. Chapter sections can be similarly numbered 1.1, 1.2, and so on, but higher numbers might be considered ambiguous if there are more than nine sections (e.g. 1.11). The main thing is to decide the details of the system and then to be consistent in its application. Similar systems can conveniently be used for the numbering of figures and tables.

Keeping to the point

A second principle is to keep, more or less strictly, not just to the topic under discussion, but to the particular aspect of the topic. Accounts of procedures, results, inferences and discussion all need to be distinct, not just for reasons of academic rigour and objectivity, but for clarity. It is easy when describing procedure to slip in a related point about results, or when discussing results to jump to conclusions. But these points can easily develop into paragraphs and assume lives of their own which soon disrupt the flow of the main argument. This is not an absolute principle of course and, as above, a little cross linking will be welcome to the reader and maintain interest. But generally it should be no more than a sentence such as: 'Problems with this question will be examined further in the discussion on the results, p.—.' Similarly, the conclusions of the research should not become mixed up with the account of the background to the work. However, an occasional sentence indicating relevance is helpful. Devices such as this help a writer to avoid being bogged down in a mass of undifferentiated material and indicate to an assessor that a student has a commanding overview of his or her material and the relationship of its parts.

A particular case where two or more topics may be better considered together is where they are to be compared. In this case the two topics may already have a parallel structure; for example, where a structured interview has been carried out with two agencies, or a survey at two sites. The comparison will consist of a number of points which relate to the same respective questions. It may be best to give separate accounts of the results from the two agencies or sites respectively and then to discuss any notable points of comparison. Alternatively, results for individual questions could be compared together in parallel. Whichever plan is adopted, it should be followed consistently and the reader at the outset informed where the comparisons are to be expected. If a question is allowed to arise, explicitly or implicitly, in an assessor's mind, which is not answered or for which there is no indication that an answer is forthcoming, this is likely to detract from the assessor's appreciation of what is being said meanwhile. Careful thought should be given to questions which the reading of the dissertation might reasonably arouse, and these questions should be acknowledged and dealt with. This may be by an immediate answer, by the promise of an answer, or by admitting, but not too often, that the questions are outside the scope of the present work.

The importance of conclusions

While the quality of all aspects of a dissertation is important, it is the quality of the concluding discussion which is likely to be the most important single influence on an assessor's mind. The conclusions are where most opportunity for critical and original thought lies. Possibly for this reason, but more usually because of lack of time, the conclusions are often short, in fact weak. Students are often unsure whether to 'save' all their conclusions for the end. The answer is yes and no. As indicated in Chapter Eight, the term conclusions covers in practice several types of argument. There are those which look back to the procedures and results, which may be properly called inferences, and those which look forward to discuss the wider meaning of the work and may consist of speculation, implications and conceptualization. In a short dissertation these aspects may all be included in a single section or chapter of conclusions, though intellectually they should be kept distinct. It is reasonable, however, at the end of each stage of the account (background, method, interviews and surveys), to produce interim conclusions relating to that section only; indeed it would be a weakness not to do so. These interim conclusions may then be brought together, related and compared in a final concluding chapter.

Dissertation format

The components of a dissertation

In addition to general principles of organization of the dissertation, above, which to some extent must be matters of choice and style, the main components of a dissertation and their order have been standardized (see recommended reading on p.230). The format is summarized here; each component will be discussed briefly in turn.

-   title page
- i   Abstract(s) (Some institutions require a long as well as a short abstract)
- ii   Contents
- iii   List of tables
- iv   List of figures
- v   List of plates
- vi   List of appendices
- vii   Preface
- viii   Acknowledgements
- ix   List of abbreviations (and glossary if necessary)
- 1   Introduction
- 2   Chapters, 1, 2, etc. (main text)
- 3   Plates (alternatively, these may usefully be included in the text at appropriate locations)
- 4   Appendices
- 5   References

The *Title page* must show the full approved title of the research, the student's name, the degree for which the dissertation is submitted, the validating institution, and the submission date.

The *Abstract* carries as a heading the same information as the title page. The main part of the abstract is a matter-of-fact summary, usually of about 500 words, of the aim, methods, arguments, results and conclusions of the research. This clearly is a succinct piece of writing. Particular care should be taken over the abstract since it is the first thing an assessor will read, though it is usually the last to be written.

The list of *Contents* itself (item ii) looks just like the format for the list of components (above) except that the title page is not listed in the contents. Individual chapters and their titles are of course shown under item 2, Chapters, in the list of contents itself; titles of tables, etc. are shown separately in their respective lists (items iii to ix) which follow the complete list of contents. Pages are numbered from Abstracts to List of abbreviations in lower-case Roman numerals; Arabic numbers are used thereafter, starting from the introduction, or from Chpater One if there is no separate introduction. The numbers of the actual pages on which the various items begin should be shown, usually in a column to the right.

The *chapter headings*, shown in the contents, should be short but as informative as possible, rather than sensational. Sub-headings and their page numbers may also usefully be shown. A good contents list can give a clear picture of the scope of the study. The same is true of the titles of tables, figures and, where used, plates (that is, photographs). Tables are matrices of numbers, words or other symbols; figures are graphic material other than tables or photographs. In each case items should be numbered consecutively, preferably using the numbered paragraph system, above. Titles should be informative so that relevant information can be quickly found from the lists: not, for example, *Results for 1992*, (what results?), but, *Listed buildings demolished (10 per cent sample) County of Buckinghamshire 1992*; not, *Professionals versus public views*, but, *Comparison of attitudes to new development: general public and professional architects*. Elementary phrases in titles such as *A map (or photograph, or graph) to show . . .*, are quite unnecessary; everyone knows what a map or graph is, and its function.

Tables and *illustrations* should be integrated as much as possible with the text, that is placed near to the relevant passage and referred to in the text itself. It is customary for the title of a table to be placed above the table, and that of a figure at the bottom. The source and date of the item should always be given, whether from the researcher's own survey or from some other publication; the standard reference format, (see p.221, below) is usual. Captions, (short explanations of the figures), are optional but useful (for photographs, see below). If figures are of such a size that they have to be bound and viewed sideways they should always be bound to be viewed from the right of the dissertation volume. Sufficient space, about 30mm, should be allowed along the binding edge so that figures are not partly obscured. Larger figures may be folded *neatly* or placed in a pocket within the back cover but these inconvenient formats should be avoided if possible. Photographs will add interest and impact to any dissertation and in some cases may be essential.

Each photograph should be selected for a purpose and the relevance must be stated in a caption or title; photographs can be interpreted in many different ways and are not always so self-explanatory as other illustrations.

Appendices are used to include information which might need to be referred to but whose inclusion in the main text would disrupt the flow. (Footnotes serve the same function in a minor way but should be used very sparingly). Questionnaires, raw results, statistics, short documents or long notes may all find their place in appendices, though once a decision has been taken to relegate material from the main text in this way further thought may discard it altogether. Strictly, appendices do count towards the total word limit though this requirement is often waived. It is wise to check the relevant regulations here.

A *Preface* is optional. It is a personal introduction where the writer may speak subjectively about his or her own interest in the topic. For this reason a preface may be quite revealing; to know the point of view from which a book has been written is always valuable and sometimes cautionary. A student may have become interested in a case-study while on a visit to Granny – but this is not part of the justification above; the point could be stated in the preface if so wished. Since acknowledgements are personal thanks these are often subsumed into a preface. Acknowledgements cost little and are appreciated by those, often busy people, who have helped, but care should be taken that sources of confidential or critical information are not exposed in this way.

In a work of any length an alphabetical reference *List of abbreviations* should be provided at the beginning. Frequent abbreviations make for tiresome reading and sometimes seem to be used to save the writer's hand and paper, or to make a certain sort of impression, rather than for the benefit of the reader. Nevertheless abbreviations are necessary. The first time, only, that an abbreviation is used it should be enclosed in brackets and preceded by the full term. A *Glossary* may be desirable to explain the meanings of any unfamiliar terms.

Use of references

The nature of the introduction and of the main text has been dealt with in a previous section so the next item to be considered here is the *References*. Since, in academic circles, networks of knowledge are considered particularly valuable, evidence of deep and wide reading relevant to the research topic will enhance the value of a dissertation. Substantial reading is shown principally by the content of the writing itself but, for a student both to obtain full credit for this reading and to satisfy more general academic requirements, the work needs to be fully and properly referenced. The academic requirements for a dissertation are that every important statement, assertion, fact or argument should be accompanied or supported by evidence (Chapters Three and Four), especially if the statement is contentious. Clearly this does not apply to very well known or self-evident facts. In some cases the evidence will come from the student's own empirical work or from his or her own argument; if so this should be made clear (for example, by reference to survey work) and will particularly enhance the value of the dissertation. But much of the information, especially in the early stages of the work, will in effect be second-hand. Even the great Sir Isaac Newton acknowledged this, so students' fears of 'copying' are groundless. Copying, or plagiarism, occurs when ideas are *not* acknowledged by reference, particularly when passages are taken word for word from others' work and put forward as a writer's own. This is a culpable misdemeanour in a dissertation and will result in failure. Writers of serious books, however, often choose to omit formal referencing (and acknowledge this in the preface) because references can interrupt the flow of reading and may appear pedantic. But for a dissertation the more references which are included, within reason, the better. There is no rule about this, but depending on the topic, a bachelors dissertation might have thirty references and a doctoral three hundred.

References thus have two academic functions. First, they are a form of argument. The writer may be saying in effect, 'I have read the work of X, I accept his arguments and use the conclusions as part of my own argument'. Or the simple argument from authority may be implied (Chapter Five). Second, the reader can check for him- or herself the original work referred to on a point of fact or argument. Often, however, the writer refers to other work not because it is accepted but because it is questionable; or several points of view may be compared. But always the reader is able to check. Frequently, of course, a reader, and particularly the assessor of a dissertation, will already be acquainted with the referenced work.

Proper use of references adds considerably to the authority of the writing. Compare, for example:

'Modern farming techniques have done much damage to our National Parks and many people think it is a big problem'.

with:

'Surveys had shown that 20 per cent of heather moorland on Exmoor had been ploughed up in ten years (MacEwen and MacEwen, 1981, p. 175). Public opposition was so great that the government appointed a special inquiry headed by Lord Porchester (1977).'

The second example is a much more authoritative and informative piece of writing which indicates a better acquaintance with the topic and a more rigorous mind. A reader is informed about the sources and authority of the statements made, of when and by what sort of people concern was shown, and the references enable details to be checked and expanded.

There are two main ways of giving references. The first is the traditional one of *historical writing* whereby superscripts in the form of numbers, like this[3], are placed at the end of the referenced information. Full details of references are then provided at the end of the chapter, or grouped by chapter at the end of the book, against the relevant numbers (for use of the abbreviation *op. cit.* in this system, see below). The system has the advantages that it does not much interrupt the text and can also be used for other short comment in the form of notes, replacing footnotes, but it is rather cryptic.

The second method, known as the *Harvard system* or the *Author–Date system*, is on the whole to be preferred and is now more common in academic work, at least in the physical and social sciences. It shows, in brackets, the author and the year of publication thus: (Smith, 1971). This system has the advantages of showing at a glance the authority used, who may well be recognized, and how recent or contemporary the information might be. Another advantage is that, since the references are identified by name and not by number, the authors' names are conveniently arranged in alphabetical order at the end of the work. In the main text, initial letters are not normally necessary except where two or more authors have the same name, in which case they should be identified by initials. If two or more works of one author are cited from the same year these are distinguished by letters, for example: (M. Smith, 1972a). Two joint authors normally have both names shown: (Smith and Brown, 1973); for more than two the Latin abbreviation of *et alii* (and other people) is used (Smith *et al.*, 1973). If a work is referenced twice in close succession the abbreviation for *opere citato* (in the work cited) may be substituted (*op. cit.*, 1973) or, alternatively, if another reference has intervened (Smith, *op. cit.*). (This last form is also used in the lists of references and notes for the historical method of referencing, above.)

Author and date are normally all the information that need be given in the main text when a work is referred to for its general influence or subject matter. Occasionally a title may be used for stylistic purposes, but is not strictly necessary: 'In his influential work, *The Origin of Species*, Darwin argued . . .'. But a proper reference must also be shown at the end of the passage: (Darwin, 1859). However, if use is made of a particular point then the reader should be directed to the page, pages or, in the case of documents or statutes, a section number. A reader will not want to read the whole reference just to find one point. The abbreviations used are: page (p.), pages (pp.), section or sections (s., ss.). If a number of references to different parts of the same work are made then these details will need to be given in each case in the main text, for example (Smith, 1973a, pp. 117–30); otherwise, if just one reference is made, such details need be shown only in the cumulative list of references at the end of the dissertation.

It is the full reference, included in the final alphabetical list, which enables a reader to trace the original work. If this primary purpose is borne in mind, as well as any secondary ones such as making a good impression on an assessor, the format required for a reference will make sense. Experience of attempting to locate references which are incorrect or incomplete will soon make this point. What needs to be known is: who wrote the item (author's correct name and initials); when the item was published (year); where can the item be read (the title of the publication which contains the item); where was it published (place and name of publisher), and any other helpful details such as volume number, edition number, series title or page numbers, above. A typical reference looks like this:

Hebborn, E., 1991, *Master Faker: The Forging of an Artist*, London, Pan Books.

This information will enable the book to be located in a library or ordered from a publisher. A common error is to confuse the name of the contributor to a book of collected writings with that of the editor. This should be distinguished by the following format (the 'in' is optional):

Keynes, J.M., 1938, 'Art and the State', in Williams-Ellis, C., (ed.), 1938 *Britain and the Beast*, London, J.M. Dent and Sons, for the Readers' Union, pp. 1–7.

Articles or papers in journals are also referenced in this format; the title of the paper is put in inverted commas, the name of the journal is underlined. In both cases the name underlined is the published work, the complete book, report, journal or newspaper, which is being sought. The volume and number of the journal would also be given, and the relevant page numbers. Where two or more works of the same author are shown in the alphabetical list a long dash is often used in place of the author's name for second and subsequent entries. It is sometimes difficult, especially with official reports, to decide who, strictly, are the authors and publishers; here the practice of a good library catalogue may be followed, or advice sought from a librarian. It is, for example, a common mistake to show Her Majesty's Stationary Office (HMSO) as author of government publications of which it is in fact the publisher.

It is often of great interest and importance in an argument to know when and where an idea or a text was first published. On the other hand, a reader may wish to know if a more recent, revised or current edition of the work is available. One way of achieving this is to reference the original date, e.g. (Partridge, 1947) in the text, but to add information about a later edition in the list of references:

Partridge, E., 1947, *Usage and abusage: a guide to good English*, London, Hamish Hamilton; revised edn, 1973, Penguin, Harmondsworth, pp.10-14.

Note also that when any details such as page numbers are given it is important that the relevant edition is referred to, in this case the 1973 Penguin edition. An alternative format is to give the original and, where relevant, later dates both in the text thus, Partridge 1973 [1947]. The full reference then becomes:

Partridge, E., 1973 [1947] *Usage and abusage: a guide to good English*, revised edn, Penguin, Harmondsworth, pp.10-14.

References should never be attributed second-hand (that is based solely on a second author's interpretation) without this being made quite clear. If at all possible the original author's work should be consulted (or even the author); often the interpretation will then seem rather different.

References are what their name implies, works referred to *in the main text*. A *bibliography* is a list of relevant books which may not be referred to specifically but which have been used for general background reading. If the relationship between a bibliography and its text appears too remote an assessor may wonder if the books have been read at all. In a dissertation it is usually best to have a list of references only.

There are many other finer points of referencing which cannot be dealt with here. Nevertheless the subject has been treated at some length because it is an area which students find confusing and where they often do not do themselves justice. Again, it is not some peripheral task, but one which lies at the heart of the efficient exchange, storage and retrieval of academic and other knowledge world-wide.

Writing

Good communication in a work of any length involves, as has been seen, much more than correct grammatical structure. Nevertheless, unambiguous and, preferably, clear sentences are important. Whole books have been written (see recommended reading p. 230) on just the fundamentals of English language. These books are interesting to study and are invaluable for reference on particular points. They also reveal how subtle, complex and indeed wonderful any language is, and how the ability to communicate and express ideas is largely taken for granted. Even articulate people will find themselves struggling sometimes to express complex ideas, and any loss of the precision of words and their usage which enable such expression is to be deplored (which is not to say that language cannot change). There is however a curious idea that the less people understand about language the better they will be able to express themselves, a proposition that would scarcely be applied to any other skill or activity. For every hedge poet who might have been thrown up by such a system there are many others who regret their lack of skill with language and powers of expression. Even the A-level Examination Boards and Her Majesty's Inspectorate of Schools, who have long countenanced if not actually encouraged such attitudes, are now belatedly deploring the state of language in what is after all the top 10 per cent of the educational product, some of whom, on entering higher education, require remedial teaching in their native language.

There is not space here to deal with such problems exhaustively. Discussion will be confined, briefly, to a few points on the nature of communication. An analysis of some of the more frequent errors in both grammar and style will be found in Appendix II. Most writers acknowledge the link between clear thinking and clear writing. Clear writing requires that ideas have been well thought through; on the other hand, the act of writing helps to clarify thought. It is for this last reason that it is advantageous to start writing early in research work, and to try as soon as possible to write down accurately and grammatically the aims of the research. Students should not be surprised to find that writing is hard work and, as pointed out above, can be very time consuming.

Ambiguity

While good style is pleasing and clarity convenient, it is important above all that academic writing, when analysed, should be found to be unambiguous and that it should actually have something of value to say. It might be supposed that to write about intangible or abstract ideas would be more difficult than to describe objects or procedures. In fact, a good test of writing is to describe, say, an experimental or survey procedure, or even a travel route, in such a way that someone else can follow it with confidence. Students frequently find such writing more difficult than the treatment of abstract ideas. On the face of it, it seems highly unlikely that to write clearly about abstract ideas should be easier than to write about concrete situations. The truth is that it can be easier to be sloppy when dealing with abstract situations since so many interpretations are possible, depending on previous knowledge and pre-conceptions. A reader can more easily jump to conclusions, even if they are the wrong ones, or can read lazily and not feel a need to understand thoroughly.

An art critic has pointed out how mere splashes of white paint on a picture of a lawn will be seen as daisies; but if the context is different, say under a cherry tree in blossom or beside a dustbin, the splashes become flower petals, or waste paper. So the artist paints daisies, and the viewer sees waste paper, and each thinks that communication has taken place. Not until the viewer says, 'What lovely daisies', and the other replies, 'I thought they were cherry petals', does the confusion become evident: which is why discussion of ideas and of writing is so important. The A-level Examination Boards have drawn attention to the unfortunate examples frequently set by the media and the advertising industry. A recent TV news headline announced, 'The government has reversed the cuts in the armed forces it had announced to meet UN commitments'. Is that a rose-petal or a cigarette butt? Was it the cuts or the reversal that were to meet U.N. commitments? In writing, it is only correct grammatical order, or syntax, which will make ideas unambiguous without reliance on an assumed previous knowledge. It is very helpful to get someone else to read drafts of a dissertation. This person does not have to be an expert in the field, indeed may be better not so, but should have a fresh, objective and logical mind. Any student whose writing has been criticized should first of all study Appendix II, below, and then, if necessary, the several books on good writing listed in recommended reading at the end of this chapter.

Submission and the spoken examination

Submission is the final handing-in of the dissertation, complete in every respect. Each institution has specific requirements for submission and for the exact form of binding, format of contents, documentation and number of copies of the dissertation. These requirements should be studied at an early stage and then checked thoroughly at the submission stage. In most cases, the dissertation having been read by the assessor, the writer will have an opportunity to explain the dissertation further at a spoken examination. This is usually a friendly and enjoyable, though necessarily critical, affair. Borderline marks, whether high or low, can be significantly influenced by this interview. It is a sobering though not unusual experience to find that meaningful thoughts written down some weeks or even months before seem far from clear, not to say unrecognizable, when an examiner asks a candidate to turn to a certain page and explain the meaning. For this reason a student should always keep a personal copy of the dissertation and should read and study it thoroughly for a few days before the spoken examination. A clear idea is necessary of where in the dissertation certain topics or questions have been dealt with so that points can be answered promptly. It is valuable also, during the period between submission and examination, to keep up with new developments in the field since an assessor may reasonably wish to discuss these.

Conclusions

It is true of research, as of many other fields of activity that only experience makes things real. As pointed out in the Introduction, the student who has successfully completed a substantial dissertation will have made a significant step forward in terms of intellectual maturity. Unfortunately, many students regret that it is only towards the end of preparing the dissertation, or even afterwards, that they begin to achieve an awareness of the nature of research, feeling that their dissertation could have been better if they had developed this understanding and synthesis earlier. It is to be hoped that the study of this book, which is not a substitute for experience, might bring this process of intellectual development forward and so make the experience more rewarding.

CHECKLIST: Chapter 9

You should know and understand:

- the relation between clear writing and clear thinking
- the relation between language and thought
- the psychological problem of starting to write a dissertation
- the need to start writing a dissertation early
- the benefits of discussing your writing with someone else

- how to
    - organize the dissertation
    - write to length
    - write in stages
    - organize time
    - set the scene
    - deal with more than one topic at a time
    - cross-reference
    - number paragraphs
    - keep to the point
    - keep the reader informed
    - reach meaningful conclusions
- the conventional dissertation format and the requirements and function of each stage
- how best to incorporate figures, tables and pictures
- how to use references correctly
- how to avoid ambiguity
- how to meet the requirements for submission
- how to prepare for your interview
- how to feel good about your dissertation

Further reading

Andrewski, S., 1972, *The social science as sorcery*, André Deutsch, London.

Barzun, J. and Graff F., 1970 [1957], *The modern researcher: the classic manual on all aspects of research and writing*, 2nd edn, Harcourt Brace and World, New York, Part III.

Bates, J.D., 1978, *Writing with precision: how to write so that you cannot possibly be misunderstood*, Acropolis Books, Washington D.C.

British Standards Institution, 1972, *Recommendations for the presentation of theses*, The Institution, London.

British Standards Institution, 1989, *Recommendations for references to published materials*, The Institution, London, BS1629:989.

Freeman, T.W., 1971, *The writing of geography*, Manchester University Press, Manchester.

Gowers, Sir E., 1973 [1954], *The complete plain words*, 2nd edn, revised by Sir Bruce Fraser, Pelican, Harmondsworth.

Leedy, P.D., 1980, *Practical research: planning and design*, 2nd edn, Macmillan, New York, pp. 181–201.

Marwick, A., 1971, *The writing of history*, Humanities: a foundation course, Unit 7, Open University Press, Milton Keynes.

Newman, R., 1989, *Study and research: a systematic approach for all students*, Bookmarque Publishing, Minster Lovell.

Partridge, E., 1973 [1947], *Usage and abusage: a guide to good English*, revised edn, Penguin, Harmondsworth.

Swan, M., 1992, *Oxford pocket basic English usage*, Oxford University Press, Oxford.

Turabiam, K.L., 1982, *A manual for writers of research papers, theses and dissertations*, 5th edn (1st edn in Britain), Heinemann, London.

Appendix I: STATISTICAL TESTS

Some of the formulae shown here appear complex and forbidding; in fact it can be seen that they are all built up from a few simple values obtained from the sample population. Today, the calculations would usually be performed by a computer or advanced calculator but it is useful to understand how variations in the sample data affect the test values and hence the significance of the results and the inferences which can be made from them. The principles set out in Chapter Seven should be studied before these formulae can be properly understood or used.

Student's *t* test for the correlation coefficient *r*.

It was seen in Chapter Seven how the closeness of a number of points to a straight line, in this case the regression line, could be summarized and expressed by a single statistic, *r*, the correlation coefficient. It was also explained that the chances of a number of points falling on or near to a line decreased as the number of points increased.

Having produced a correlation or regression line for two variables we need to know what is the probability of that particular value of *r* occurring by chance with that particular number of points (*n*). To do this, *r* and *n* are converted to another test statistic known as *student's t*. Statisticians have already computed the probability of any particular value of *t* occurring for any one of a range of sample sizes. Sample size (*n*) is modified slightly to allow for errors arising from the use of relatively small samples. Sample size is thus reduced to a factor known as the *degrees of freedom* which basically is (*n*–1). Since, in a correlation, each point represents two values, *n* is corrected here to (*n*–2) (with large samples clearly the difference between *n* and *n*–2 becomes negligible). The value of *t* for the particular experiment or survey is then looked up in a table, to be found in most statistics texts, which shows the probability (p) of any value of *t* occurring by chance for any value of the degrees of freedom (*n*–2). If the particular value of *t* is greater than the value shown for a selected probability, say p = 0.05, then the probability of the value of *r* occurring by chance is less than this. This can be thought of either as the probability of the value of r occurring by chance being less than $p = 0.05$ (less than 1 in 20) *or* as the probability of r not occurring by chance (ie. being 'true') being more than $p = 0.95$ (more than 19 in 20). Tables may show either or both of these options.

To summarize:

1. the computer produces a value of r
2. t is calculated as $t = r - \sqrt{\dfrac{n-2}{1-r^2}}$
3. degrees of freedom $= n - 2$
4. find the value of t in the t-table in the row showing degrees of freedom $= n - 2$
5. read off the column headings showing the probability p (interpolate the value of t if necessary, taking the next lower value of p).

Most statistical packages will produce values for r and t.

Student's *t*-test for the difference between means

Student's t-test can be used to find more precise probabilities for the difference between means than those given by the simple standard error test (Chapter Seven). The value is calculated as shown below and then applied to the t-tables as described above for the correlation coefficient. The degrees of freedom in this case are again $n - 2$. The resulting p value is the probability that a sample difference of that size could have occurred by chance.

$$t = \frac{(x_1 \sim x_2)}{\sqrt{\dfrac{\left(s_1\sqrt{\dfrac{n_1}{n_1-1}}\right)^2}{n_1} + \dfrac{\left(s_2\sqrt{\dfrac{n_2}{n_2-1}}\right)^2}{n_2}}}$$

where x_1 = mean of sample 1
x_2 = mean of sample 2
n_1 = size of sample 1
n_2 = size of sample 2
and s_1 = sample standard deviation for sample 1

$$= \sqrt{\frac{\Sigma (x - \bar{x})^2}{n}}$$

and s_2 is calculated similarly for sample 2.

Chi-squared test for comparing sample frequencies

As outlined in Chapter Seven, the chi-squared procedure is a test for whether or not the particular frequencies or proportions of a variable observed in a sample differ to such an extent from the frequencies which might be expected that the differences can be accepted as more than just a chance occurrence. The expected frequencies for a single variable may be calculated by comparison with some general characteristic of a population of an area or of a locality, such as the proportion of males to females, or of upland to lowland. For example, if girls were as likely as boys to take up opportunities in higher education then we would expect the numbers of boys and girls in a sample of higher education students to be proportional to the ratio of boys and girls in the appropriate age group.

Chi-squared is most commonly used however for comparing frequencies of two or more variables from two samples or sub-samples, as in the tables on p.179. In this case, the expected values for cells in the table are calculated on the hypothesis that the proportion or frequencies for the two variables are the same. Arithmetically this is so if the number in a cell is equal to its row total multiplied by its column total divided by the overall total or sample size. In this way an expected value is calculated for each cell in the table.

In the next stage the difference between the observed value O and expected value E is calculated. Each difference is squared (to eliminate negative values) and expressed as a ratio of the expected value. The sum of all the squares, chi-squared, is an expression of the total variation from expected values.

The familiar procedure is now followed of testing whether this total variation is greater than would be expected by chance in relation to the number of cells in the table. The size of the table is expressed as the number of degrees of freedom which is given by the number of rows, minus one, multiplied by the number of columns minus one, $(n_r - 1) \times (n_c - 1)$.

The probability that the differences in the tables have been produced by chance is given by locating the value of χ^2 against the appropriate degrees of freedom in a table of the χ^2 distribution. The procedure is similar to that for the t-test, above.

To summarize:

1. calculate expected values E:
   for a single variable; by reference to some external proportion;
   for a table; by $E = \dfrac{row\ total \times column\ total}{total}$
2. for each cell calculate difference $(O - E)$
3. square each difference $(O - E)^2$
4. divide each square by its own $E \dfrac{(O - E)^2}{E}$
5. add all squares; $\chi^2 = \Sigma \dfrac{(O - E)^2}{E}$
6. calculate degree of freedom; d.f. $= (n_r - 1) \times (n_c - 1)$
7. look up probability p in the χ^2 table.

Assumptions
1. Where d.f are greater than 1, E must not be less than 5 for more than 20 per cent of cells. Computer printouts may draw attention to this condition.
2. Where d.f $= 1$, use Yate's Correction (i.e. substract 0.5 from the value of each O-E *before* squaring).
3. Observed values must be expressed as counts and not as percentages.

Confidence limits for predictions from regression lines

Like the predictions from other statistical relationships which are based on samples, the calculation of a value based on a regression equation is expressed as a range or series of ranges, based on standard errors, with associated probabilities. Thus the true value of y for a given value of x, using a linear regression equation, would have a 95 per cent probability of lying within plus or minus two standard errors of the calculated value of y. The standard error of the estimate of y is given by $SE_y = \sigma_y \sqrt{1 - r^2}$

$$\sigma_y = s\sqrt{\dfrac{n}{n-1}}$$

$$s = \sqrt{\dfrac{\Sigma(y-y)^2}{n}}.$$

Appendix II: CLEAR WRITING

A dissertation has to be of a standard suitable for publication, that is it should have no categorical errors, though there may be room for differences of opinion over matters of style.

Outlined here briefly are some of the most common errors which frequently result in ambiguity in student writing. For more detail the books listed at the end of Chapter Nine should be consulted.

Sentence construction

The basis of writing is the *sentence*. Apparently many A-level candidates do not understand what a sentence is. The only absolute agreed grammatical definition of a sentence is that it should start with a capital letter and end with a full-stop. But general usage is that a sentence should have a subject, that is a word that represents a thing which, broadly, takes some action, and an active verb which expresses something which the subject has done, does or will do. A sentence may also, and usually does, have an object, a thing to which something is done. Good writers, occasionally, deliberately produce sentences which do not conform to these conventions, but it is done for a purpose and not by mistake.

'The government passed the Bill in 1992' is an example of a sentence which has a subject (the government), an active verb (passed) and an object (the Bill); there is also an extra bit of information in the short phrase 'in 1992' which tells us when the passage took place. It is incorrect to lapse into a sort of note-taking style such as, 'Passed in 1992' which has no subject or object, or even, 'Bill passed in 1992', where the object appears, wrongly, to be the subject and the verb is inactive. It is also incorrect to add the ending '-ing' to the main part of the verb, thus making 'passing', and to use this as a verb. It is not. Thus, 'Passing the Bill in 1991' is not a sentence, nor is even, 'The government, passing the bill in 1992'. The phrase can, however, be used as a bit of extra information in a sentence: 'The government, passing the bill in 1992, resigned', but this is unclear as to whether the government resigned during or after the passage. 'The government, having passed the Bill in 1992, resigned', is better. If all this causes problems it would be better still to say simply, 'The government passed the Bill in 1992 and resigned', though too much of this will make rather bland reading.

The use of note form and the use of -ing plus a verb as though it were a verb are the most common examples of the misuse of a non-sentence. They are most frequently found, wrongly, after a *semi-colon*: 'The government resigned; passing the Bill in 1992'. A semi-colon is normally used to join two sentences which are closely related. Some writers prefer not to use semi-colons at all, but if used, what follows the semi-colon should usually be a sentence in its own right. Another mispractice with sentences is to string several increasingly unrelated sentences together separated only by commas. As stated, two clearly related sentences may be linked with a semi-colon; beyond that, full-stops should be used.

Elementary grammar

Another problem is in the use of *commas*. Here practice varies between those writers who prefer not to use any and those who put commas in every natural pause in a sentence. It is probably best to use commas as little as possible except when necessary to make clear the structure of the sentence. It was said of Oscar Wilde that he could spend a whole morning putting in a comma and a whole afternoon taking it out. In the construction given above, 'The government, having passed the Bill in 1992, resigned' the central part between the commas could be removed and a short but conventional sentence would remain. Commas are often used to enclose extra information like this, rather like brackets; if so, as with brackets, when the first one is put in, the second should be also. Alternatively, this form of sentence often can read reasonably well with no commas at all.

The choice of commas depends on the sense. 'Having passed the Bill in 1992, the government resigned' is another form of construction where inclusion of the comma is a matter of judgement. In this particular example omission of the comma would leave some doubt as to whether the passage or the resignation occurred in 1992. However, if the comma is instead placed just before the word 'in', the meaning of the sentence is changed. With the exclusion of the phrase 'in 1992' use of the comma becomes unnecessary though optional since there is a natural break in the reading at this point.

A particular case where a comma is essential is in the use of 'however' at the start of a sentence. 'However, it is done . . .,' means, 'Anyway, it is done now . . .' 'However it is done', means 'In whatever way it is done', which is fine if that *is* what is intended. The first use is by far the more common. Whether commas should enclose 'however' within a sentence is again a matter of judgement depending on the sense of the words which immediately follow. As can be seen, there are few absolute rules about use of commas but the ultimate meaning should not be ambiguous or misleading. An expensive court case once rested on the effect of a comma in a sentence. Lawyers are notorious for placing non-ambiguity above immediate clarity in their writing.

Some rules however should be followed. The English language does not rely so much on the particular endings, or inflections, of words as do many other languages. But *singular* and *plural verbs* are differentiated in many cases, though not all: he need*s* (singular), they need (plural) are different; however, he resigned and they resigned are the same. The differentiation usually is made in the present tense and not in the past; compare for example: he resign*s*, they resign, he resigned, they resigned. A singular form is often used, wrongly, in place of the plural when two or more subjects are separated in a long sentence of the following type: 'John, who has since resigned over the affair, and Peter *need* (plural) help': that is, John and Peter need help. This error is particularly easy to make when the subjects are not simple names, as in this case, but are themselves phrases consisting of several words.

Another rule which should be followed, but often is not since students mistakenly feel it is confusing, is the use of the *apostrophe* to indicate ownership. Simply, if a word or name ends in a letter which is not *s*, an apostrophe and an *s* are added: John's file. If the word already ends in *s*, it is sufficient to add an apostrophe: James' computer. James's is also correct, although some people consider it unwieldy. Whichever form you decide to use, the important thing is to be consistent throughout. The rule is inviolable for plural words: the student's car (one student), but the students' car (jointly owned), *never* the students's. For plural words that do not end in 's', the apostrophe must be inserted before the possessive 's': men's, women's, children's, people's, etc.

Pronouns can be a subtle but important source of ambiguity. Pronoun is the term used for words such as 'it', 'they', 'he' or 'she', which are used to avoid repeating the names of things. Strictly a pronoun represents the last preceding thing, or noun, of the same number (singular or plural) or gender as itself. Excessive use of pronouns is confusing in any case, and if this rule (which?) is not followed it (what?) is even more so. As can be seen from the previous sentence this is another rule which sometimes is not used as strictly as it ought to be, provided the sense is felt to be clear; some confusion exists here as to whether 'it' refers to 'excessive use' or to 'rule'. If the meaning might be unclear, use of a noun is safer. A better sentence would be: '. . . if the rule is not followed, the result is even more confusion'. As a general rule paragraphs should not begin with a pronoun alone.

Style

This discussion has covered some of the more common causes of the ambiguity which occurs in dissertations. It is the variety and choice of construction and the judgement involved which help to make language such a rich experience. Consultation of the relevant books in the recommended reading will show just how great this complexity is. A few points of style may be mentioned also. It is for example unoriginal, but easy, to start every sentence with 'The'. It can also be easy, but irritating, to repeat certain words or phrases two or more times in a sentence or paragraph. If a word is unusual the repetition will jar even over several pages. English is rich in synonyms and these should be used to the full if not too esoteric or obscure. (A good thesaurus will help if you become lost for words.) Long sentences are another potential object of criticism. There is in fact nothing wrong in principle with an occasional long sentence provided the meaning is clear. Indeed nineteenth-century writers often produced very long sentences which, because of their careful construction, were perfectly understandable. But if there is any doubt about clarity or style then it is wise to use shorter sentences though, as seen above, even these can be ambiguous. A mixture of short and long sentences adds variety.

It is usual in formal academic writing, as in a dissertation, not to use the personal pronouns, I, we and you. This custom, like the priest's robes perhaps, symbolizes that the generality of knowledge should be above personal views. Use of phrases such as, 'I believe', raises questions about a writer's impartiality and maturity. It is naive also to suppose that much information gained from a dissertation is absolute; hence 'soft' phrases rather than 'hard' should be used in most cases: not, for example 'this proves', but 'this suggests', or 'this tends to show'.

Student writers are often cautioned against use of jargon. Jargon is the term for technical words for which there is no short substitute. Sailors use the term 'sheet' to distinguish, from the many other ropes on a boat, a rope which controls the set of a sail. But there is no point in using jargon to people who are not familiar with it; if necessary, include a glossary. As a famous professor of botany and Fellow of the Royal Society once said, 'If it's got a little lump on it, say it's got a little lump on it; don't call the thing a tubercle'. What should be avoided is unnecessary pseudo-jargon, used like teenagers' slang merely to impress and to identify status: complex hyphenated words, or words tortured into forms previously unknown to grammatical science, or obscure phraseology which is pseudo-scientific or bureaucratic in style. Another professor, of sociology, has pointed out that much academic writing, when put into plain words, says nothing original and sometimes nothing at all. If the ideas in a dissertation are sound, the best impression will be produced by the use of plain language, together with the necessary minimum of technical or professional terms.

REFERENCES AND BIBLIOGRAPHY

American book publishing record cumulative 1876–1949, 1950–1977, 1980–1984, R.R. Bowker, New York (published annually).

Andrewski, S., 1972, *The social sciences as sorcery*, André Deutsch, London.

Ayer, A.J., 1956, *The problem of knowledge*, Penguin, Harmondsworth.

Barzun, J. and Graff, F., 1985 [1957], *The modern researcher: the classic manual on all aspects of research and writing*, 4th edn, Harcourt Brace Jovanovich, New York.

Bates, J.D., 1978, *Writing with precision: how to write so that you cannot possibly be misunderstood*, Acropolis Books, Washington D.C.

Berlin, I., 1956, *The age of enlightenment: the eighteenth century philosophers*, Books for Libraries Press, New York.

Books in print, 1948– , R.R. Bowker, New York (published annually; formerly Publisher's Trade List Annual).

British books in print, 1874– , J. Whitaker and Sons, London (published annually; formerly *The reference catalogue of current literature*).

British humanities index, 1962– , Bowker-Sauer, London (published quarterly; formerly *The subject index of periodicals*, 1915–1961).

British Standards Institution, 1972, Recommendations for the presentation of theses, The Institution, London.

British Standards Institution, 1989, *Recommendations for references to published materials*, The Institution, London, BS1629:989.

Brown, P., 1992, 'Breast cancer: turning facts into figures', *New Scientist*, 18 Jan., pp. 16–17.

Bryman, A., 1988, *Quantity and quality in social research*, Contemporary Social Research Series, Martin Bulmer, London Unwin Hyman.

Bulmer, M. (ed.), 1984 [1977], *Sociological research methods: an introduction*, 2nd edn, Macmillan, Basingstoke.

Campbell, D.T., and Stanley, J.G., 1963, *Experimental and quasi-experimental designs for research*, Rand McNally, Chicago.

Central Statistical Office, 1976– , *Guide to official statistics*, HMSO, London.

Chapman, M., and Mahon, B., 1986, *Plain figures*, HMSO, London.

Copi, I.M., 1978, *Introduction to logic*, 6th edn, Macmillan, New York.

Current research in Britain, 1985– , Longman, Harlow (published annually; formerly *Research in British universities and polytechnics and colleges*, 4 sections including humanities and social sciences).

Dalton, R., et al., 1975, *Sampling techniques in geography*, George Philip and Son Ltd., London.

de Vaus, D., 1992, *Surveys in social research*, 3rd edn, UCL Press, London.

Dale, A., and Marsh, C., 1993, *The 1991 census user's guide*, HMSO, London.

Dissertation abstracts international: A; the humanities and social sciences, University Microfilms International, Godstone.

Dixon, B.R., et al., 1987, *A handbook of social science research: a comprehensive and practical guide for students*, Oxford University Press, Oxford.

Dominowski, R.L., 1980, *Research methods*, Prentice-Hall, Englewood Cliffs.

Drew, C.J., 1980, *Introduction to designing and conducting research*, C.V. Mosby, St Louis.

Easthorpe, G., 1974, *A history of social research methods*, Longman, London.

Eysenck, H.J., and Nias, D.K.B., 1978, *Sex, violence and the media*, Maurice Temple Smith, London.

Fearnside, W.W., and Holther, W.B., 1959, *Fallacy, the counterfeit of argument*, Prentice-Hall, Englewood Cliffs.

Fenner, P., and Armstrong, M.C., 1981, *Research: a practical guide to finding information*, William Kaufman, Los Altos, CA.

Festinger, L., et al., 1950, *Social pressures in informal groups*, Harper & Row, London.

Field, G.C., 1949, *The philosophy of Plato*, Oxford University Press, London.

Fisher, S., and Greenberg, R., 1977, *The scientific credibility of Freud's theories and therapy*, Harvester Press, Hassocks.

Freeman, T.W., 1971, *The writing of geography*, Manchester University Press, Manchester.

Gash, S., 1989, *Effective literature searching for students*, Gower, Aldershot.

Gowers, Sir E., 1973, *The complete plain words*, 2nd edn, revised by Sir Bruce Fraser, Pelican, Harmondsworth.

Gregory, S., 1963, *Statistical methods and the geographer*, Oxford University Press, Oxford.

Grigg, A., 1978, *A review of techniques for scaling subjective judgments*, Supplementary Report 379, Transport and Road Research Laboratory, Crowthorne.

Hansen, N.R., 1965, *Patterns of discovery*, Cambridge University Press, Cambridge.

Harrison, M., 1961, *London beneath the pavement*, Peter Davis, London, pp. 63–79.

Hawkins, G.S., 1966, *Stonehenge decoded*, Souvenir Press, London.

Henckel, R.E., 1976, *Tests of significance*, Sage, Beverley Hills.

Hobbes, T., 1968 [1651], *Leviathan* (ed. C., Macpherson), Pelican, Harmondsworth.

Hodgart, M.J.C., 1962, *Samuel Johnson and his times*, Batsford, London.

Hodges, L., 1981, *Logic*, Penguin, Harmondsworth.

Hoinville, G., et al., 1978, *Survey research practice*, Heinemann Educational, London.

Hoskins, W.G., 1972 [1959], *Local history in England*, 2nd edn, Longman, London.

Howard, K., and Sharp, R.A., 1983, *The management of a student research project*, Gower, Aldershot.

Hume, D., 1896 [1739], *A treatise of human nature*, (ed. Selby-Bigge), Clarendon Press, Oxford.

Index to theses with abstracts accepted for higher degrees in the universities of Great Britain and Ireland and the Council for National Academic Awards, ASLIB and Expert Systems, London (published quarterly).

Irvine, J., et al. (eds.), 1979, *Demystifying social statistics*, Pluto Press, London.

Kerlinger, F.N., 1973, *Foundations of behaviourial research*, Holt, Rinehart and Winston, London.

Leedy, P.D., 1980, *Practical research; planning and design*, 2nd edn, Macmillan, New York.

Locke, J., 1924 [1690], *An essay concerning human understanding* (ed. Pringle-Pattison), Oxford University Press, Oxford.

Locke, L.F., 1987, *Proposals that work: a guide for planning dissertations and grant proposals*, 2nd edn, Sage, Newbury Park.

Losee, J., 1993, *A historical introduction to the philosophy of science*, Oxford University Press, Oxford.

Marwick, A., 1970, *Primary sources*, Humanities: a foundation course, Unit 6, introduction to history, part 2, Open University Press, Bletchley.

Marwick, A., 1971, *The writing of history*, Humanities: a foundation course, Unit 7, Open University Press, Milton Keynes.

McCrone, J., 1993, *The myth of irrationality: the science of the mind from Plato to Star Trek*, Macmillan, London.

Mead, M., 1930, *Growing up in New Guinea, a study of adolescence and sex in primitive societies*, Penguin, Harmondsworth.

Mill, J.S., 1929 [1859], *On liberty*, Watts and Co., London.

Mill, J.S., 1972 [1843], *A system of logic*, Book III, Longman, London.

Mort, D., 1990, *Sources of unofficial UK statistics*, 2nd edn, Gower, Aldershot.

Murdoch, I., 1992, *Metaphysics as a guide to morals*, Chatto & Windus, London.

Newman, R., 1989, *Study and research: a systematic approach for all students*, Bookmarque Publishing, Minster Lovell.

Newton, E., 1962, *The meaning of beauty*, Pelican, Harmondsworth.

Nicholson, H., 1960, *The age of reason (1700–1789)*, Constable, London.

Norcliffe, G.B., 1982, *Inferential statistics for geographers*, 2nd edn, Hutchinson, London.

O'Brien, R.B., 1992. 'Was the voter soup stirred long enough?' *Daily Telegraph* (London), 3 April.

Ogburn, W.F., 1912, 'Progress and uniformity in child labour legislation', reproduced in Duncan, O., 1964, *On culture and social change*, University of Chicago Press, Chicago, pp. 110–130.

Oppenheim, A.N., 1969, *Questionnaire design and attitude measurement*, Heinemann, London.

Partridge, E., 1973 [1947], *Usage and abusage: a guide to good English*, revised edn, Penguin, Harmondsworth.

Phipps, R., 1983, *The successful student's handbook: a step by step guide to study, reading and thinking skills*, University of Washington Press, Seattle.

Popper, Sir K., 1982 [1959], *The logic of scientific discovery*, Hutchinson, London (first published as Logik der Forshung, 1934, Springer).

Popper, Sir K., 1972 [1963], *Conjectures and refutations*, 4th edn, Routledge & Kegan Paul, London.

Preece, R.A., 1990, 'Development control studies: scientific method and policy analysis', *Town Planning Review*, 61 (1) pp. 59–74.

Quetelet, J.A.L., 1846, *Sur la theorie de probabilite appliquée aux sciences morales et politiques*, Hayez, Brussels.

Read, H., 1926, *Reason and romanticism*, Faber & Gwyer, London.

Renfrew, C., 1973, *Before civilisation: the radiocarbon revolution and prehistoric Europe*, Jonathan Cape, London.

Reynolds, P.D., 1971, *A primer in theory construction*, Bobbs Merrill, Indianapolis.

Rhind, D., 1983, *A census user's handbook*, Methuen, London.

Rowntree, D., 1991 [1981], *Statistics without tears: a primer for non-mathematicians*, 2nd edn, Penguin, Harmondsworth.

Salmon, W.C., 1984 [1963], *Logic*, 3rd edn, Prentice-Hall, Englewood Cliffs.

Scott, J., 1990, *A matter of record; documentary sources in social research*, Polity Press, Cambridge.

Scottish Tourist Board, 1993, *Standardized questions for tourism surveys*, STB Edinburgh.

Severin, T., 1985, *The Jason voyage*, Hutchinson, London.

Siegel, S., 1956, *Non-parametric statistics for the behaviourial sciences*, International Student edn, McGraw-Hill Kogakusha, Tokyo.

Skinner, Q., (ed.) 1985, *The return of grand theory to the social sciences*, Cambridge University Press, Cambridge.

Social and Community Planning Research, 1972, *Questionnaire design manual*, SCPR, London.

Stevens, A., 1980, *Clever children in comprehensive schools*, Penguin, Harmondsworth.

Strong, L.A.G., 1951, 'Thomas Hardy', in Strong, L.A.G. (ed.), *Sixteen portraits*, Naldrett Press, London, pp. 66–79.

Summers, G.F., 1977, *Attitude measurement*, Kershaw Publishing, London.

Sutherland, S., 1993, *Irrationality; the enemy within*, Constable, London.

Swan, M., 1992, *Oxford pocket basic English usage*, Oxford University Press, Oxford.

Trustead, J., 1979, *The logic of scientific inference: an introduction*, Macmillan, London.

Turabiam, K.L., 1982, *A manual for writers of research papers, theses and dissertations*, 5th edn (1st edn in Britain), Heinemann, London.

Van Dalen, D.B., 1979, *Understanding educational research*, McGraw-Hill, Maidenhead.

Walker, K., 1950, *Meaning and purpose*, Pelican, Harmondsworth.

Wasserman, P. et al., 1980, *Statistical sources: a subject guide to data on industrial, business, social educational, financial and other topics for the United States and internationally*, 6th edn, Gale Research, Detroit.

Wilson, S., 1973, *Truth*, Arts: a third level course, problems of philosophy, Units 9–10, Open University, Milton Keynes.

Woodrow, M. (ed.) *Clover newspaper index*, Clover, Bigglesworth.

Yeomans, K.A., 1968, *Statistics for the social scientist 1: introducing statistics*, Penguin, Harmondsworth.

Zeisel, J., 1984, *Inquiry by design: tools for environment-behaviour research*, Cambridge University Press, Cambridge (originally published in 1981 by Wadsworth, Belmont, CA).

INDEX

Principal references and definitions are indicated by bold type page numbers.